Rhino 7.0 for Jewelry
Volume I: 2-D

Intro to Rhino
Basic Rhino Commands
2-Dimensional Drawing Tutorials

Dana Buscaglia

ISBN# 978-1-716-03535-7

INTRODUCTION

The chapters in this book were conceived as step-by-step tutorials to be used for Rhinoceros™ courses for jewelry students and professionals.

This book will cover the creation of 2-dimensional drawings and layouts.

(A following book will cover the creation of 3-dimensional models and strategies.)

- Go through this book from the beginning and, slowly and thoughtfully, take yourself through the step-by-step chapters. Repeat a chapter if you feel that you had a struggle getting through it. The extra time spent will pay off! Stay calm and understand that everyone goes through this stage!
- Avail yourself of the Help Menu in Rhino. The reader is urged to take advantage of this resource. If you are in a command described in a tutorial that you may not fully understand, press "F1" and you will be taken to the Help menu *for that command.*
- Take Rhino courses. You will always learn something more in each course.
- Avail yourself of the tutorials on the Rhino website - www.rhino3d.com.
- There are many Rhino tutorials on the Internet. If you do a search, you will find free videos on sites like YouTube. Also, check out the Rhino website,
- Understand that most of the learning starts at home, working on your own computer. Don't feel that you have to keep taking courses to continue learning. The hard work is done by you alone, applying commands to your own needs and doing your own problem solving. Repetition is important. It is how you become comfortable in the Rhino workspace and how you get used to drawing and modeling certain shapes.
- Start using Rhino in your own work. The sooner you do that, the faster you will learn.

Table of Contents

Introduction to the Rhino Workspace

Opening Rhino

- **Double-click** on the Rhino icon that is placed on your desktop when you install the program.

Fig. 1

The Rhino Splash Screen

- The Rhino Splash Screen will open, giving you some options and information.

- <u>**Recent**</u> tab:
    - This shows title and thumbnails of the Rhino files most recently opened.
    - You have the option of clicking on one of these thumbnails to select a file to open.

- <u>**Open**</u> tab:
    - This is a browse button for finding a file that was already saved on your computer.

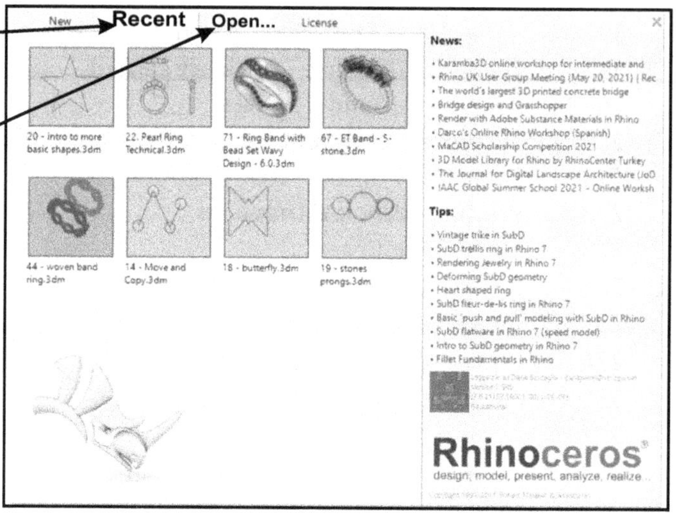

- <u>**New**</u> tab:
    - Shows a list of templates with different settings for scale and unit measurement.

    - Notice that the cursor is hovering over the last template on the list, **Small Objects - Millimeters.**
        - A description of the template's characteristics appears in the yellow box to the right.
            - **Measurement units**: millimeters
            - **Absolute tolerance**: .001mm
                - Absolute tolerance is the smallest distance recognized by the settings of this template.

    - Click on this template to choose it as it's small scale and millimeter unit measurement are good for creating small objects.

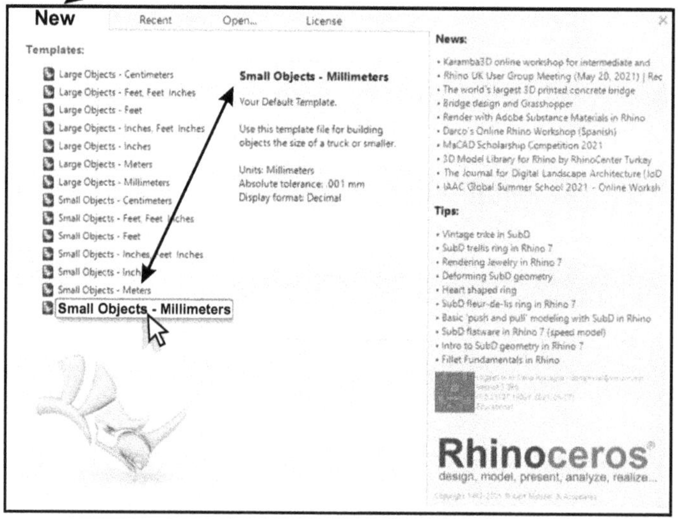

Fig. 2

1

- Notice that Rhino is opening behind the Splash Screen. ***Don't worry if you have not yet clicked on your choice of file or template.***

- As long as you **keep your cursor inside the Splash Screen**, the Splash Screen will not go away.

- When you click on the Template or File that you want to open, *the Rhino screen will update to your selection* and the Splash Screen will go away.

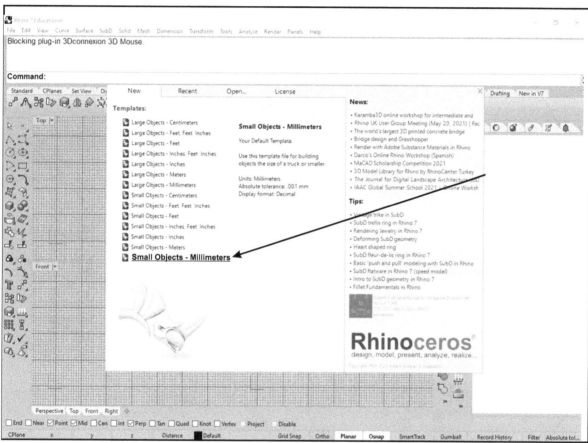

Fig. 3

- If you want the splash screen to appear again, click on **Help ❶** in the top menu and click to choose the **About Rhinoceros...** option. ❷
- You can also just type **"about"** in the **Command Line** and the Splash Screen will appear.

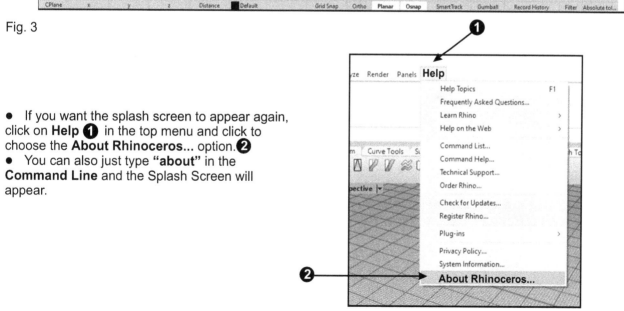

The Rhino Workspace
A brief tour

The Rhino Screen

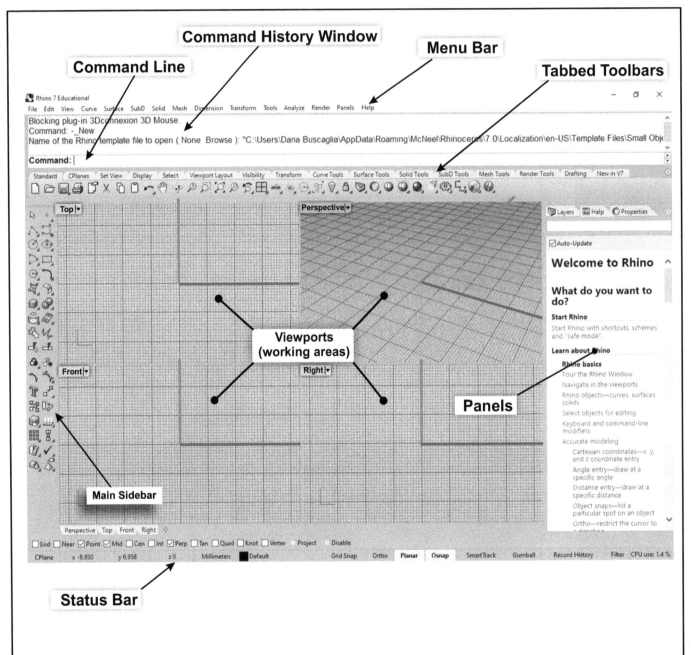

*   You can also read an excellent description of the Rhino Workspace in the Rhino Help menu which is available in the Menu Bar in the Rhino workspace. Type **"Rhino Window"** in the help menu..

Fig. 1

Viewports

- **Viewports** are the working areas of Rhino.

- **Double-click** on a viewport title to maximize the viewport. **Double-click** again to minimize the viewport and show more than one viewport at a time.

- The **Grid** units are specified in the title of the chosen template.
  - In this template, each grid intersection represents 1mm.
  - The **Grid** rests on the **Construction Plane.**
    - The **Construction Plane** is an imaginary surface upon which objects are created by default.
  - The grid has X and Y axes. Where these two axes meet is called, in terms of absolute coordinates, **"0,0"**, or just **"0". This organizes the workspace.**

- Click on the little arrow on the right side of the viewport title.

  - A context menu will drop down with many options and settings that will be covered in later chapters.

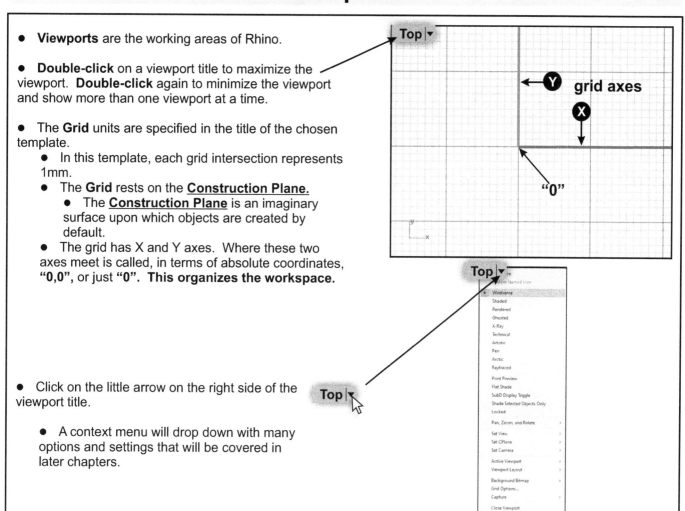

Fig. 2

Menu Bar

- Just about every Rhino tool and command can be found in the drop-down menus in the menu bar at the top of the workspace.

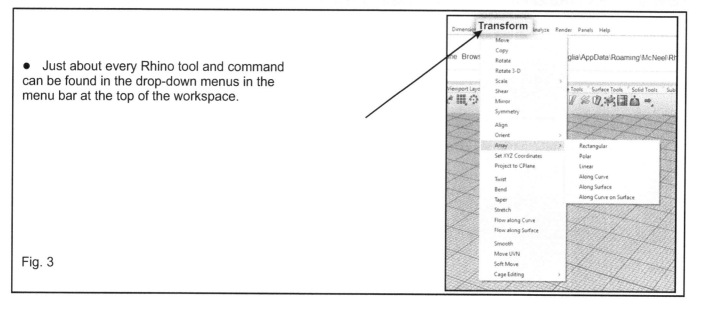

Fig. 3

Command Line
Guides you through the commands with step-by-step prompts.

- This is how the **Command Line**, or **Command Prompt**, looks when there is no command active.

- In this example, the **Circle** command is has been activated. The **Command Line** is "prompting" for the location of the **Center of the circle.**

- Within the parentheses are **links** that give you options to tailor the command to your needs.

- To cancel out of a command, press the Esc key on your keyboard.

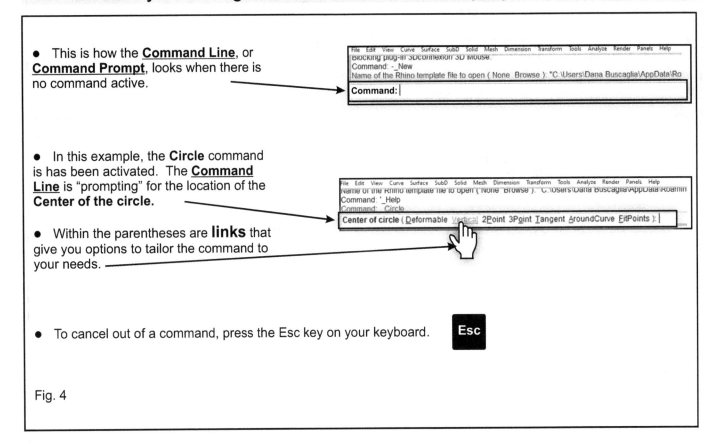

Fig. 4

Command History Window

- The **Command History Window** displays the commands that immediately preceded the current command.

- It is also a source of information, depending on the command.

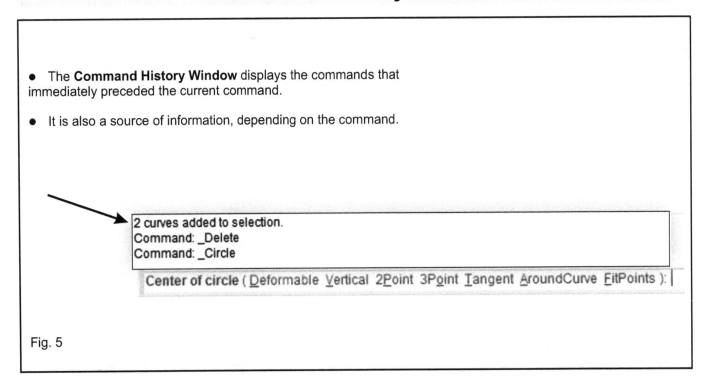

Fig. 5

5

Toolbars

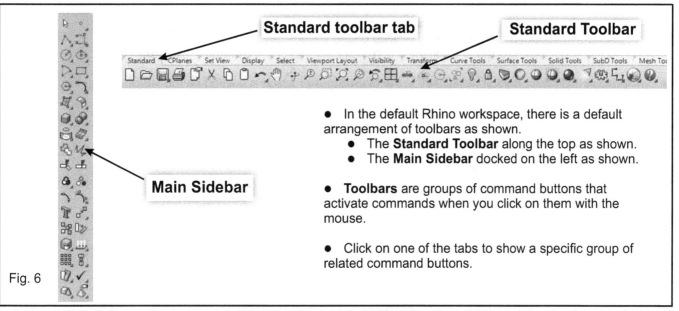

- In the default Rhino workspace, there is a default arrangement of toolbars as shown.
  - The **Standard Toolbar** along the top as shown.
  - The **Main Sidebar** docked on the left as shown.

- **Toolbars** are groups of command buttons that activate commands when you click on them with the mouse.

- Click on one of the tabs to show a specific group of related command buttons.

Fig. 6

Toolbar Flyouts

- A little black triangle at the lower right corner of a button means that if you **right-click on this button** (or hold **down the left mouse button**), another toolbar will appear - a **"toolbar flyout"**.

  - Click the dark band **❶** on the top of the toolbar and drag the toolbar out further into the viewport.
  - It's appearance will change and it will remain on the workspace as a **"floating toolbar"** until you choose to close it by clicking the **"X" ❷** in the upper right corner.

Fig. 7

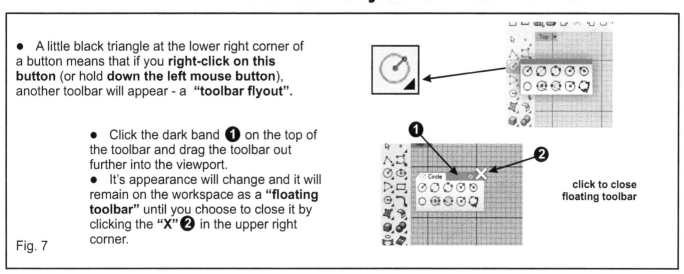

click to close
floating toolbar

Tooltips

- If you hover the cursor over a single button, a little text box will appear - **a "Tooltip"**.

- Tooltips describe the commands enabled by the button.

- In this example, notice that there are two lines to the tooltip, indicating functionality for **both left and right mouse buttons.**
  - The little symbols indicate the left and right mouse buttons.

Fig. 8

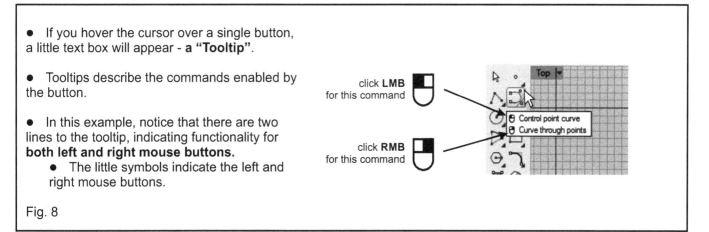

click LMB
for this command

click RMB
for this command

Toolbar Groups & the Default Rhino Workspace

- The default Rhino window features the **Standard Toolbar Group**.
  - Individual toolbars are accessible by clicking on the various tabs shown.
  - Click on the **Standard** tab to display the command buttons of the **Standard Toolbar**.

- Included in this Rhino default workspace is the **Main Sidebar** which is docked on the left whenever the Standard Toolbar is displayed on top.

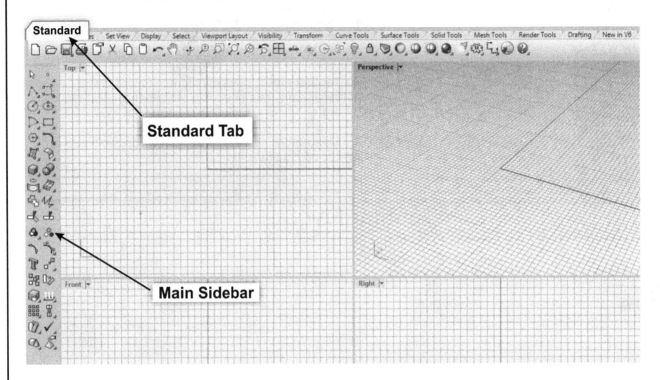

Standard Tab

Main Sidebar

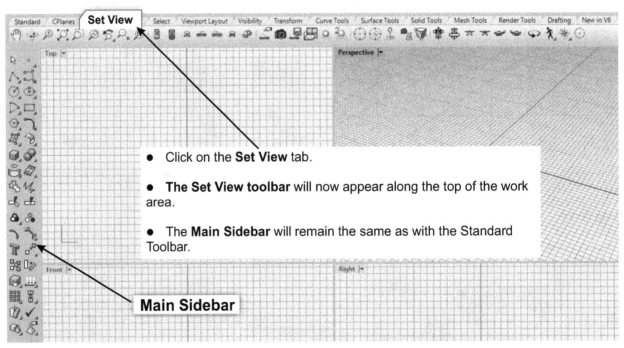

- Click on the **Set View** tab.

- **The Set View toolbar** will now appear along the top of the work area.

- The **Main Sidebar** will remain the same as with the Standard Toolbar.

Main Sidebar

Fig. 9

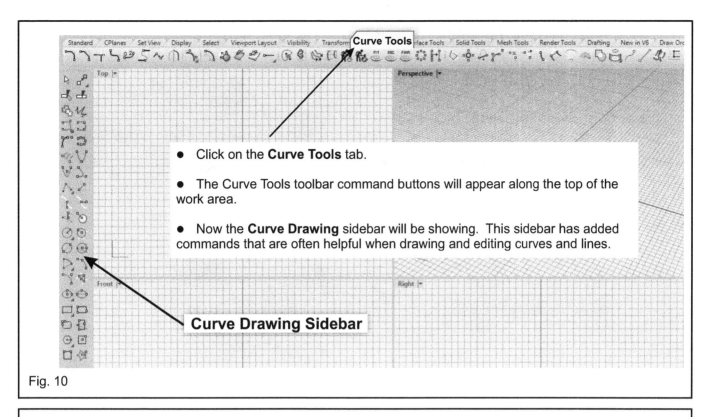

- Click on the **Curve Tools** tab.

- The Curve Tools toolbar command buttons will appear along the top of the work area.

- Now the **Curve Drawing** sidebar will be showing. This sidebar has added commands that are often helpful when drawing and editing curves and lines.

Curve Drawing Sidebar

Fig. 10

- Click on these tabs and you will see sidebars that compliment them, usually pertaining to further relevant editing and transformation commands.

| Curve Tools | Surface Tools | Solid Tools | Mesh Tools | Render Tools | Drafting |

Fig. 11

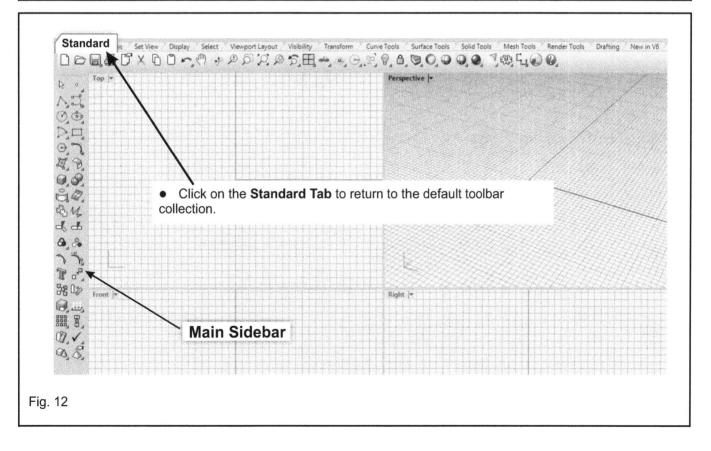

- Click on the **Standard Tab** to return to the default toolbar collection.

Main Sidebar

Fig. 12

Adding Tabbed Toolbars to the Workspace

- **Right-click** on any tab. ❶

- Click on the **Show or Hide Tabs** option in the drop-down menu. ❷

- Click on the **Analyze** tab option in the sub menu that appears from the **Show or Hide Tabs** option. ❸

- The **Analyze Tabbed Toolbar** will now be added to the toolbar collection.

- Note: click on a checked item in the drop-down to close that tabbed toolbar.

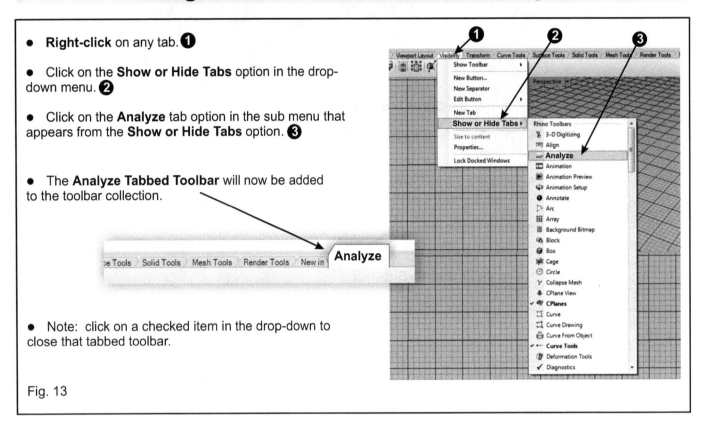

Fig. 13

Adding a Floating Toolbar to the Workspace

- **Right-click** on any Tab. ❶

- Click on the **Show Toolbar** option in the drop-down menu. ❷

- Click on the **Analyze** toolbar option in the sub menu that appears from the **Show Toolbar** option as shown. ❸

- The **Analyze** toolbar will appear as a **Floating Toolbar** that can be closed out by clicking on the **X** on the top right.

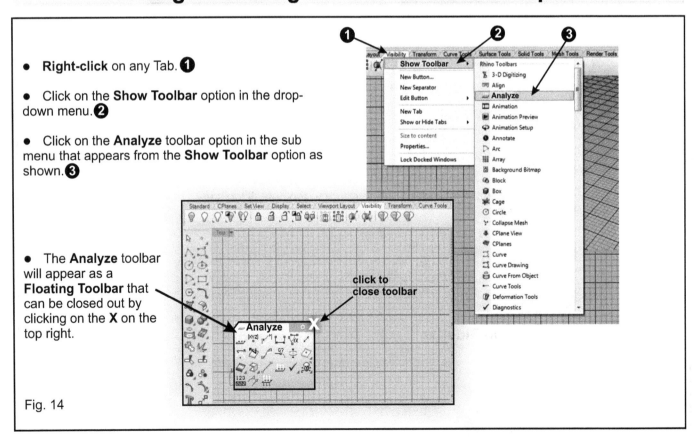

Fig. 14

Panels

- Many Rhino settings and controls are contained in the **Panels** that dock on the right of the workspace.

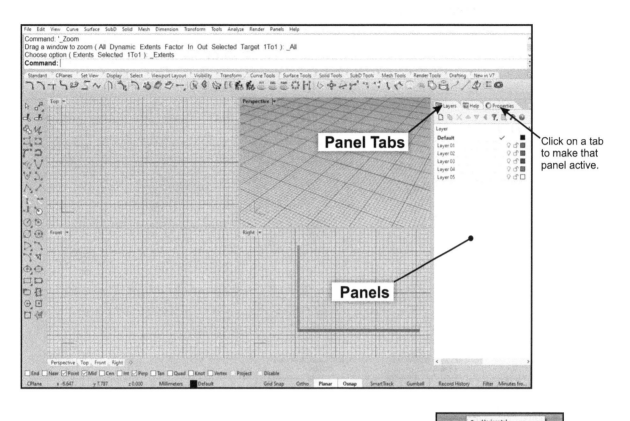

Panel Tabs

Click on a tab to make that panel active.

Panels

- **Right-click** on one of the tabs ❶ to get a drop-down menu. Click on one of the categories ❷ and it's tab will become accessible.

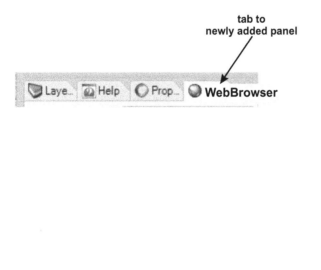

tab to newly added panel

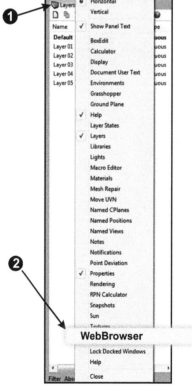

Fig. 15

If No Panels are Showing in the Workspace

- The **Panels** drop-down ❶ in the **Menu Bar** at the top of the workspace offers most of the available categories that can be included in the panels grouping.
- Click on the **Layers** category as shown. ❷

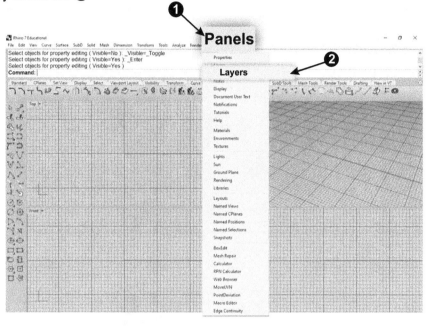

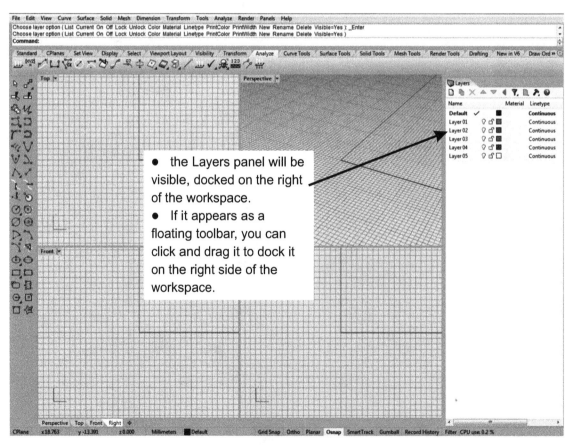

- the Layers panel will be visible, docked on the right of the workspace.
- If it appears as a floating toolbar, you can click and drag it to dock it on the right side of the workspace.

Fig. 16

- To add more panels, **right-click** on any panel tab to get the drop-down list of other categories.

- Click on the **Help** category and that panel will be added to the panels.

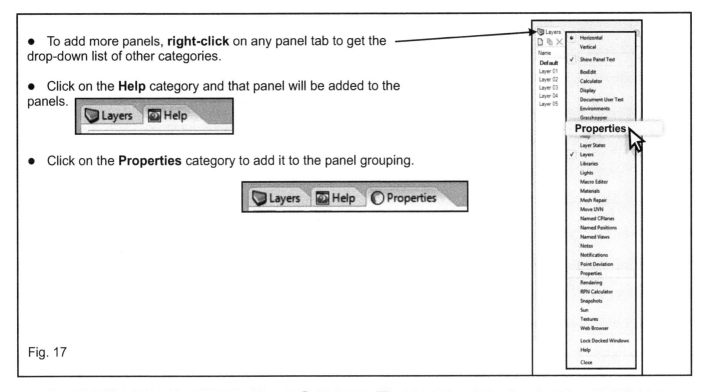

- Click on the **Properties** category to add it to the panel grouping.

Fig. 17

Status Bar

- The **Status Bar** is at the bottom of the workspace. It has two general functions:
  - A source of information and status.
  - Toggles for Modeling Aids

A Different colored pane indicates that this function is active.

Info Pane

- **CPlane:** a toggle between the default World Coordinates and the Coordinate of another Construction Plane. Keep this setting on **CPlane**.

- **X, Y, and Z buttons:** indicates the position of the cursor at any given time in the X, Y, and Z directions, expressed in absolute coordinates..

- **Millimeters:** this pane shows the unit of measurement for the project in which you are working. When you are drawing, this box will also show the distance the cursor is moving from the previously designated point.

- **Default:** clicking on this pane will open a useful pop-up list of layers. (see **Layers** chapter)

- **Grid Snap**, **Ortho**, **Osnap**, **Record History:** click to toggle on modeling aids covered in later chapters.

- **SmartTrack**: toggles on a system of temporary reference for lines and points. May be confusing for beginners.

- **Gumball:** a Widget that can perform move, scale and rotate commands.

- **Filter:** enables the filtering of the types of objects that can be selected.

- **Info Pane:** Information cycles on this pane. This illustration shows the unit of measurement for the model. Right-click for a pop-up list from which you can choose what pieces of information you want to see cycled on this pane.

Fig. 18

- Click on **Help** ❶ in the **Menu Bar** to see many helpful links. **Help Topics** will bring you to the Rhino Help window. The **F1 key** ❷ will also open this window.

F1

- If you are in a command and press **F1**, *Rhino Help will open up to explain the same command that is active in your workspace.*

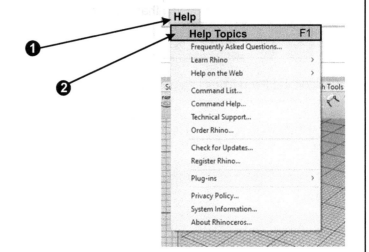

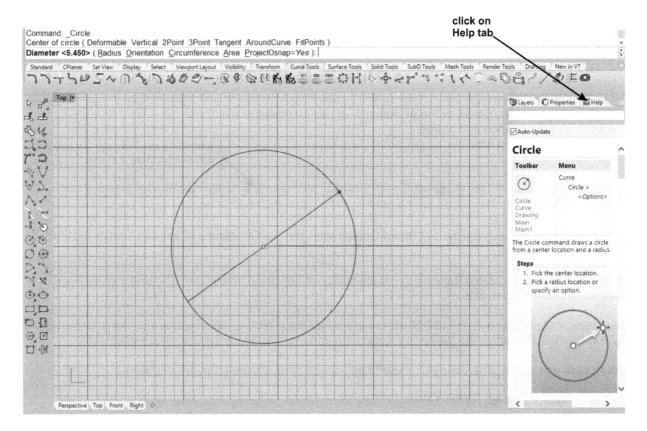

- Click on the **Help** tab to activate the **Help Panel.**

- Click on a command and the panel will display the help chapter that describes the command in which you are working.

- This illustration shows the Circle command in progress with the help panel displaying information about the Circle command.

Fig. 19

Document Properties

- Click on the **Tools** category ❶ in the **Menu Bar** at the top of the workspace.
  - Click on **Options** ❷ in the drop-down menu.

- The **Rhino Options** box will open.

- Click to highlight the **Units** category. ❸
  - Millimeters ❹ are the unit of measurement for this Rhino file.
    - This is the unit of measurement in the **small objects - Millimeters** startup template file that you originally opened in Rhino.
  - Notice that **Absolute Tolerance** ❺ is set to .001mm as this is another setting in the template that you opened.

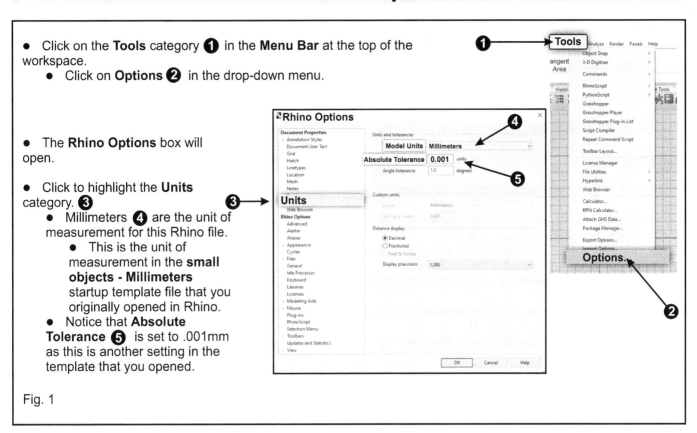

Fig. 1

- Click to display the **Grid** category.
  - The **Minor Grid Lines** setting is set at **1mm**.
    - **Minor grid lines** ❷ will show every millimeter.
  - Change the **Major Grid Lines** ❸ setting to **every 5 grid lines.**
    - The darker thicker grid lines will show as **every 5th grid line.**

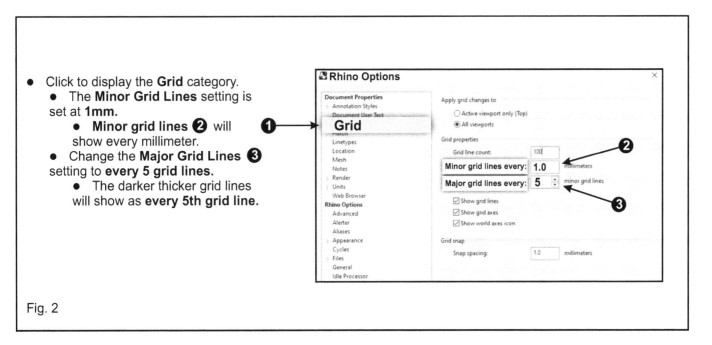

Fig. 2

- Save the **Document Properties** settings by creating a new Rhino template file.

- Click on the **File** category in the **Menu Bar** at the top of the workspace. ❶
  - Click to select the **Save As Template** option in the drop-down context menu. ❷

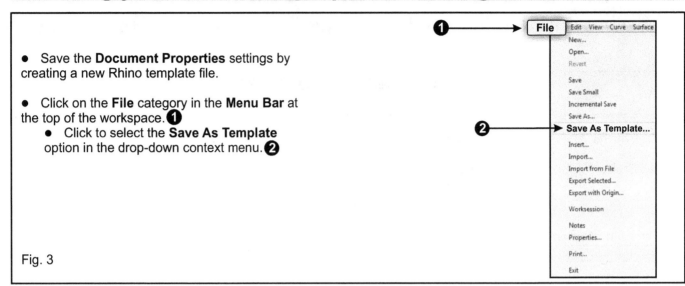

Fig. 3

- The **Save Template File** will open

- Name the file as suggested in this example.
  - **CUSTOM - millimeters**

- If you are working on your regular working computer, save this template in the file that contains the other templates as shown. This is the default location.

- If you are working at another location, save this to a flash drive or other storage medium and load it onto you regular computer.

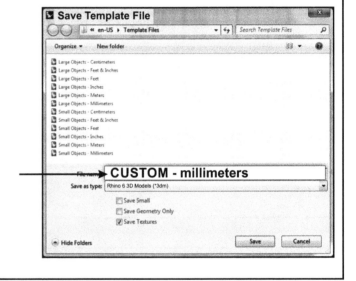

Fig. 4

- When you open Rhino again to start a new file, your new custom template will be included in the list of templates.

- If you have saved your template to another location on your computer, go directly to that location and open the file from that location.

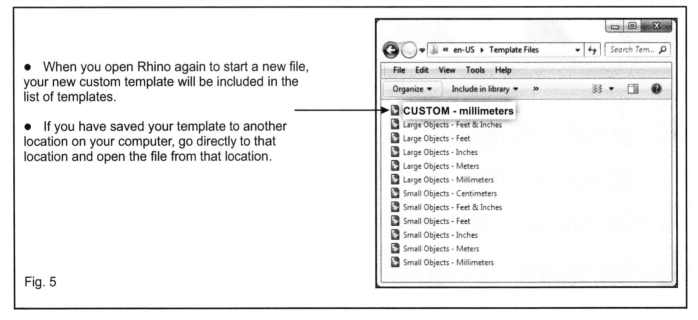

Fig. 5

Rhino Options: Basic Settings
Settings that will remain each time Rhino is opened

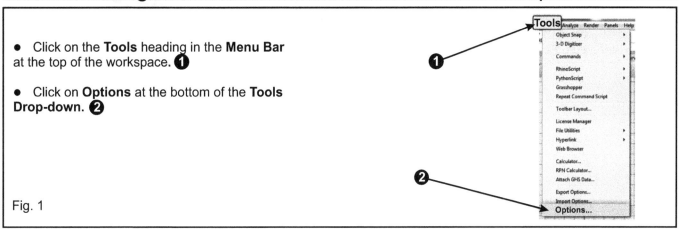

- Click on the **Tools** heading in the **Menu Bar** at the top of the workspace. ❶

- Click on **Options** at the bottom of the **Tools Drop-down**. ❷

Fig. 1

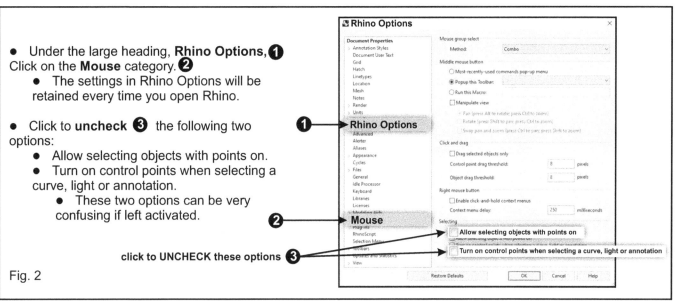

- Under the large heading, **Rhino Options,** ❶ Click on the **Mouse** category. ❷
  - The settings in Rhino Options will be retained every time you open Rhino.

- Click to **uncheck** ❸ the following two options:
  - Allow selecting objects with points on.
  - Turn on control points when selecting a curve, light or annotation.
    - These two options can be very confusing if left activated.

click to UNCHECK these options ❸

Fig. 2

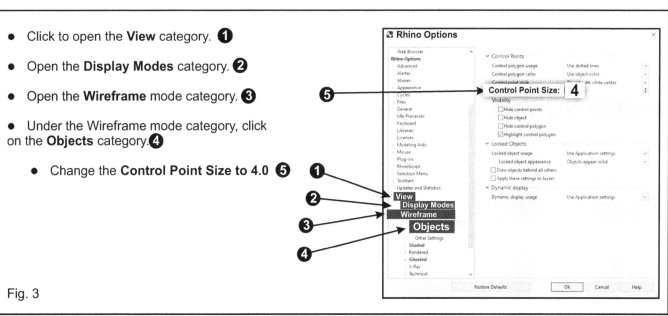

- Click to open the **View** category. ❶

- Open the **Display Modes** category. ❷

- Open the **Wireframe** mode category. ❸

- Under the Wireframe mode category, click on the **Objects** category. ❹

  - Change the **Control Point Size to 4.0** ❺

Fig. 3

- Under the **Objects** category, click to open the **Points** category.❶

- **Point Objects settings:** ❸
  - Change the **Point Object Size** to **4.**

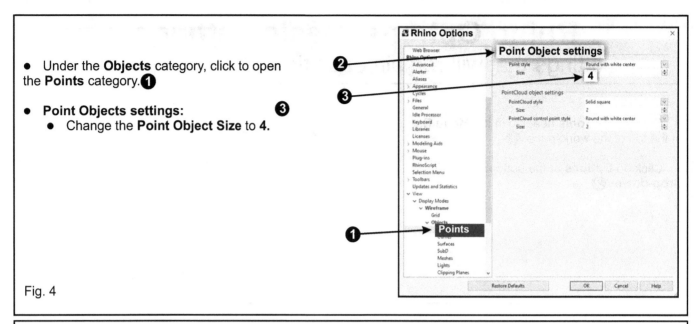

Fig. 4

- Under the Objects category, click to select the **Curves** category.❶
  - Change the **Curve Width** to **3.0 pixels.**❷

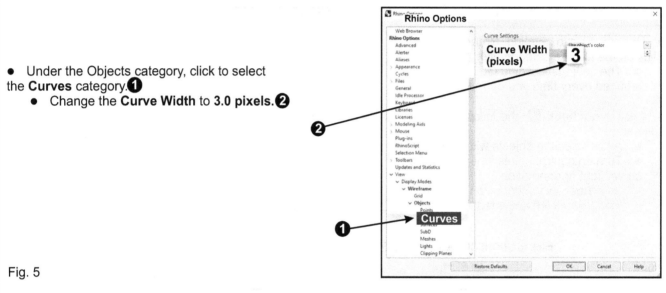

Fig. 5

- Click on the **Surfaces** category❶

  - Change the **Edge Thickness** to **3.0** ❷ **pixels.**

- Click on the **OK button** ❸ to exit the Rhino Options box.
  - You must click on the **OK button** to retain the options you have just set.
  - *If you just "X out" of the box, the settings will not be retained.*

- Use the above settings for these additional display modes:
  - **Shaded**
  - **Ghosted**

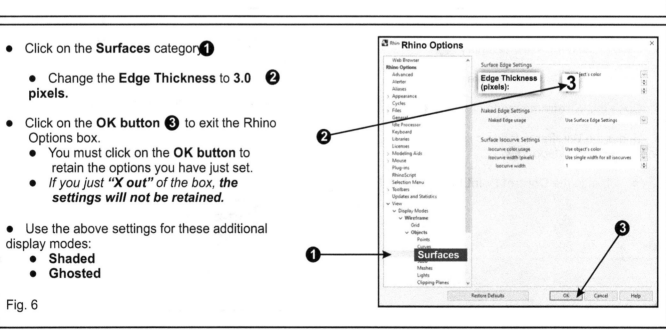

Fig. 6

- **RIGHT-CLICK** on the **History** button ❶ at the bottom of the workspace.
  - Select the options ❷ shown in the context menu.
  - This will change the default setting that has History always enabled.

- Note: Keeping History on all of the time can lead to complications as you don't always want to use it.

Fig. 7

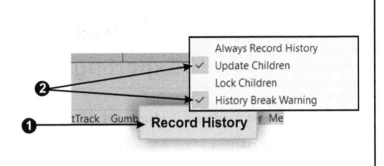

Exporting & Importing Rhino Options
Loading your Rhino Options into another Computer

Exporting Rhino Options

- Click on the **Tools** heading in the **Menu Bar.** ❶

- Click on **Export Options** at the bottom of the **Tools Drop-down.** ❷

- Save your Rhino options to a designated location in your computer when the **Save As** box opens. ❸

- Click the **Save button** to save your Rhino Options file and exit.

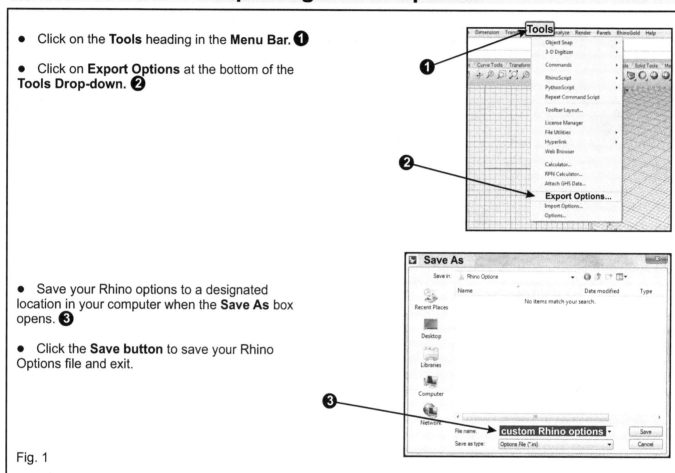

Fig. 1

Importing Rhino Options

- Click on the **Tools** heading in the **Menu Bar.** ❶

- Click on **Import Options** at the bottom of the **Tools Drop-down.** ❷

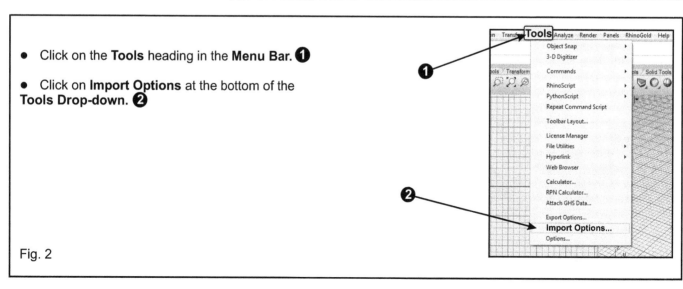

Fig. 2

- The **Import Options** dialog box will open.

- Click on the **browse button** ❶ to navigate to the **custom Rhino options** file that you saved from another computer onto a flash drive or some other storage media. ❷

- Navigate to your **custom Rhino options** file and click on the **Open button.** ❸

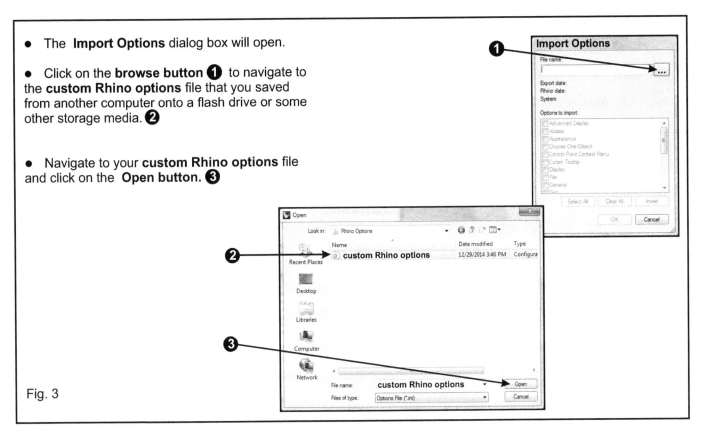

Fig. 3

- The **custom Rhino options** file will now be showing in the **file name** line at the top of the **Import Options** box. ❶

- Click on the **Select All button** so that all of the categories of options will be checked for importing into the Rhino workspace. ❷

- You can drag the bottom edge of the box down to see that all options have been checked.

- Click on the **OK button** to exit out of the box. ❸

- The options will be imported into the Rhino workspace.

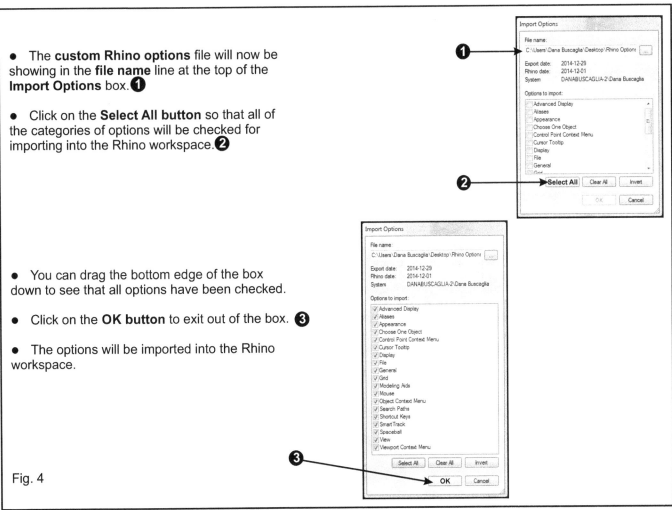

Fig. 4

Downloading Supporting Files from the rhinoforjewelry website
Saving the supporting files to a file on your computer.

- Type this URL address to access the opening page of the website: **www.rhinoforjewelry.com**

- In the Navigation Menu on the left, click on the **support files for textbook** link. ❶

Fig. 1

- You will arrive at a page with the following links:
  - **Files for the textbook**
  - **Textures and Environment maps used in the textbook**

- Click on the **Files for Textbook** link. ❷

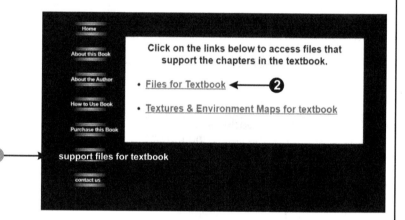

Fig. 2

- A new window will open up, showing a list of the files that support the chapters in the textbook.
  - If you click on any of these files, a Rhino file will open (after a moment).
    - Save each file to a designated folder on your computer.

- The last link is a ZIP file that contains all of the above files.

Note: files may be different from the illustration shown.

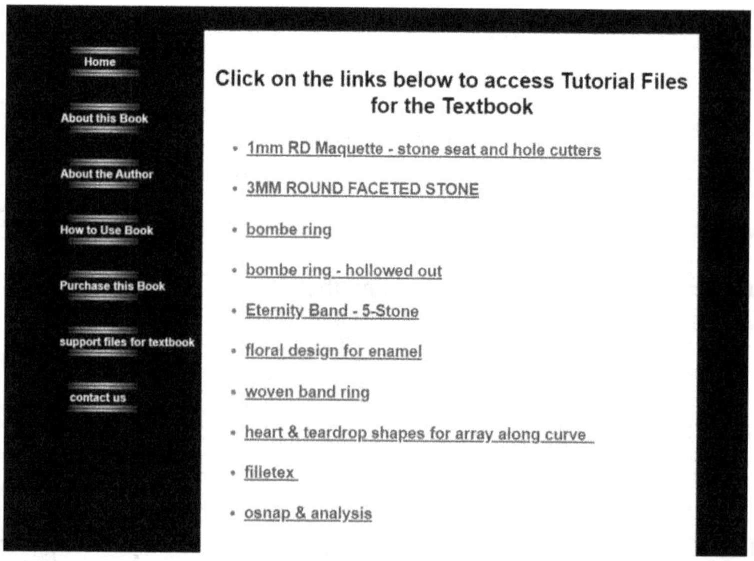

Fig. 3

- Navigate back to the page with the main list as shown.

- Click on the **Textures & Environment Maps for textbook** link.

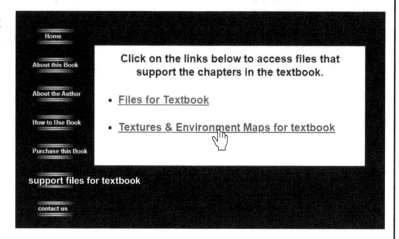

Fig. 4

- You will now see Textures and Environment maps for Diamonds, Polished Silver, Polished Gold, and texture bitmaps that will be used to generate textured surfaces in the 3D section of the textbook.
    - When the jpeg image opens, right-click on the image and choose **"save as"** or **"save image as"** in the context drop-down menu.

- As before, open and save these files to a designated folder in your computer.

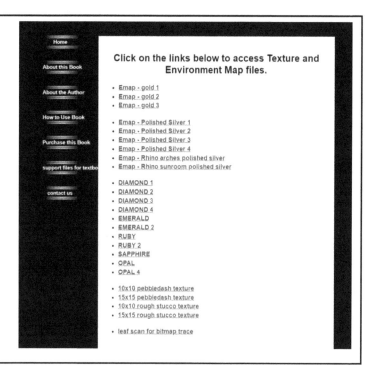

Fig. 5

- These files will be imported into Rhino files in the course of this book.

- It is easier if you have these files saved to your computer because the Import command in Rhno will not be successful at importing them directly from the website.

Downloading Rhino Training Files
Rhino's Basic Manual and Accompanying files

- This is the link to access the Rhino website.

Fig. 1

- Click on the **learn** link

Fig. 2

- The **Learn** page will open.

- On this page you will find a rich assortment of Rhino tutorials.

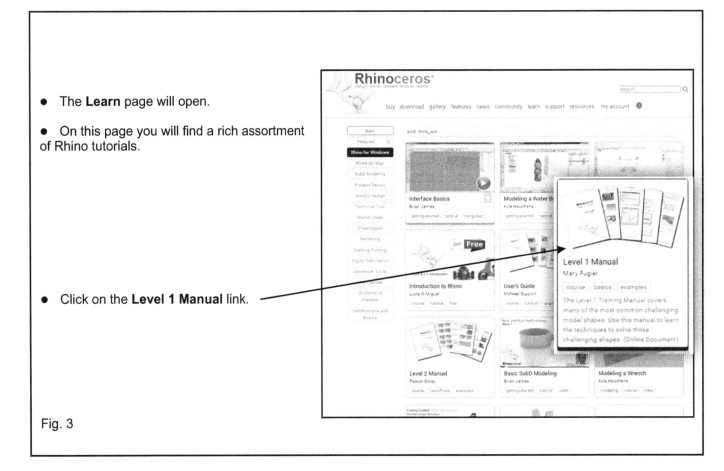

- Click on the **Level 1 Manual** link.

Fig. 3

- The **Introduction** page will open.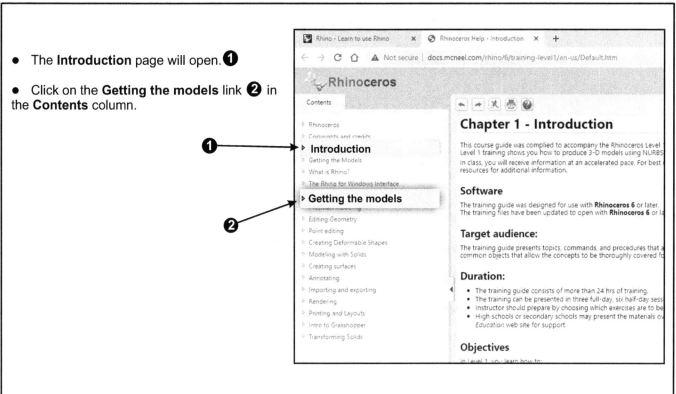

- Click on the **Getting the models** link ❷ in the **Contents** column.

- The page will open, explaining how to download Rhino models for the tutorials.

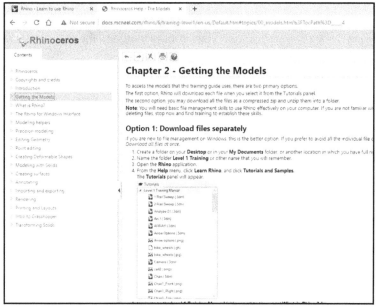

Fig. 4

Viewport Navigation for 2D Drawings
Panning and Zooming in 2D Drawings

Zooming the View - using the Mouse Wheel

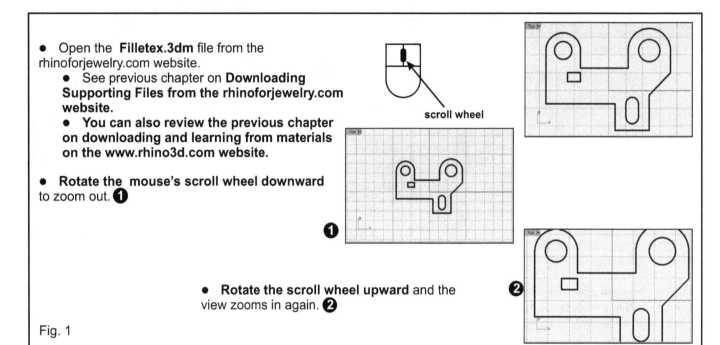

- Open the **Filletex.3dm** file from the rhinoforjewelry.com website.
  - See previous chapter on **Downloading Supporting Files from the rhinoforjewelry.com website.**
  - **You can also review the previous chapter on downloading and learning from materials on the www.rhino3d.com website.**

- **Rotate the mouse's scroll wheel downward** to zoom out. **①**

  - **Rotate the scroll wheel upward** and the view zooms in again. **②**

Fig. 1

Zooming the View - a Smoother Method

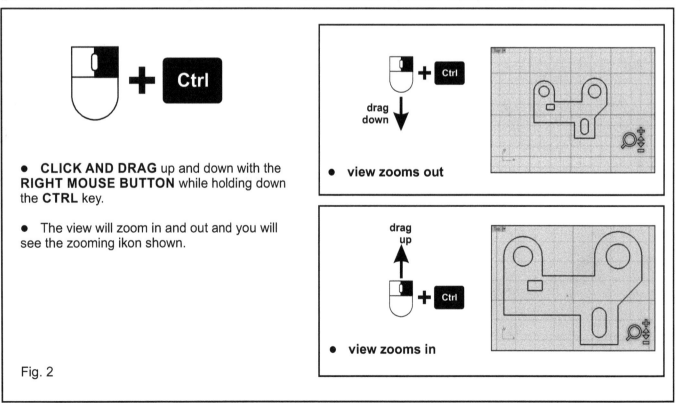

- **CLICK AND DRAG** up and down with the **RIGHT MOUSE BUTTON** while holding down the **CTRL** key.

- The view will zoom in and out and you will see the zooming ikon shown.

- **view zooms out**

- **view zooms in**

Fig. 2

Specific Zoom Commands

- **Standard tabbed toolbar.** Standard

- Select the small oblong line shown and click on the **Zoom Selected** command in the Standard Toolbar.

Zoom Selected
command

- The view will zoom in so that the selected object fills the viewport as shown.

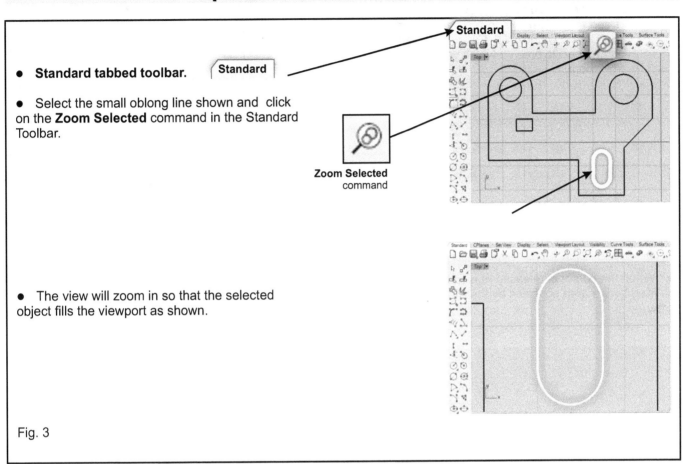

Fig. 3

- **LEFT-CLICK** on the **Zoom Extents** command.

Zoom Extents
command

- The view will zoom out so that you can see all of the objects in the workspace.

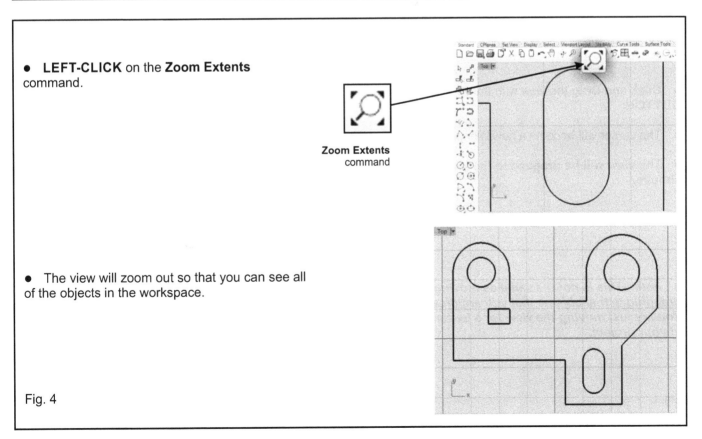

Fig. 4

- **Left-click** on the **Zoom Window** command.
  - **Drag a window to zoom** prompt:
    - Drag a window **❶ ❷** to delineate a specific area on which you want to zoom.

Zoom Window
command

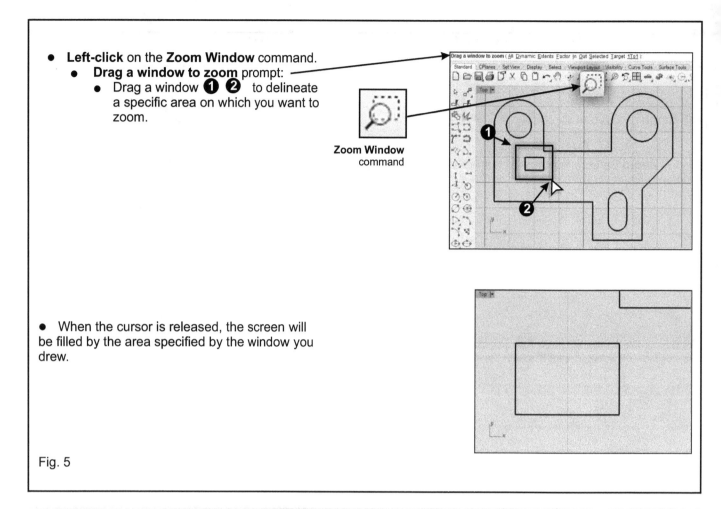

- When the cursor is released, the screen will be filled by the area specified by the window you drew.

Fig. 5

Moving ("Panning") the View

- **Click and Drag** the view with the **RIGHT MOUSE BUTTON.**

- The cursor will become a hand shape.

- **The view will be dragged to the location you choose.**

- *note: This is not the same as moving or dragging actual objects that you are creating. You are just moving the view for a better look at your project.*

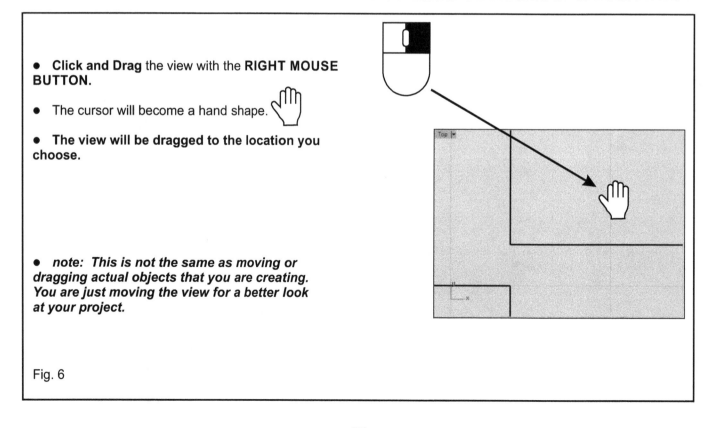

Fig. 6

Getting Back Into Top View
When you accidentally tip the view into 3D space

- Ways that you can accidentally tip the view into 3D space.
    - Panning with both shift and ctrl keys held down.
    - Clicking on the Perspective button in the Set View commands.

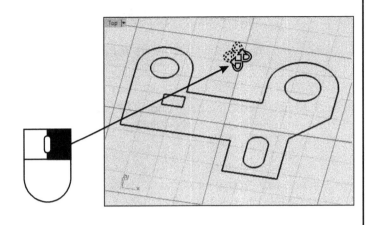

- In this illustration, clicking and dragging has resulted in a tipped, or rotated view.
    - **The hand cursor has been replaced by a rotate cursor when you try to Pan the view and the view will rotate and spin, rather than panning.**

Fig. 7

- *The Grid seems to be made of diagonal lines, instead of a horizontal and vertical configuration.*

- Click on the **Set View** tab to access the **Set View** toolbar.

- Click on the **Top View** command.

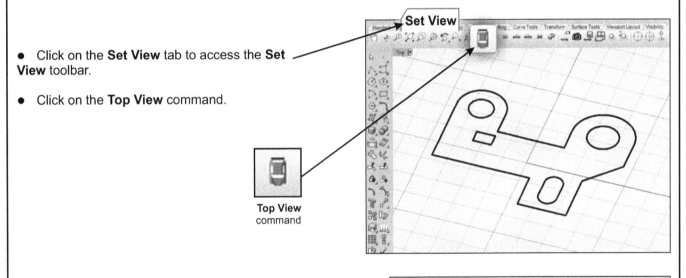

Top View
command

- The Top View has been restored.

- Notice how the grid looks squared up again because you are now looking straight down on it.

- **When you Pan, you will see the Hand Cursor once again.**

- This is called a *Plan, or Parallel, View.*

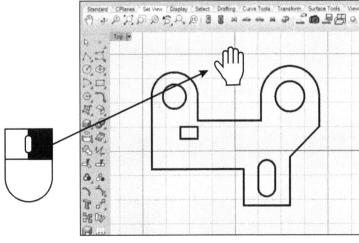

Fig. 8

Selecting and De-Selecting Objects
Clicking to Select and Using Selection Windows

Simple cursor selecting and de-selecting

- Open the **Filletex.3dm** file from the **rhinoforjewelry.com** website or the rhino3d.com website.

- **Left-click** to select the circle shown. ❶
- The circle will turn yellow, indicating that it has been selected.

- Click away ❷ from the selected object to immediately de-select it.
- The circle is now its original black color.

Fig. 1

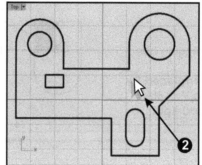
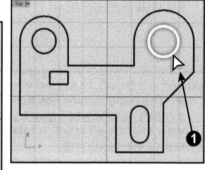

- Hold the **Shift** key down and click to multi-select each of the 4 objects shown. ❶

- Hold the **Ctrl** key down and select one of the selected objects to de-select it. ❷

Fig. 2

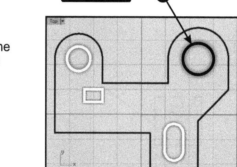
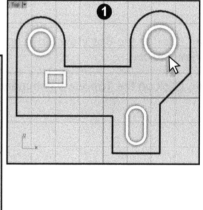

- Click and Drag (❶ & ❷), to create a window that intersects with two of the curves that make up the drawing as shown.
- This **"Crossing Window"** will have a dashed outline.

- The two curves that were touched by the selection window (**"Crossing Window"**) will be selected.

- Click away to de-select.

Fig. 3

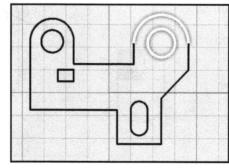
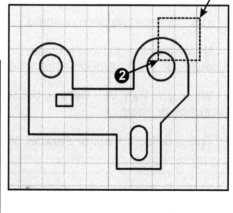

- Click and drag (**①** & **②**), to create a window that encloses the circle and square shown.

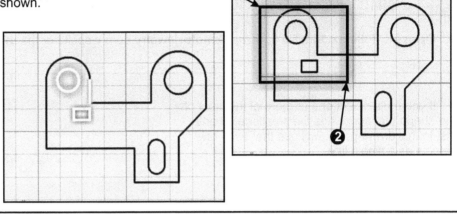

- Only the objects that were **totally enclosed** by the **Enclosing Window** will be selected.

- Click away to de-select

Fig. 4

The Selection Menu

- If you click to select an object at the point where it is very near to another object or objects, **①** Rhino will open a **Selection Menu.**

- The purpose of this menu is to ascertain which object you wanted to select.
  - When the **Selection Menu** appears, if you press **Enter,** the highlighted name at the top of the list will be selected **②** and the list will disappear.

- Click on the intersections of the two lines again to get the **Selection Menu** back.

- This time, roll the cursor over the list in the **Selection Menu** and notice how it's line or other object turns pink. **③**
  - If you click on that item on the list, it's object will turn yellow **④** because you will be choosing it for selection and the Selection Menu will disappear.

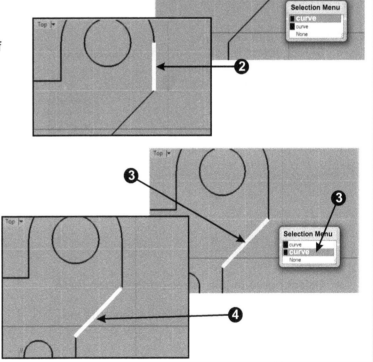

Fig. 5

- To avoid having to deal with the **Selection Menu** which is a nuisance because it holds up your workflow:
  - When you select an object, select it at a location in which it is not near to other objects, if possible.
  - The cursor in this illustration is located where it can select the line and you will not have to deal with a **Selection Menu.**

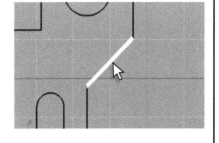

Fig. 6

Join Command
Joining curves together end to end to create a Polyline.

- Open the **Filletex.3dm** file from the **rhinoforjewelry.com** website or the rhino3d.com website.

- If you multi-select one or more of the lines of the shape that surrounds the smaller elements inside this drawing, you will see that each one selects as a single line.

- Click away to de-select.

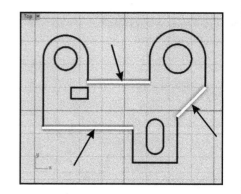

Fig. 1

- Click on the **Join** command.
  - **Select object to join. Curves, surfaces and polysurfaces must be open** prompt:
    - Select the line shown. ❶

Join
command

- **Select curve to join. Press Enter when done** prompt:
  - Select another line ❷ that is touching the previously selected curve.

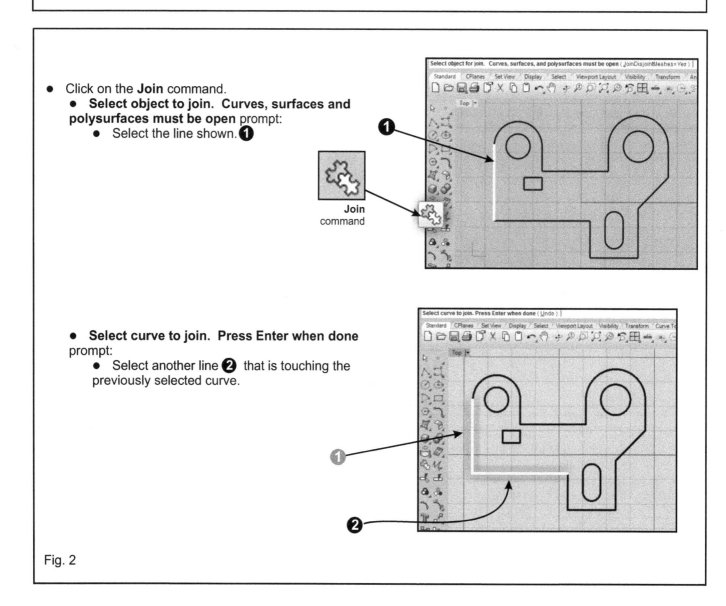

Fig. 2

- Continue to select curves as the **Command Line** prompts.

- If you select the last line in the frame drawing, the curves will all de-select because no more lines can be added to a **Closed Curve.**

- Notice that the History window is informing you that you have joined 12 curves into 1 closed curve.

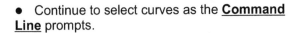

Fig. 3

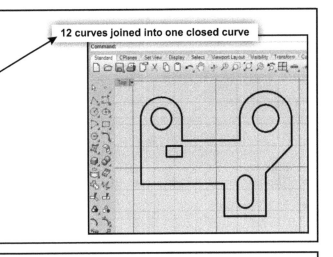

- If you press **Enter** before selecting all of the lines of the frame, the **Join** command will be finished and you will have created an **open curve.**

selected lines show an open curve

this line was not selected

Fig. 4

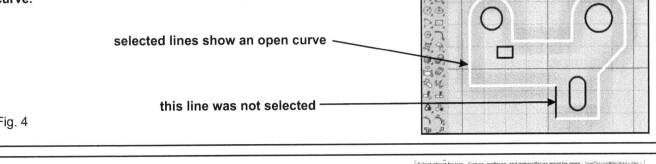

- **Standard tabbed toolbar.**   `Standard`

- Click on the **Join** command.
  - **Select object to join. Curve, Surfaces and polysurfaces must be open** prompt:
    - Click to select one of the lines as shown. ❶

Join command

- **Select object to join. Press Enter when done** prompt:
  - Click to select another line or curve that is not touching the first curve.❷

- The **Rhinoceros 7 Join** box will appear, warning that the ends of the two selected curves are not touching.
- Click the **No button** ❸ as it is not a good idea for Rhino to try to join these curves together as the result is usually not what you want.

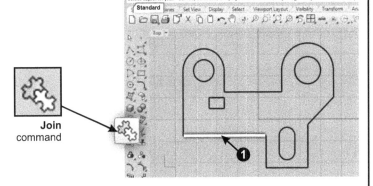

Fig. 5

32

Anatomy of a Line & a Polyline
Basic Rhino Line Commands

Line Command

- **Curve Tools tabbed toolbar.**
  - The curve tools group of command buttons will display on both **Curve Tools Toolbar** and the **Curve Drawing Sidebar**.

- **Top Viewport.** `Top|▼`

- **LEFT-CLICK** on the **Single Line** command.

Single Line command

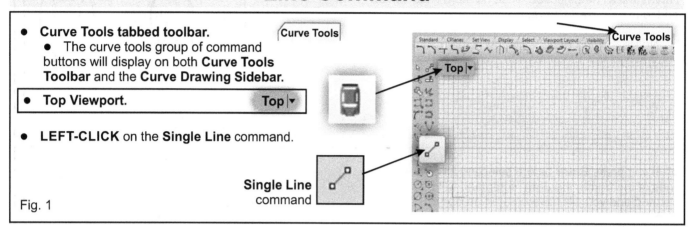

Fig. 1

- **Start of Line** prompt:
  - **LEFT-CLICK** on a location on the construction plane as shown. ❶
  - This will set the location of the start of your line.

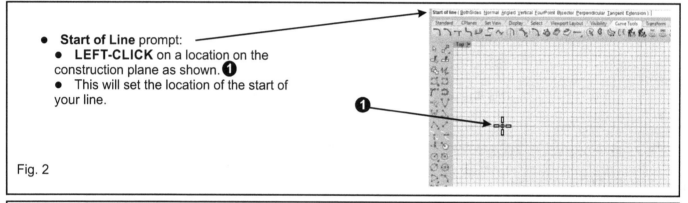

Fig. 2

- **End of Line** prompt:
  - Draw the cursor across the construction plane to arrive at the location that you want to choose for the end of the line
  - A "rubber band" preview line will follow the cursor.
  - **LEFT-CLICK** to set the location of the end of the line. ❷

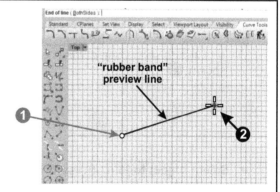

Fig. 3

- The new line has been created and the Line command is finished.

- Notice that the **<u>Command Line</u>** is now prompting for the next command.

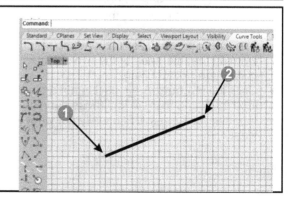

Fig. 4

Line with Specified Length of 15mm

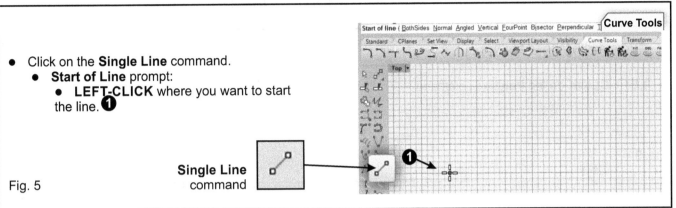

- Click on the **Single Line** command.
  - **Start of Line** prompt:
    - **LEFT-CLICK** where you want to start the line. ❶

Single Line
command

Fig. 5

- **End of Line** prompt:
  - Type the number "**15**" in the **Command Line**. ❷
  - Press the **"Enter"** key.

    - Note: after specifying a number in Rhino, **you always need to press "Enter" to tell Rhino that this is the number you want.**

Fig. 6

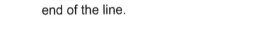
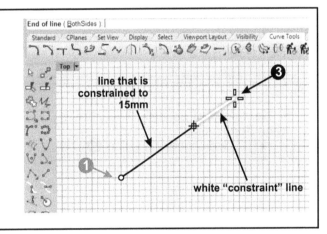

- **End of Line** prompt continues:
  - The line is now constrained to a length of 15mm.
  - If drag the cursor out past the end of the preview, you will see a **white constraint line.** ❸
  - **LEFT-CLICK** to set a location for the end of the line.

Fig. 7

- A 15mm line has been created.

- Notice that the **Command Line** is now prompting for the next command.

- The **Aligned dimension** added here is described in the chapter on **Applying Dimensions.**

Fig. 8

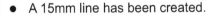

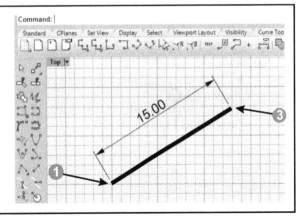

Polyline Command
A Polyline is a line with more than one segment.

- **Curve Tools tabbed toolbar.**   Curve Tools

- **LEFT-CLICK** on the **Polyline** command.

Polyline command

Fig. 9

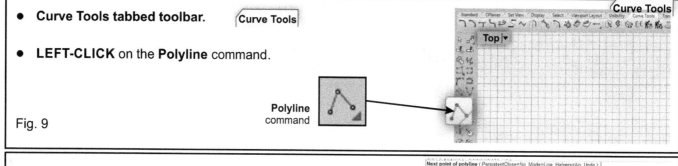

- **Start of Polyline** prompt:
  - **LEFT-CLICK** on the desired location for the start of the polyline. **1**

Fig. 10

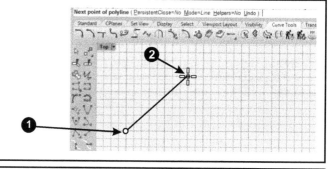

- **Next Point of polyline** prompt:
  - **LEFT-CLICK** on a location for the end of the first line segment. **2**

Fig. 11

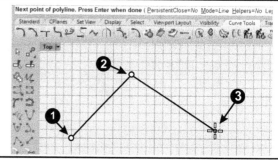

- **Next point of polyline. Press Enter when done** prompt:
  - Click on another location. **3**

Fig. 12

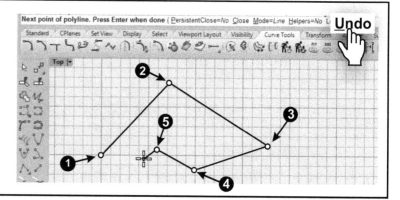

- **Next point of polyline. Press Enter when done** prompt:
  - Click on a couple more locations as shown. **4** **5**
  - Click on the **Undo** option in the **Command Line** as shown.

Fig. 13

- The most recent location **5** has been removed. If you continue to click on **Undo,** the locations will disappear in the order in which they were created.
- Click on the **Close** option in the **Command Line** as shown.

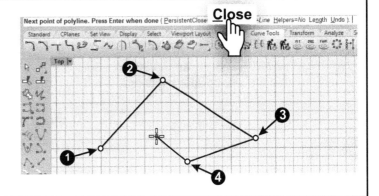

Fig. 14

- A new line segment has been created that joins the first line segment. **1**

- This is now a **closed polyline**.

new line segment

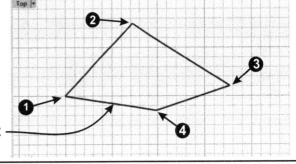

Fig. 15

Length & Angle Constraints

- **LEFT-CLICK** on the **Polyline** command on the Main Sidebar.
  - **Start of polyline** prompt:
    - Click to select a location for the start of the polyline. **1**

Polyline command

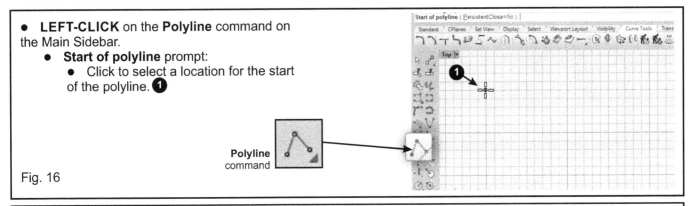

Fig. 16

- **Next point of polyline** prompt:
  - Type **"10"** in the **Command Line.**
  - Press **"Enter"** to tell Rhino that this is the number you want.

Next point of polyline (PersistentClose=*No* Mode=*Line* Helpers=*No* Undo) : **10**

Fig. 17

- Your line will be constrained to a length of **10mm**.

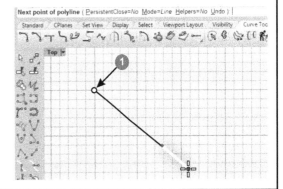

Fig. 18

- Now type **"<45"** in the **Command Line** and press **Enter.**
  - The **"<"** symbol is the upper case on the Comma key on your keyboard.

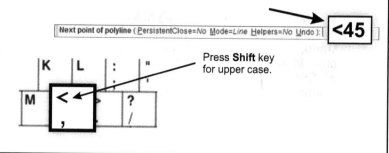

Press **Shift** key for upper case.

Fig. 19

- Now the line will not only be constrained to a length of 10mm but will also be constrained to a 45° angle.

- Draw the cursor around so that the line's angle is as shown and click to set location. ❷

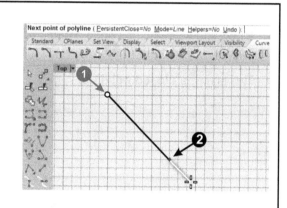

Fig. 20

- Type **"10"** again and press **"Enter"**.
- Type **"<45"** again and press **"Enter"**.
- Move the cursor around to choose the angle shown .
- Click to set the location of the end of the line segment as before. ❸

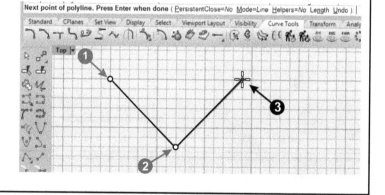

Fig. 21

- **Next point of polyline. Press Enter when done** prompt:
  - Press **"Enter"** to end the command.
  - The result is an **Open Polyline.**

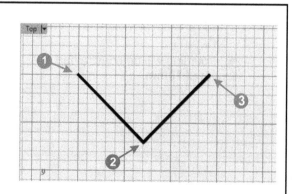

Fig. 22

Anatomy of a Circle
Basic Rhino Line Commands

Circle: Center, Radius command

- **Curve Tools tabbed toolbar**.

  Curve Tools

- **LEFT-CLICK** on the **Circle: Center, Radius** command.

Circle: Center, Radius command

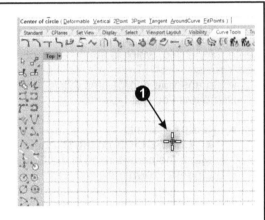

Fig. 1

- **Center of circle** prompt:
  - Left-click to set the desired location of the center of the circle. **①**

Fig. 2

- **Radius** prompt:
  - Draw the cursor out and notice that the preview of the circle follows it.
  - **LEFT-CLICK** to set the radius of the circle. **②**

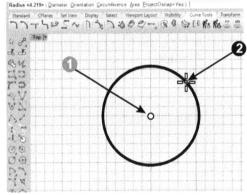

- The command is ended.

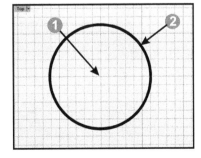

Fig. 3

Creating a Circle with a Specified Radius or Diameter

- **Curve Tools tabbed toolbar**.

- **LEFT-CLICK** on the **Circle: Center, Radius** command.

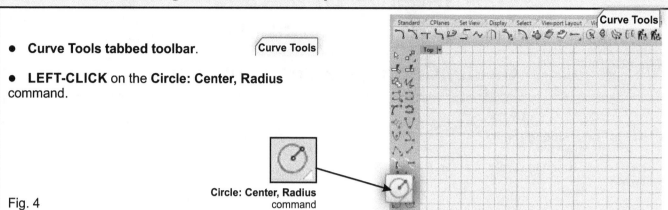

Circle: Center, Radius
command

Fig. 4

- **Center of circle** prompt:
  - Type **"0"** in the **Command Line.**
  - Press **"Enter"**.

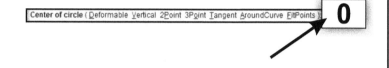

Fig. 5

- The circle is now centered around the exact center of the grid, which is the meeting of the X and Y axes.
  - In absolute coordinates this is "0,0". Rhino lets you just type **"0"**.

  - **Radius** prompt:
    - **LEFT-CLICK** on the **Diameter** option within the parentheses in the **Command Line** as shown.

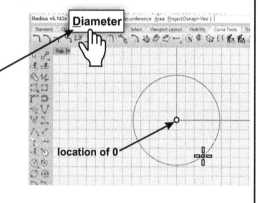

Fig. 6

- **Diameter** prompt:
  - You are now being prompted for the **Diameter**, not the Radius because you changed the option in the Command Line.
  - Type **"15"** in the **Command Line** and press **"Enter"**.

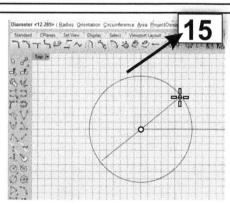

Fig. 7

- You have created a circle around "0" with a diameter of 15mm.

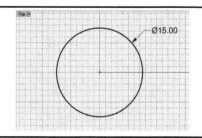

Fig. 8

Circle: Diameter command
A circle command defined by the diameter.

- **LEFT-CLICK** on the **Circle:** Diameter command.

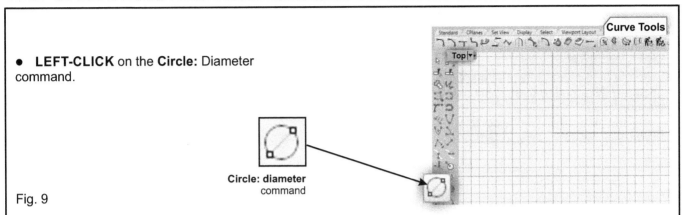

Circle: diameter
command

Fig. 9

- **Start of diameter** prompt:
  - Type a **"0"** in the **Command Line** and press **"Enter"**.

Start of diameter (Vertical): **0**

Fig. 10

- The start of the circle passes exactly through "0" ❶

- **End of diameter** prompt:
  - When you pull out the cursor, notice that the space between it and the start point is defined by the **Diameter** or the circle, not the Radius.
  - Type **"15"** in the **Command Line** and press **"Enter"**.

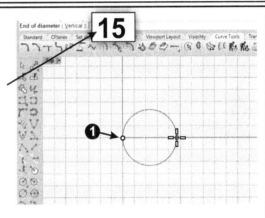

Fig. 11

- **End of diameter** prompt continues:
  - The diameter of the circle is constrained to 15mm.
  - **LEFT-CLICK** on the location that places the circle the way you want it to be.

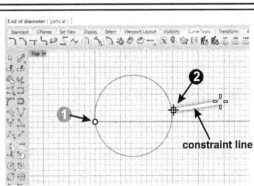

constraint line

Fig. 12

- A 15mm diameter circle has been created by defining the start and end points of its diameter as well as the exact measurement of the diameter.

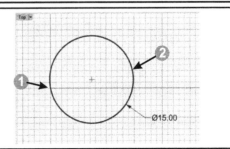

Ø15.00

Fig. 13

Ortho and Grid Snap Modes
Constraining the Movement of the Cursor

Ortho Mode

- On the Status Bar at the bottom of the workspace, click on the **Ortho** button to turn on **Ortho mode.**
  - The button will change color, showing that you will now be working in **Ortho mode.**

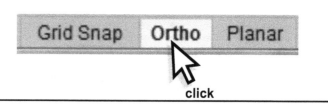

click

Fig. 1

- **Curve Tools tabbed toolbar.**

- Click on the **Polyline** command and start to click on locations for your line segments.

- Notice that you can only create lines that are either perfectly horizontal or perfectly vertical.

- **Ortho** is constraining the placement of the lines to 90° directions.
  - Your settings may allow you to draw lines in a 45° directions as well.

Polyline
command

Fig. 2

- Click on the **Ortho** button again to *toggle off Ortho mode.*
  - Notice that the appearance of the **Ortho** button reverts to its original gray color.

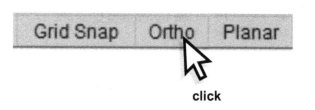

click

Fig. 3

- Click to create some more line segments and you will see that you are not longer constrained by **Ortho.**
- If you toggle **Ortho** on again, line segments that you will create will again be constrained to 90° directions

  - Other ways to *Toggle Ortho on and off.*

    - *Tapping the F8 key.* F8

    - *Holding down and releasing the Shift key to temporarily toggle ortho on or off.*

Shift

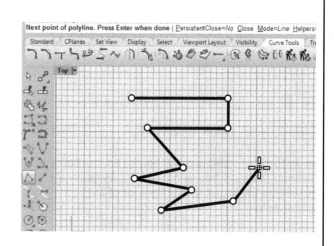

Fig. 4

Grid Snap Mode

- On the Status Bar at the bottom of the workspace, click on the **Grid Snap** button to turn on **Grid Snap mode.**
    - The button will change color, showing that you will now be working in **Grid Snap mode.**

Fig. 5

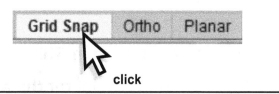

click

- Click on the **Polyline** command.
    - **Start of polyline** prompt:
        - When you start clicking on locations for your line segments, notice that *you can only click on GRID INTERSECTIONS.*

Fig. 6

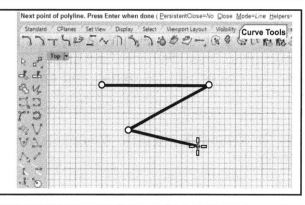

- **LEFT-CLICK** on the **Grid Snap** button again to toggle off **Grid Snap** mode.
    - Notice that the appearance of the **Grid Snap** button reverts to its original gray color.

Fig. 7

click

- Click on some more locations.

- Notice that now that the last 4 clicks are in locations that were not constrained to grid intersections because *Grid Snap was toggled off.*

- If you toggle **Grid Snap** on again, any lines that you continue to create, will once again be constrained to grid intersections.

Fig. 8

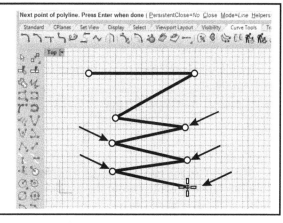

- **Grid Snap** makes certain tasks very easy.

- The polylines in the illustration were all made with easy accuracy in **Grid Snap** mode.

- Another way to *Toggle Grid Snap on and off:*

    - *Tapping the F8 key.* **F9**

Fig. 9

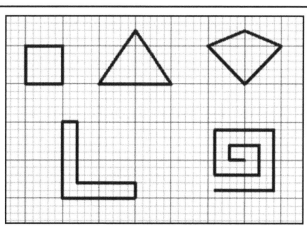

42

Object Snap "OSNAP"
Accurate Placement of Objects in Relation to Each Other

- **There is no function in Rhino that is more important than Object Snap.**

- **Object Snap is crucial for the accuracy of drawings and models.**

- Save this file as **osnap & analysis.3dm.** We will use this file again in the next exercise for measuring lines, distances and angles.
- You can access the **osnap and analysis** file on the **rhinoforjewelry.com** website.

- The **Object Snap** pane will appear when you click on the **Osnap button** in the **Status Bar** as shown.

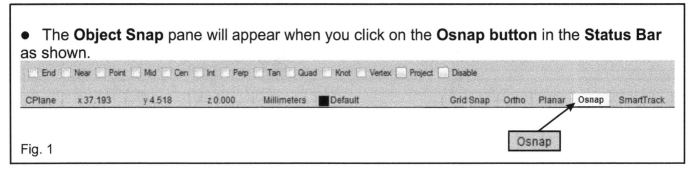

Fig. 1

- **Curve Tools tabbed toolbar.**

- Toggle on **Grid Snap** at the bottom of the workspace.

- Use the **Circle: center, radius** and the **Polyline** commands to create the simple circles and squares shown.
  - **Circles: 10mm diameter**
  - **Squares: 10mm sides**
  - **placement: All objects are 5mm apart.**

- **Grid Snap** makes these objects easy to create.

- Toggle off **Grid Snap** when you are done creating the circles and squares.

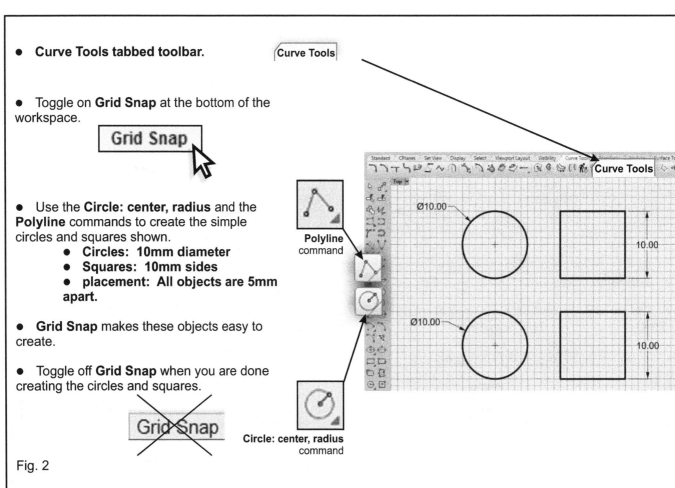

Fig. 2

- **LEFT-CLICK** on the box or text of **End Osnap** (**Endpoint Object Snap**) to toggle it on. A little check mark will appear in the box as shown.

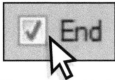

- Use the **Line** command to draw a line from the corners of the two boxes as shown.

- As the cursor is drawn over the corners of the squares, the cursor will be pulled to them (will "snap" to them) - the corners are **End Points** of lines that make up the squares.
    - Click for the locations of the start and end of the line **when you see the little tool-tip that says "End".** ❶ & ❷

- The Line's placement will accurately start and end exactly on the end points that the cursor snapped to.

Fig. 3

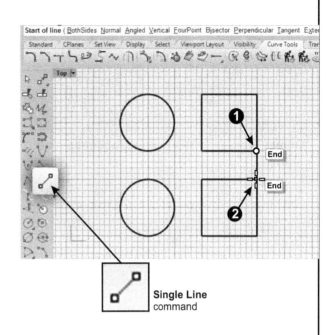

Single Line command

- Now, click on the box or text of **Mid Osnap (Midpoint Object Snap)** to toggle it on.

- Use the **Line** command to draw a line that connects an **end point** and a **mid point** as shown. ❶ & ❷

Fig. 4

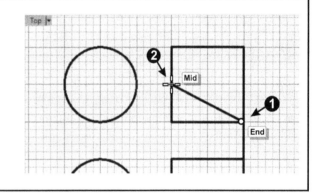

- Click on **Cen osnap (Center Object Snap)** to toggle it on.

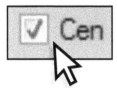

- Use the **Line** command to draw a line from the center of the lower circle to the center of the lower square as shown.

- *NOTE: Center Snap requires you to guide the cursor over the line that defines the circle or square.*

- *Click to set start and end of line ONLY when you see the little* Cen *tool-tip which is telling you that you are snapping to the center of the object.*

Fig. 5

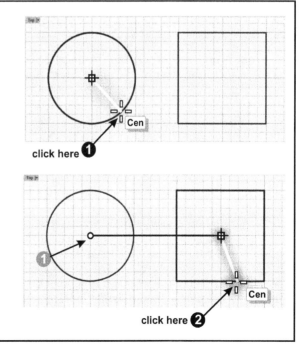

click here ❶

click here ❷

- Click again on the enabled object snaps to *toggle them off. The check marks will disappear.*

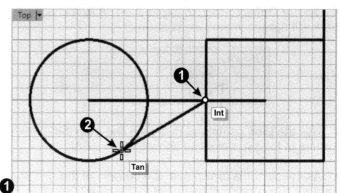

- Then toggle on both **Int osnap (Intersection Object Snap)** and **Tan osnap (Tangent Object Snap)**.

- Create a **Line** that starts at the intersection shown ❶ and ends at the tangent point on the circle shown. ❷

Fig. 6

- **RIGHT-CLICK** on the **Quad osnap (Quadrant Object Snap)**.

right-click

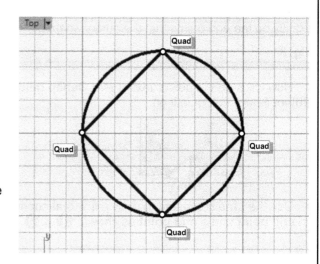

- **Quad Osnap** will be turned on and the other object snaps will be disabled because you right-clicked on one of them.

- Create a **Polyline** that connects all 4 **Quad** points of the top circle as shown.

- The **Quad** points of a circle, oval, arc or wavy curve are the locations that are at the furthest extant of the X and Y grid directions.

Fig. 7

- Toggle on the **Near Osnap (Near to Object Snap)** and **Perp Osnap (Perpendicular Object Snap)**.

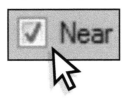 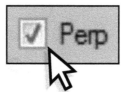

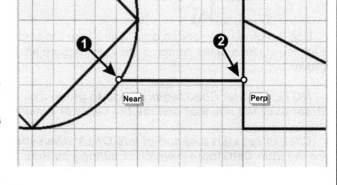

- Create a **Line** that starts somewhere on the curve of the top circle as shown. ❶
  - **Near Osnap** simply means that the cursor is in contact to an object but the exact location is not set until you click to set it.

- The end of the line will snap to a point that creates a line that is perfectly perpendicular to it's ending location. ❷

Fig. 8

Analysis Commands
Measuring Length, distance, Angle, Radius and Diameter

Measuring the Length of a Line

- Open your Rhino file, **osnap & analysis.3dm** from the previous **Object Snap** chapter.

- Access the **Analyze tabbed toolbar.**
  - Ref: **"Adding Tabbed Toolbars to the Workspace"** in the **The Rhino Workspace** chapter.

- **LEFT-CLICK** on the **Length** command.

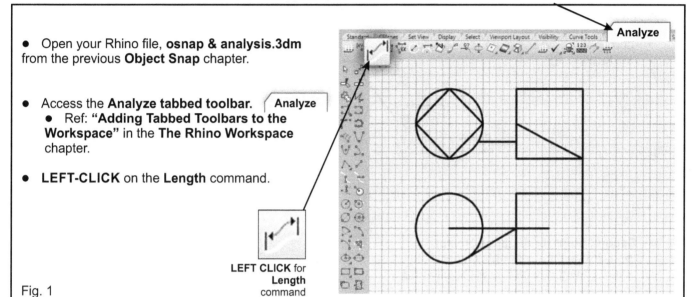

LEFT CLICK for **Length** command

Fig. 1

- **Select curves to measure** prompt:
  - Select the diagonal line in the upper right square as shown.
  - Press **Enter.**

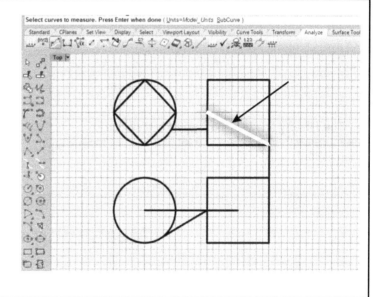

Fig. 2

- The History window will report the exact length of the line you just selected.

- *Note: If the History line only displays one line of text, drag the lower edge of the Command Line downward until three lines or more of text are visible in the History Line.*

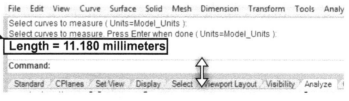

Length = 11.180 millimeters

click and drag for more lines to show in the History window

Fig. 3

Measuring the Distance Between Two Points

- To measure the **Distance between two locations**, **LEFT-CLICK** on the **Distance** command in the **Analyze tabbed toolbar**.

    - **First point for distance** prompt:
        - Use **End Osnap** to snap to the lower corner of the lower square and click to set location. ❶

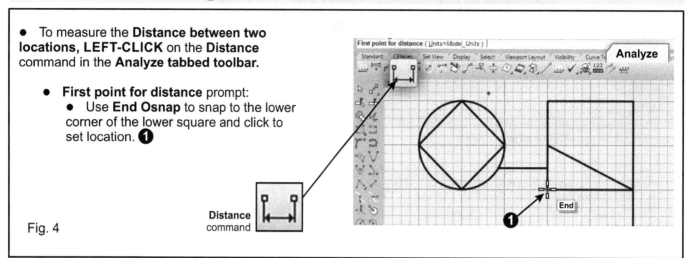

Distance command

Fig. 4

- **Second point for distance** prompt:
    - Click on the upper right corner of the same square and click to set location. ❷

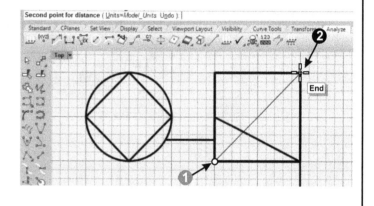

Fig. 5

- The History line will show you the distance measurement (in addition to a lot of extra information!)

Fig. 6

| CPlane angles and deltas: | xy = 45.000 elevation = 0.000 | dx = 10.000 dy = 10.000 dz = 0.000 |

Distance = 14.142 millimeters

Command:

Measuring an Angle

- To measure the **Angle formed by two lines**, **LEFT-CLICK** on the **Angle** command in the **Analyze tabbed toolbar**.
    - **Start of first line** prompt:
        - Snap to the end point of the diagonal line and click to set location. ❶

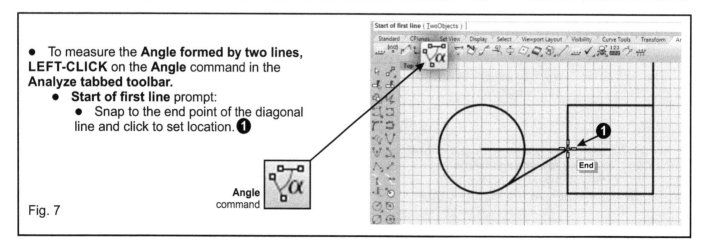

Angle command

Fig. 7

- **End of first line** prompt:
  - Snap to the other **end** of the diagonal line and click to set location. ❷

Fig. 8

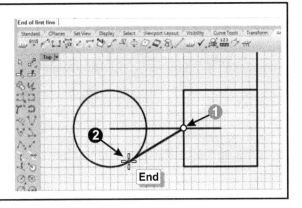

- **Start of second line** prompt:
  - Click on the **end** of the start of the horizontal line. ❸
  - *This is the same location as the start of the first line.*

Fig. 9

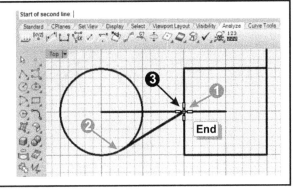

- **End of second line** prompt:
  - Snap to the **end** of the second line and click to set location. ❹
  - The History line will report the measurement of the angle.

  Start of second line:
  End of second line:
  Angle = 30
  Command:

Fig. 10

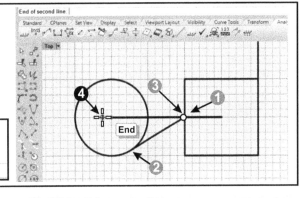

Measuring Diameter & Radius

Radius = 5.000
Diameter = 10.000

- Select one of the circles and **LEFT-CLICK** on the **Measure Diameter** command.

- The History line will display both the Radius and the Diameter of the selected circle.

Fig. 11

Measure Diameter
command

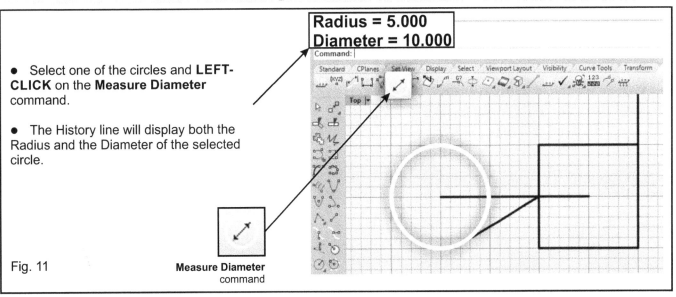

Applying Dimensions
Applying Dimensions and Adjusting Dimension Settings

- Open your previously saved file, **osnap & analysis.3dm.**

- Click on the **Drafting tabbed toolbar.**

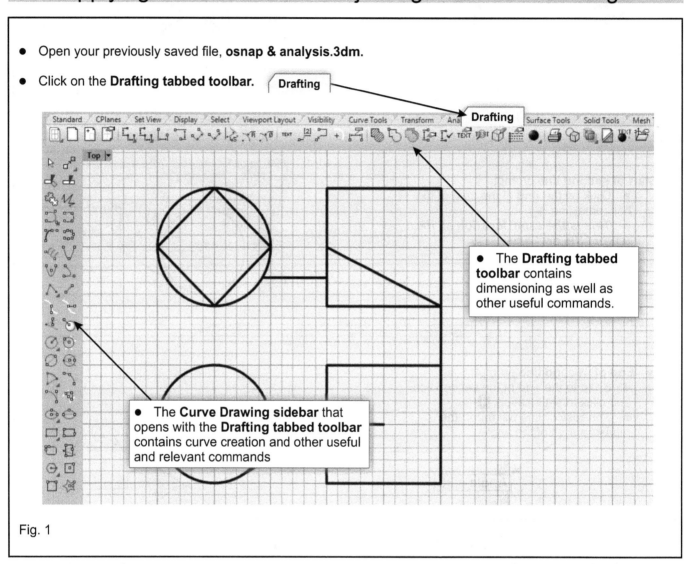

- The **Drafting tabbed toolbar** contains dimensioning as well as other useful commands.

- The **Curve Drawing sidebar** that opens with the **Drafting tabbed toolbar** contains curve creation and other useful and relevant commands

Fig. 1

Horizontal and Vertical Dimensioning

- Make sure that **End Osnap** is enabled.

✔ End

- **LEFT CLICK** on the **Linear Dimension** command as shown.

LEFT CLICK for **Linear Dimension** command

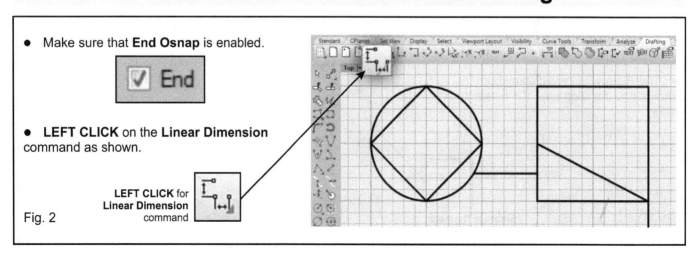

Fig. 2

- **First dimension point** prompt:
  - Snap to the one of the corners - **End Osnap** will work here because of the two lines that make up the corner. ❶

Fig. 3

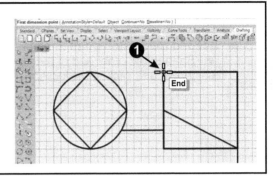

- **Second dimension point** prompt:
  - Snap to the other **End** of the line that you want to dimension and click to set location. ❷

Fig. 4

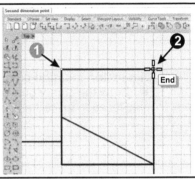

- **Dimension location** prompt:
  - Pull the cursor outward and click to set the location of the extension lines and text. ❸

Fig. 5

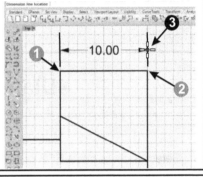

- Click on the same command again to get a vertical dimension, using **End Osnap** to click on the locations ❶ and ❷ . Click on location ❸ for placement of text and extension lines.

Fig. 6

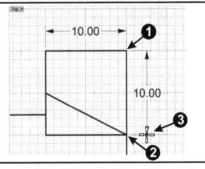

Diagonal Dimensioning - Aligned Dimension command

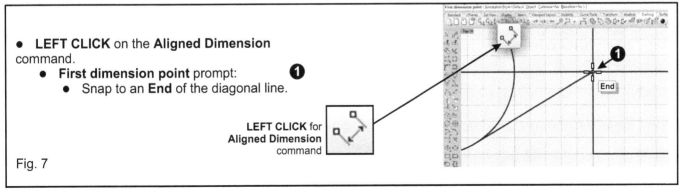

- **LEFT CLICK** on the **Aligned Dimension** command.
  - **First dimension point** prompt: ❶
    - Snap to an **End** of the diagonal line.

LEFT CLICK for
Aligned Dimension
command

Fig. 7

- **Second dimension point** prompt:
  - Snap to the other end of the diagonal line as shown and click to set location. **2**

Fig. 8

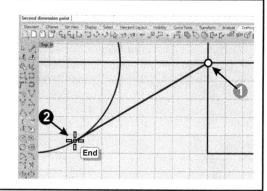

- **Dimension location** prompt:
  - Draw the cursor outward and click to set final location for text and extension lines. **3**

Fig. 9

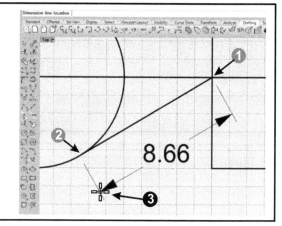

Diameter & Radius Dimensioning

- Select a circle and **LEFT CLICK** on the **Diameter Dimension** command.

LEFT CLICK for
Diameter Dimension
command

Fig. 10

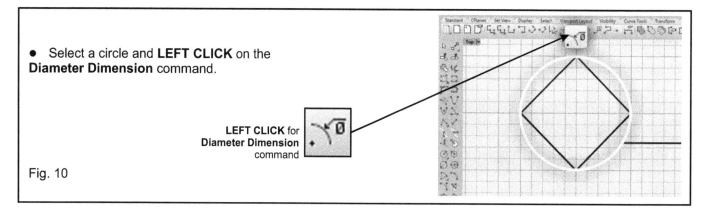

- **Diameter location** prompt:
  - Draw the cursor out and click to set desired location of the dimension text and extension line.

Fig. 11

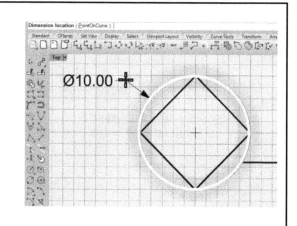

- **LEFT CLICK** on the **Radial Dimension** command to get a dimension for the **Radius** of the circle.

LEFT CLICK for
Radial Dimension
command

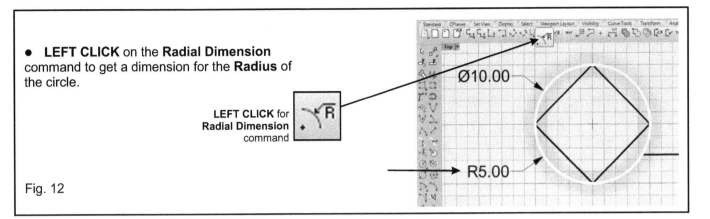

Fig. 12

Angle Dimensioning

- **LEFT CLICK** to select the **Angle Dimension** command.
  - **Select arc or first line** prompt:
    - Click to select the line shown. **1**

LEFT CLICK for
Angle Dimension
command

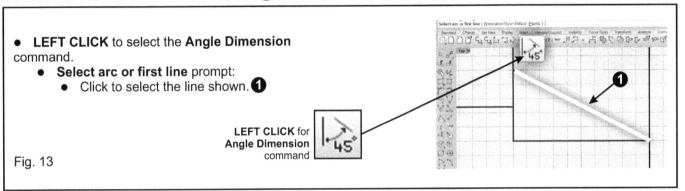

Fig. 13

- **Select second line** prompt:
  - Click on the line shown. **2**
    - The rest of the square polyline will also select because all of the segments are joined together.

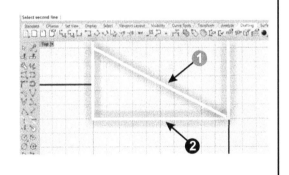

Fig. 14

- **Dimension location** prompt:
  - Pull the cursor outward and click on the desired location. **3**

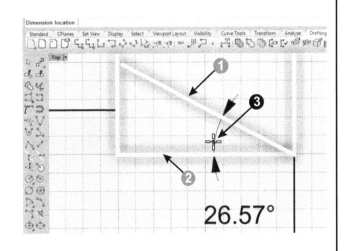

Fig. 15

Dimension Settings

- Click to open the **Tools** drop-down on the **Menu Bar** at the top of the workspace. ❶

- Click on the **Options** category at the bottom of the drop-down. ❷

- The **Rhino Options** box will open.

- Click to open the **Annotation Styles** category. ❶
  - The default annotation styles will be listed.
    - Click to select the **Millimeter Small** annotation style ❷ to make it current.

    - Click to **uncheck** the "**Enable layout space scaling**" option. ❸
      - This a better setting with layouts, which will be covered later in this book.

- Click on the **Edit button** ❹ to begin editing the current style.

- The **Millimeter Small** style window will show a column of setting categories.

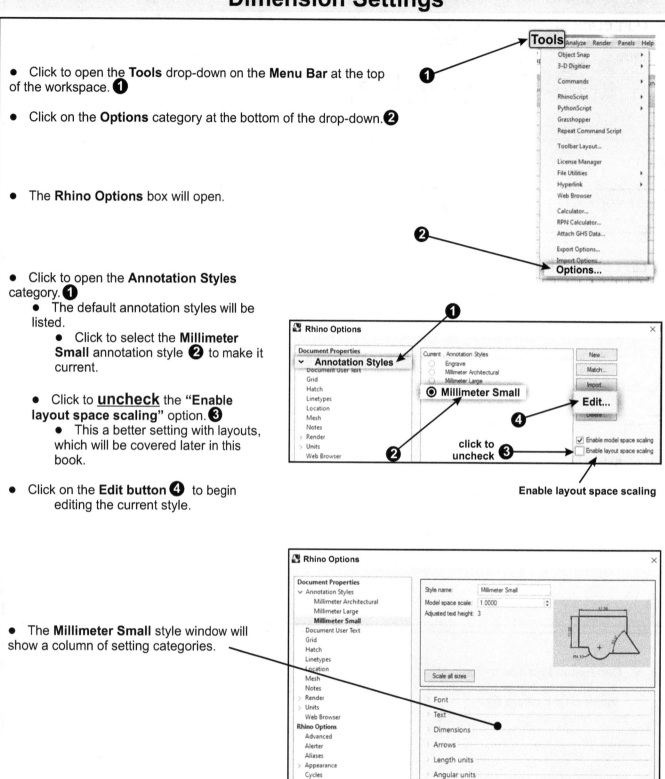

Enable layout space scaling

Fig. 16

53

- Click to open the **Font** window. **1**
  - Important settings are **Font** **2** and **Height.** **3**

- The preview illustration **4** in the upper right will update as you change the style settings.

- There are a lot of settings here. To get an explanation of each one, click on the **Help button** **5** at the bottom of the options box.

Fig. 17

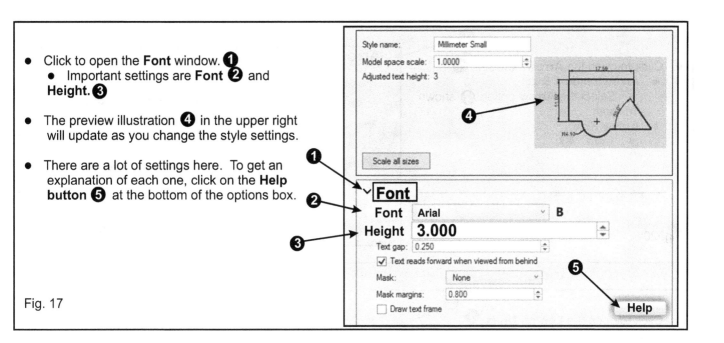

- Click to open the **Text** category. **1**
  - It is good to check the **Horizontal to View** option **2** for viewing dimension text in perspective viewports when working in 3d space.

Fig. 18

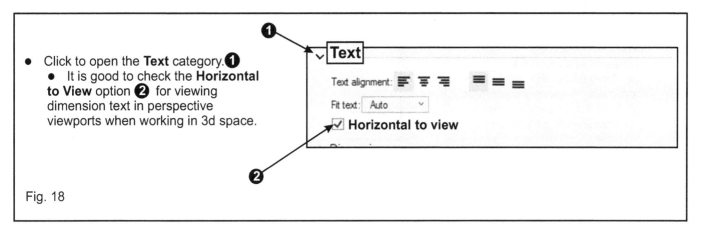

- Click to open the **Dimensions** category **1**
  - Note the settings for **Dimension Text** **2** and **Radial Dimension Text (angle dimensions).** **3**
    - Both boxes are checked for **Horizontal to View** **4** which means the text will always display horizontally.
    - **In Line** **5** means that the dimension text will be displayed within the central line of the dimension if enough space is available.

Fig. 19

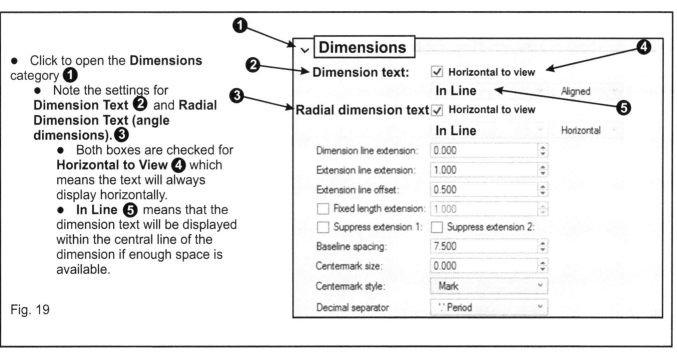

- Click to open the **Arrows** window. **1**
  - **Arrowheads 1 & 2:**
    - Select the **Arrow** option **2** shown for both.
  - **Arrow Size:**
    - **1mm. 3**

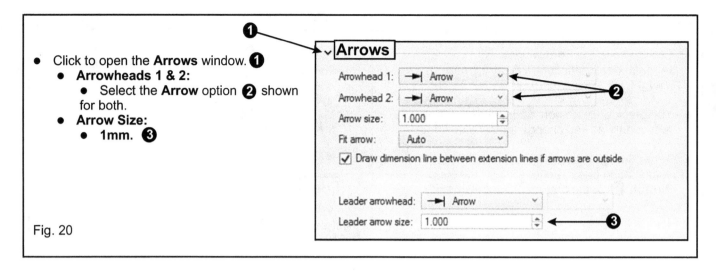

Fig. 20

- Click to open the **Length Units 1** category.
  - **Units - formats 2**
    - Designates the units for decimal or fractional format. Choose the **Model units - decimal** option.**3**
  - **Linear Resolution 4**
    - Designates the amount of precision in the measurements - note that in this setting, the measurement is accurate to .01mm.

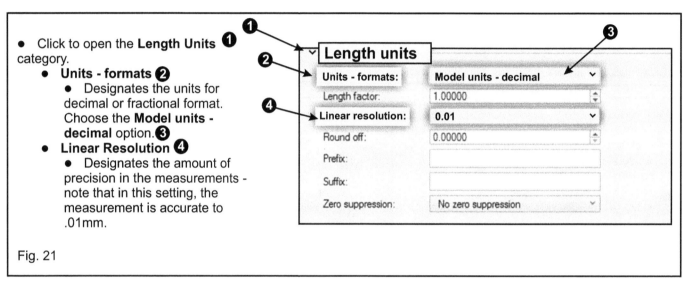

Fig. 21

Adding a New Dimension Style

- Create a horizontal line with a length of **184.15mm**.

- A new dimension style will be needed so that dimensioning this line will express a value in inches instead of millimeters.

Fig. 22

- Access the **Rhino Options** box again.

- Click on the **Annotation Styles** category ❶ to show default list of annotation styles.❷

- The next step will be to add a new dimension style that will read inches instead of millimeters.

- Click on the **New button.**❸

Fig. 23

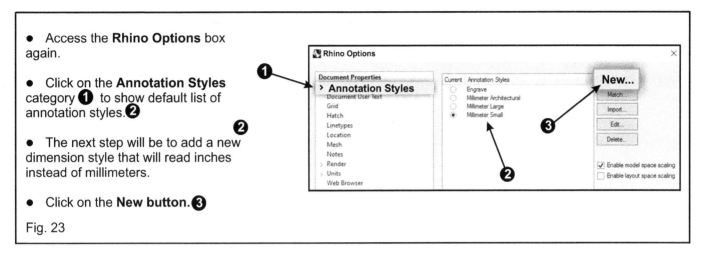

- The **New Annotation Style** box will open.

- Create a name for the new annotation style. ❶

- Select the **(built in) Template Inch Fractional**❷ annotation style which is one of Rhino's annotation templates.

- Click on the **OK button.** ❸

Fig. 24

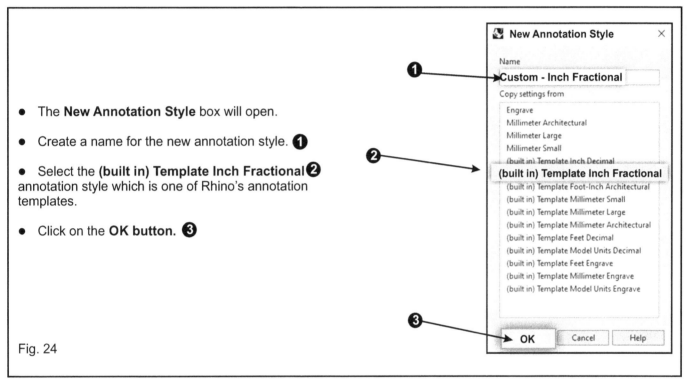

- The new style template ❶ will be added to the Annotation Styles list.

- Click on the radio button ❷ to make the **Template Inch Fractional** annotation style current.

Fig. 25

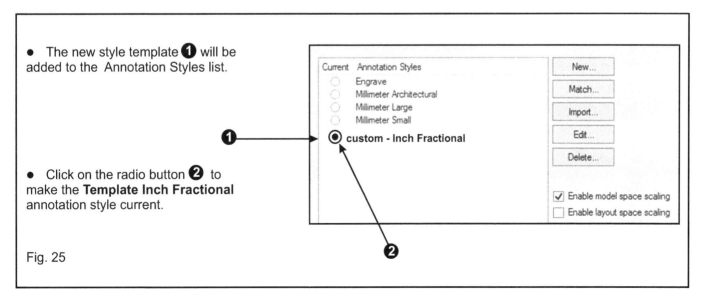

- After you have made the new annotation style current, ❶ click on the **Edit button.** ❷

Fig. 26   Template Inch Fractional ❶

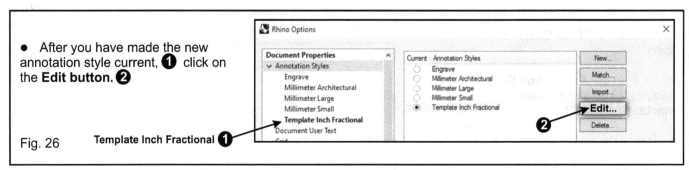

- **Font** height: **.5mm**

Fig. 27

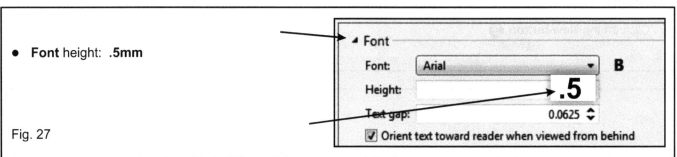

- **Dimensions** ❶
  - **Dimension text:** ❷
    - **In Line** ❸

Fig. 28

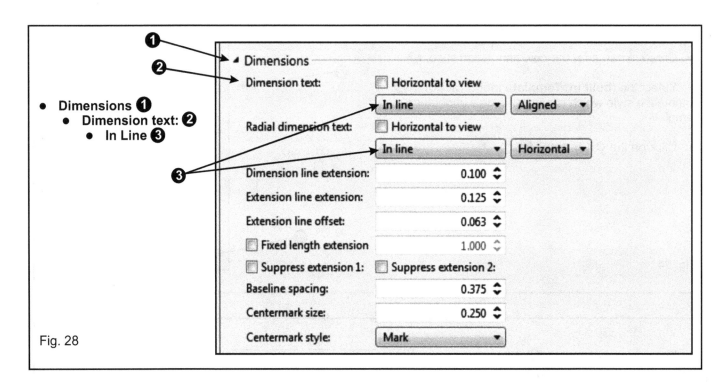

- **Arrows:** ❶
  - **Arrowheads:**
    - **Arrowheads:** ❷
  - **Arrow Size:**
    - **.5** ❸

Fig. 29

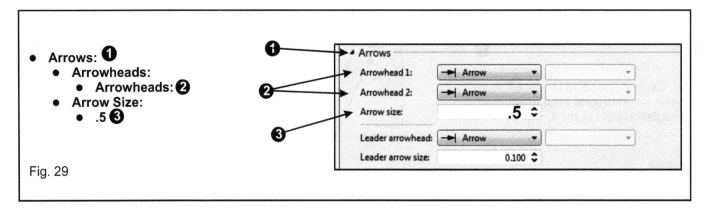

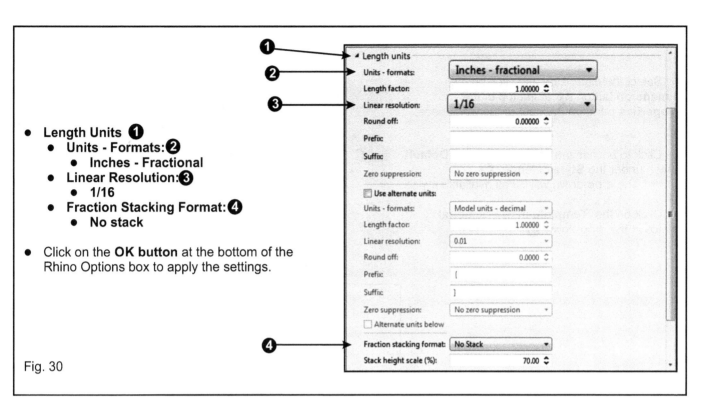

- **Length Units ❶**
  - **Units - Formats:❷**
    - **Inches - Fractional**
  - **Linear Resolution:❸**
    - **1/16**
  - **Fraction Stacking Format:❹**
    - **No stack**

- Click on the **OK button** at the bottom of the Rhino Options box to apply the settings.

Fig. 30

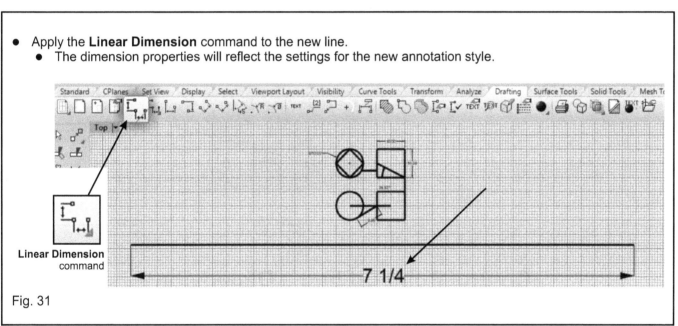

- Apply the **Linear Dimension** command to the new line.
  - The dimension properties will reflect the settings for the new annotation style.

Linear Dimension command

Fig. 31

Changing the Style of a Dimension

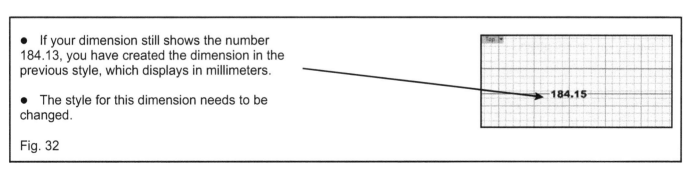

- If your dimension still shows the number 184.13, you have created the dimension in the previous style, which displays in millimeters.

- The style for this dimension needs to be changed.

Fig. 32

- Select the dimension and click on the **Dimension** button ❶ at the top of the **Properties** pane on the right of the workspace.

- Click to access the drop-down on the **Default** button under the **Style category.** ❷
    - The drop-down will list all available styles.

- Click on the **Template Inch Fractional** choice in the drop-down. ❸

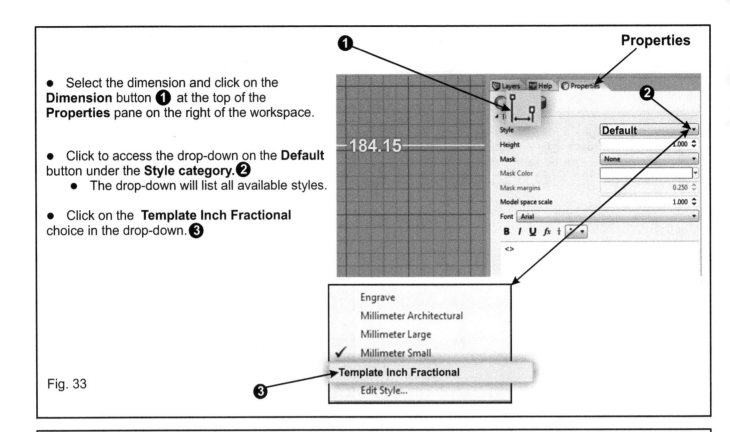

Fig. 33

- The dimension settings will show that the selected dimension has been changed to the **Template Inch Fractional** style.

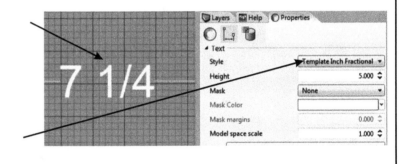

Fig. 34

Control Point Editing a Dimension

- Select the diagonal **Aligned Dimension** and press the **F10 Hotkey** to turn on that dimension's control points.
    - The **F10** key is a convenient shortcut for turning on control points.

F10

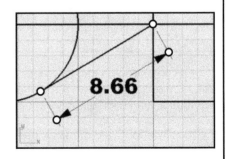

Fig. 35

- The 5 control points of the dimension will appear.

- Select the three control points shown.

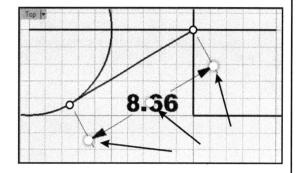

- Drag the control points and click to set a new location for the text and extension lines.

- Click away to de-select.

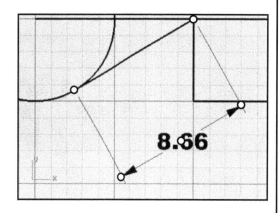

Fig. 36

- Select the single point over the text.

- Drag the text and click to set new location.

- Press the **Esc** key a couple of times to turn off control points.

Esc

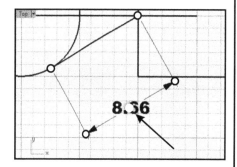

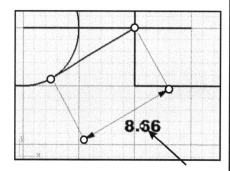

Fig. 37

- Dimensioning small distances can result in the dimension text being offset to the top or side.

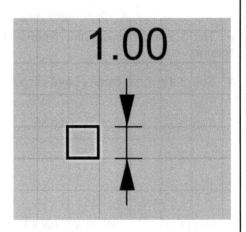

- Select the dimension and press the **F10 hotkey** to turn on its control points.

F10

- Select the middle of three control points ❶ between the dimension arrows.

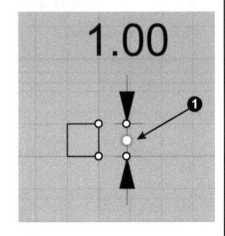

Fig. 38

- When you **Drag** the selected control point, the text will jump to a position under the cursor. ❷

- You can move the dimension text to a location of your choosing.

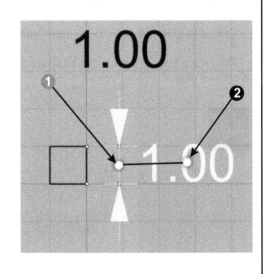

- Press the **Esc key** a couple of times to de-select and turn off control points.

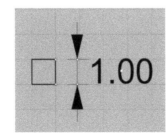

Fig. 39

Editing a Dimension Text

- **Double-click** on the dimension text **❶** and the **Edit Linear Dimension** text box will open. **❷**

- The two symbols **<>** represent the existing text. **❸**

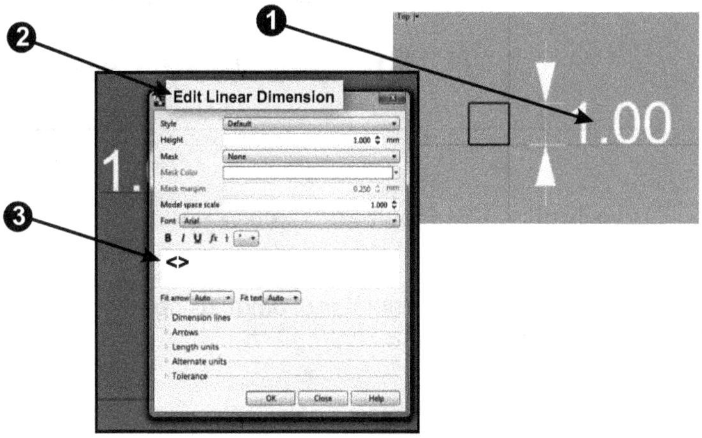

- Select the two symbols and type in **1mm.❸** This will replace the existing text with the text that you have just typed in.

- Notice other options to change the text format and size, including arrow size and other dimension characteristics.

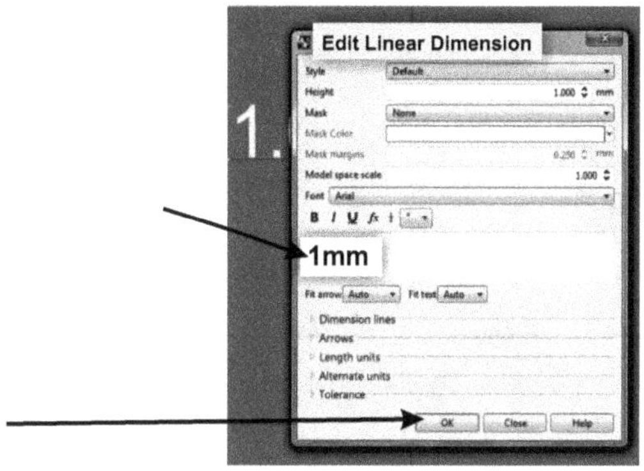

- Click the OK button to close the box.

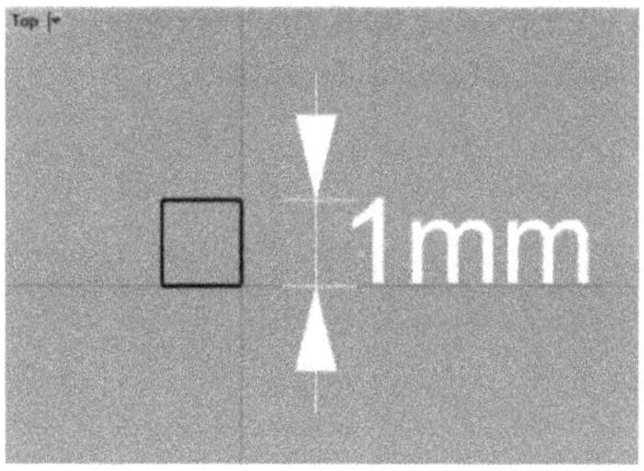

- The dimension text has been edited.

Fig. 40

Move & Copy Commands
Click & Drag, Move, Copy

Simple Move with "Click & Drag"

- **Curve Tools tabbed toolbar.**   Curve Tools

- Create a circle with a diameter of 8mm, using one of the **Circle** commands.

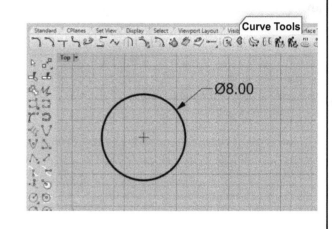

Fig. 1

- **LEFT-CLICK** on the circle and start dragging it in the desired direction.

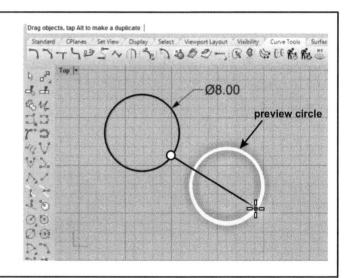

Fig. 2

- Release the cursor, when you have dragged and dropped the object to the desired location.

- The circle has been moved to a new location.

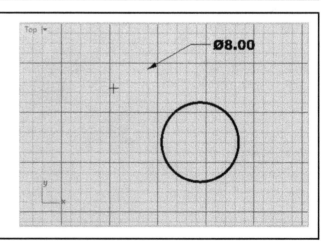

Fig. 3

Move Command

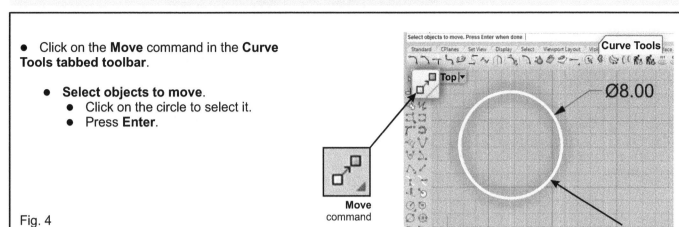

- Click on the **Move** command in the **Curve Tools tabbed toolbar**.

  - **Select objects to move**.
    - Click on the circle to select it.
    - Press **Enter**.

Fig. 4

- **Point to move from** prompt:
  - Snap to the bottom **Quad** point of the circle and **left-click.** ❶

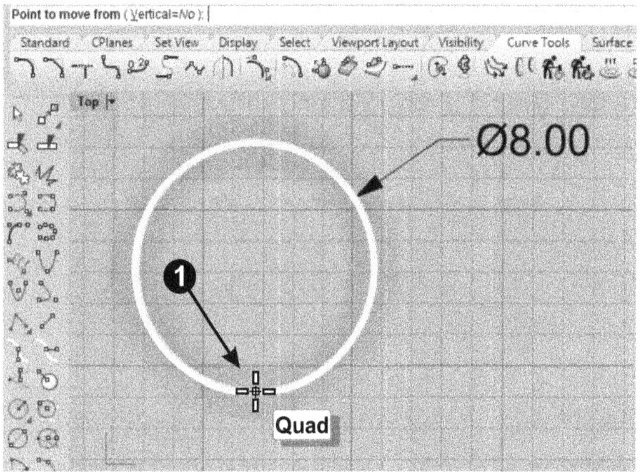

Fig. 5

- **Point to move to** prompt:
  - Move the cursor and watch the preview circle move with it as shown.
  - **LEFT-CLICK** to set a new location for the circle. ❷

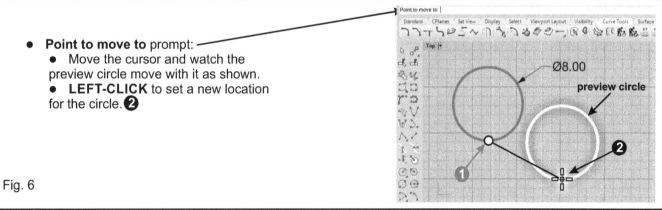

Fig. 6

- The circle has been moved to a new location.

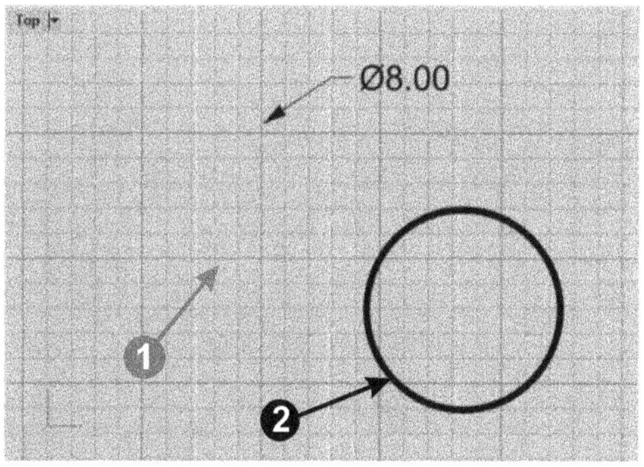

Fig. 7

Moving a Specified Distance

- **Curve Tools tabbed toolbar.** `Curve Tools`

- Select the circle and click on the **Move** command.

- *Note: pre-selection saves time by eliminating the step in a command in which you are prompted to make a selection and press Enter.*

Move command

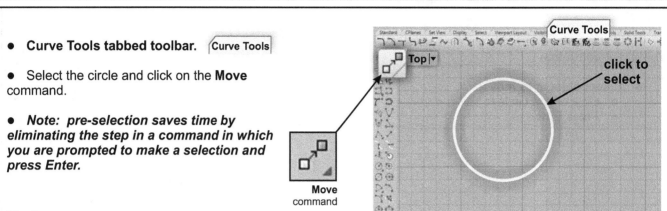

click to select

Fig. 8

- **Point to move from** prompt:
  - Use **Center Osnap** to snap to the center of the circle and click when you see the **Cen** tooltip as shown. ❶

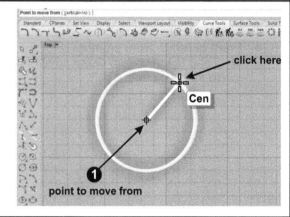

click here

Cen

point to move from

Fig. 9

- **Point to move to** prompt:
  - Type **"10"** in the **Command Line** ❷ and press **Enter.**
    - The distance of the move will be constrained to 10mm.
  - Click to set the new location for the circle. ❸

10

new location preview

❷

❸

❶

Fig. 10

- The circle has been moved **10mm**.

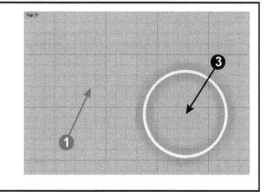

Fig. 11

Moving to a Specified Location

- Use the **Polyline** command to create a line with 3 segments, similar to the one shown, next to the 8mm diameter circle being used in this exercise.

- Specified lengths and angles are not needed for this exercise.

Polyline
command

Fig. 12

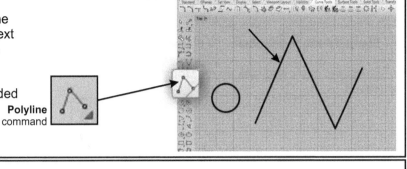

- Turn on **Center osnap** and **End osnap**.

- Select the circle **1** and click on the **Move** command.

Move
command

Fig. 13

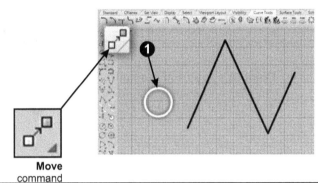

- **Point to move from** prompt:
  - Use **Center osnap** to snap to the center of the circle and **left-click**. **2**

Fig. 14

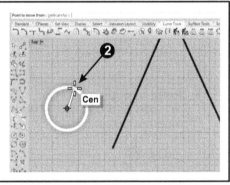

- **Point to move to** prompt:
  - Use **End osnap** to snap to the end point of the nearby polyline as shown.
  - **Left-click** to set the new location for the circle. **3**

Fig. 15

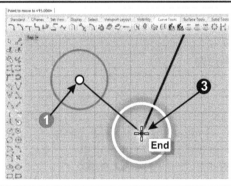

- The circle is now perfectly centered on the end of the polyline.

- *If the circle is still selected when the command is over, click on the grid anywhere to de-select.*

Fig. 16

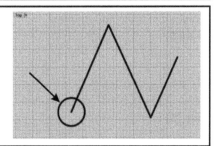

Copying to Specified Locations

- **Standard tabbed toolbar.** [Standard]

- Select the circle and click on the **Copy** command.

Copy
command

Fig. 17

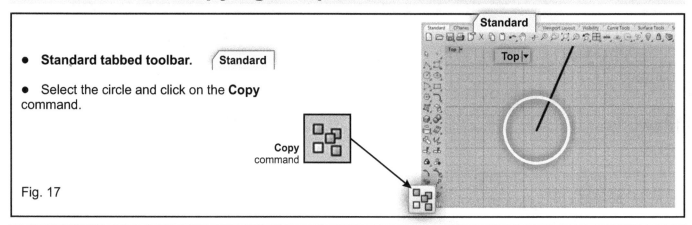

- **Point to copy from** prompt:
  - Use **End osnap** to snap to the end of the polyline and click to set this location. **1**

Fig. 18

- **Point to copy to** prompt:
  - Use **End osnap** to snap to the next end point as shown.
  - Click to set this location for the first copy. **2**

Fig. 19

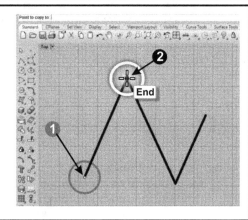

- Snap to the other end points and click to make copies at desired locations. **3** & **4**

- Press **Enter** when you have finished making the desired copies.

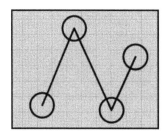

Fig. 20

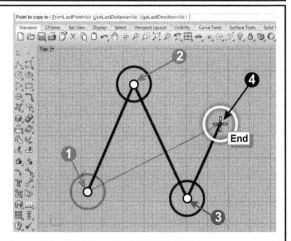

Simple Copy with Click and Drag - Using the Alt Key

- Select the circle you want to copy.

- Start to **click and drag** with the **left mouse button.**

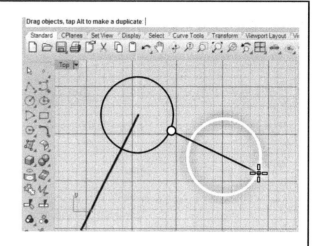

Fig. 21

- After you have started to drag the circle, **softly tap the Alt key on your keyboard once.**

- A little Plus sign will appear next to the cursor.
    - When you see this plus sign, you will know that you are making a copy!

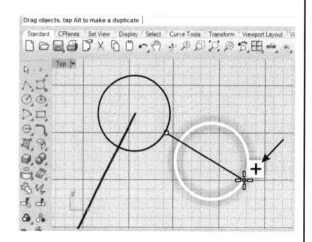

Fig. 22

- Release the left mouse button where you want to place the copy.

- If your circle copy is still selected, **left click** somewhere on the grid and the circle will de-select.

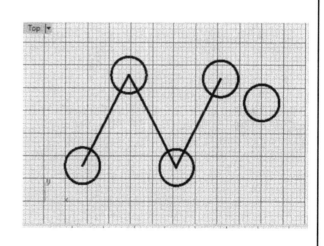

Fig. 23

Trim Command
Cutting away unwanted lines and curves for more design definition.

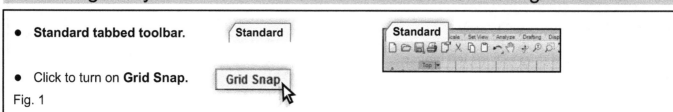

- **Standard tabbed toolbar.**
- Click to turn on **Grid Snap.**

Fig. 1

- Click on the **Circle: center, radius** command.
  - **Center of circle** prompt:
    - Type **"0"** in the **Command Line** and press **Enter. ❶**
    - Click to set location. **❷**

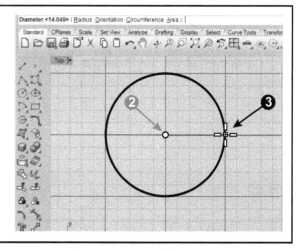

Circle: center, radius
command

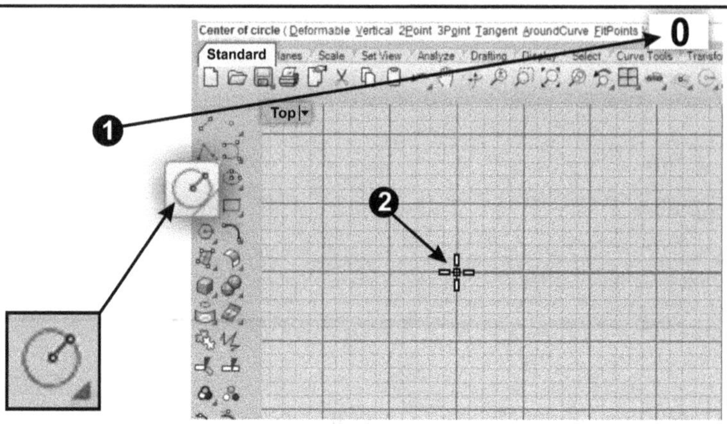

Fig. 2

- **Diameter (or Radius)** prompt:
  - Draw the cursor out 5 mm - it will snap to each 1mm grid intersection because **Grid snap mode** is turned on.
  - Click to set the radius when the cursor snaps to the 5th grid intersection. **❸**

  - Grid snap mode will ensure that your circle has a diameter of **10mm** (and a radius of **5mm**)

Fig. 3

- Select the circle and **left-click** on the **Copy** command.

  - **Point to copy from** prompt:
    - Click on the same location that you designated for the center of the circle. **❶**
    - You can also type **"0"** to designate this location.

Copy
command

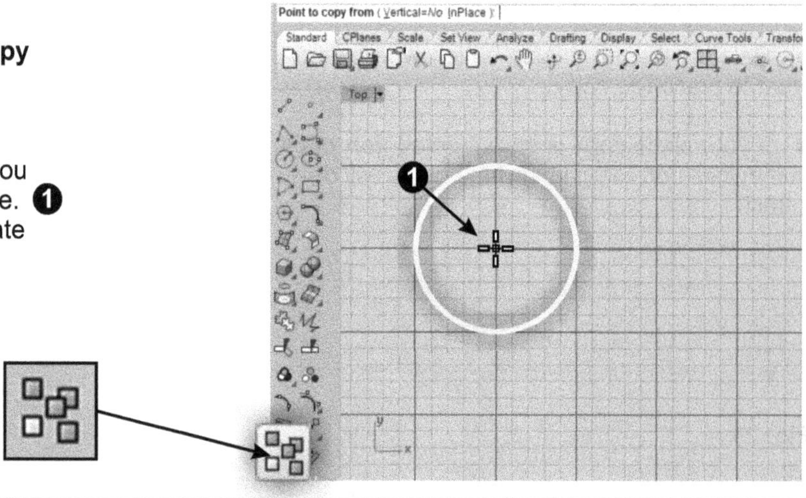

Fig. 4

- **Point to copy to** prompt:
  - Draw the cursor out and click to set the location of the copy on the **next heavy grid line** as shown.
    - Grid Snap mode will ensure that this copy is exactly 5mm away from the original circle.
  - Click to set location. ❷
  - Press **Enter** to end the command.

Fig. 5

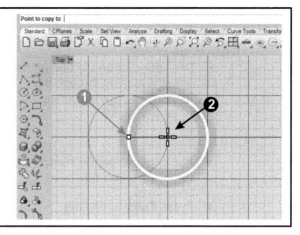

- **Left-click** on the **Trim** command.
  - **Select cutting objects. Press Enter when done** prompt:
    - Select the circle shown.
    - Press **Enter.**

left-click for **Trim** command

Fig. 6

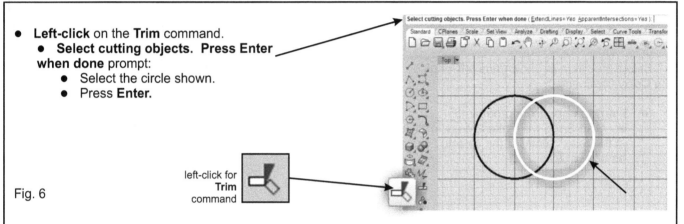

- **Select object to trim** prompt:
  - Click on the part of the circle outside the cutting object as shown. ❶

Fig. 7

cutting object

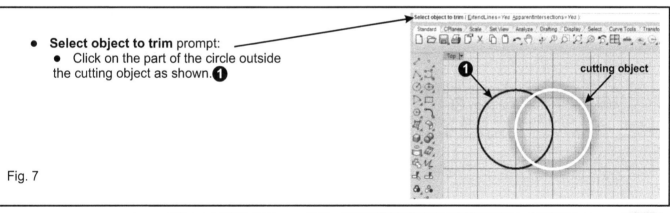

- The part of the circle that you selected to trim has been trimmed away to the boundary of the cutting object.
- Click on the **Undo** option in the **Command Line** as shown.

- The Trim has been undone and the trimmed circle has been restored.

Fig. 8

cutting object

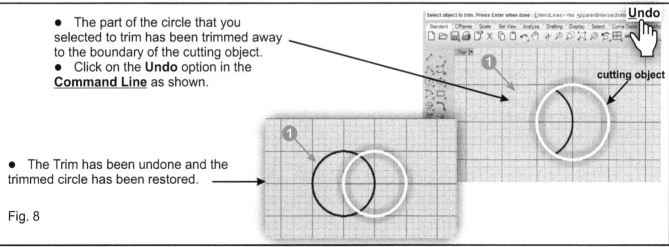

70

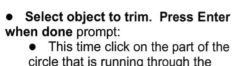

- **Select object to trim. Press Enter when done** prompt:
  - This time click on the part of the circle that is running through the inside of the designated cutting object as shown. ❷

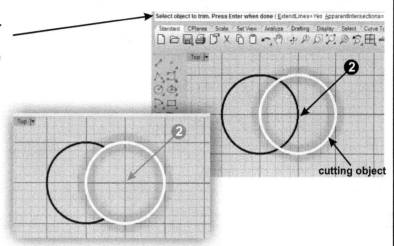

  - The segment on the inside of the cutting object has been trimmed away.
  - Press **Enter** to end the command.

Fig. 9

- Select the circle as shown and **left-click** on the **Copy** command.

  - **Point to copy from** prompt:
    - **Grid Snap** will make is easy to click in the exact center of the selected circle as shown. ❶

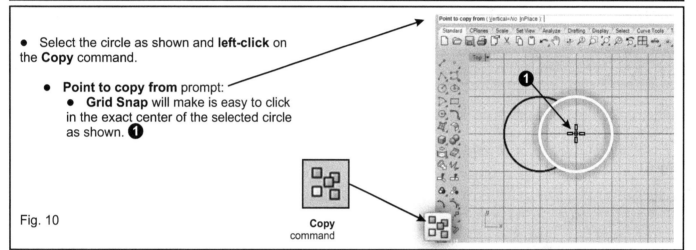

Copy
command

Fig. 10

- Drag the cursor 5mm to the right and click to make the first copy.❷
  - **Grid Snap** will make it easy to make a copy to the right, exactly 5mm away.

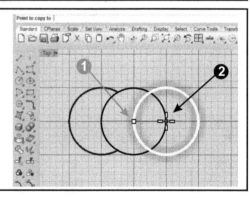

Fig. 11

- Make some more copies as shown, continuing to use **Grid Snap** for easy accuracy in placing a **copy every 5mm**.
- Press **Enter** to end the command.

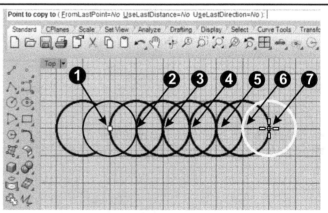

Fig. 12

- Pre-select all of the circles as shown.

- **Left-click** on the **Trim** command.

  - **Select object to trim. Press Enter to clear selection and start over** prompt:
    - Select the circle segment as shown. ❶

left-click for
Trim
command

Fig. 13

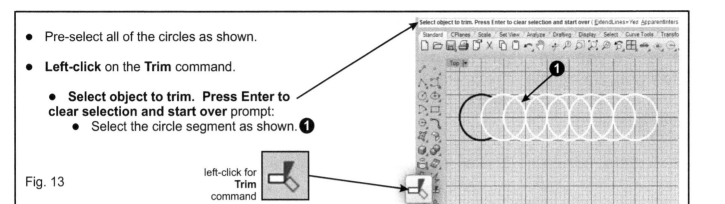

- The segment that you selected will be trimmed away. ❶
- Click on the lower segment as shown. ❷

- *Remember: if you make a mistake when you are in this command, click on the **Undo** option in the **Command Line** to go back to the previous trimming step.*

  - *You can click **Undo** as many times as you want to go back as many steps as you need.*

Fig. 14

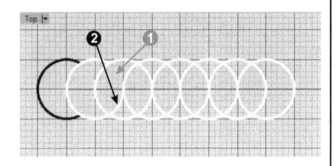

- Another segment has been trimmed away.

Fig. 15

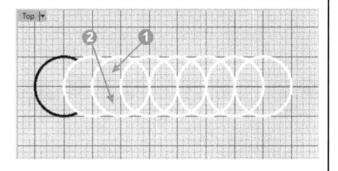

- Keep trimming away until you create the design shown.
- Press **Enter** to end the command.
- Click away to de-select all objects.

Fig. 16

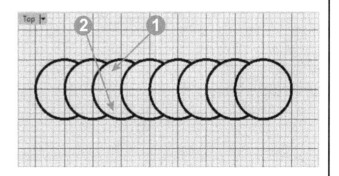

- See if you can create these simple designs, using the Circle, Polyline, Line and Trim commands. Grid snap will be useful.

- Create some designs of your own.

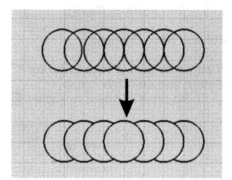

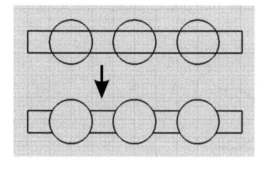

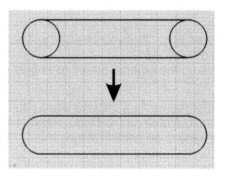

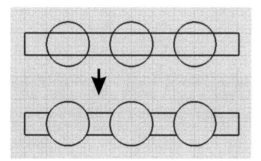

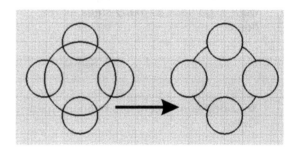

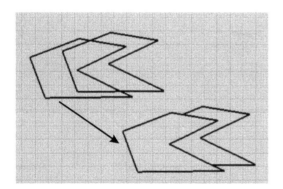

- *Try turning off grid snap and doing some more freeform designs, copying a single circle to create a more organic or freeform concept.*

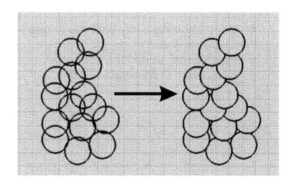

Fig. 17

From a Polyline to a Butterfly
Distance and Angle Constraints
Rebuild and Point Editing

Save this file as **polyline for butterfly.3dm** as it will be used again in a future chapter.

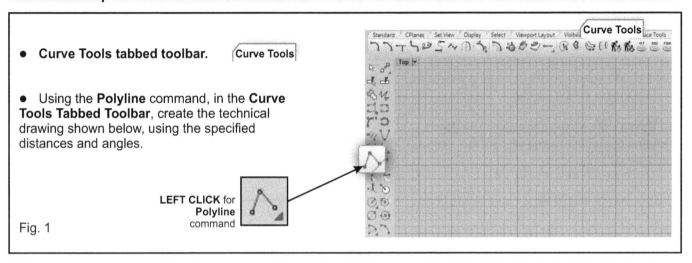

- **Curve Tools tabbed toolbar.** [Curve Tools]

- Using the **Polyline** command, in the **Curve Tools Tabbed Toolbar**, create the technical drawing shown below, using the specified distances and angles.

LEFT CLICK for
Polyline
command

Fig. 1

- Create this line drawing using **Distance and Angle constraints** described in the **Anatomy of a Line and a Polyline** chapter.

- Make sure to use **ORTHO**.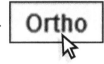

- This is a symmetrical drawing. *Dimensions applied on one side of the drawing apply to the corresponding lines and angles on the other side.*

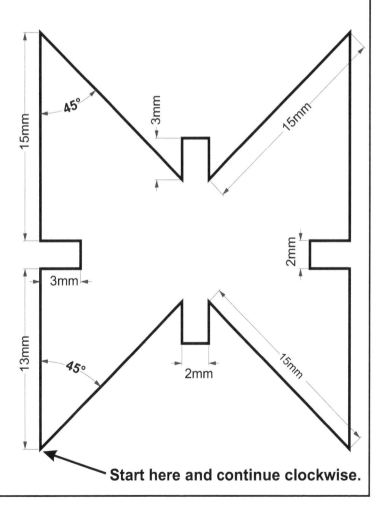

Fig. 2

Start here and continue clockwise.

- When you are creating the last line segment, draw the cursor over the starting point of the first line.

- You will snap to this starting point and you will see a little cursor tip that says **"Point"**, *even if you don't have Point osnap enabled at the bottom of the workspace.*

- Click on this point and your polyline will be automatically fully closed - it will be a **Closed Polyline.**

Fig. 3

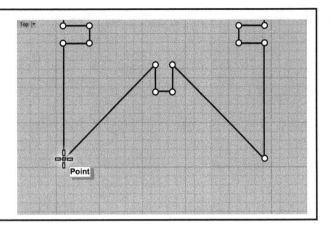

- **What if** you unintentionally end the **Polyline** command before you are finished with the drawing?

Fig. 4

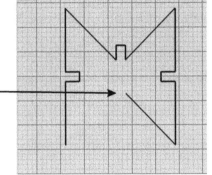

- **Left-click** on the **Continue control point curve** command.

LEFT CLICK for the **Continue control pont curve** command

Fig. 5

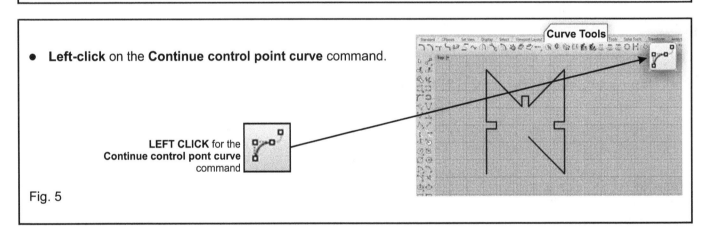

- **Select curve near end to continue** prompt:
  - Click on the line near the end from which you wish to continue as shown.

Fig. 6

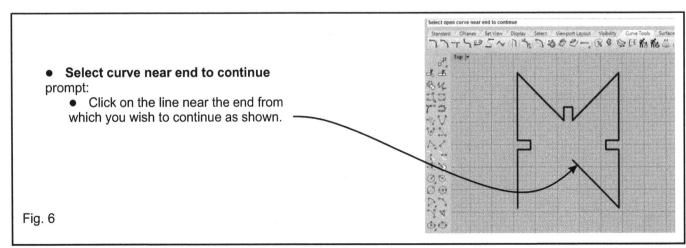

- **Next point. Press Enter when done** prompt:
  - Type **"3"** in the **Command Line** and press **Enter.**

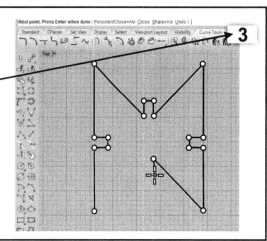

Fig. 7

- With **Ortho** enabled, click to place the next point.

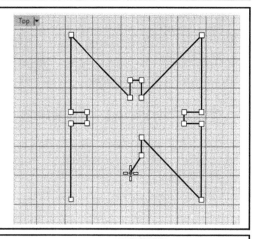

Fig. 8

- Continue with the drawing, clicking on the **Close** option in the **Command Line** when you are ready to create the last line segment.

- *Clicking on the **Close** option is another way of ensuring that you will be creating a **closed polyline.***

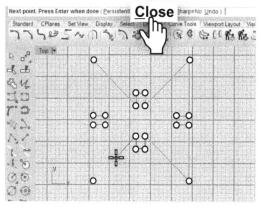

Fig. 9

- The resulting closed polyline.

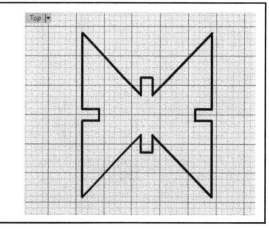

Fig. 10

Rebuilding the Polyline
Rebuilding to Create a Single Graceful Curve from a Polyline

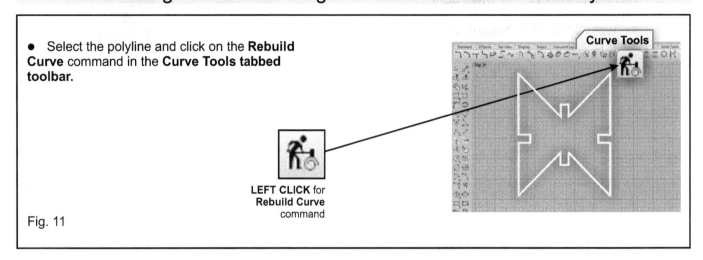

- Select the polyline and click on the **Rebuild Curve** command in the **Curve Tools tabbed toolbar**.

LEFT CLICK for
Rebuild Curve
command

Fig. 11

- The **Rebuild** dialog box will appear.

- Click on the **Preview** button and a **black Preview line** will appear showing how the line will be transformed if you use the suggested point count of 10.

- See the detailed description for the **Rebuild** dialog box below.

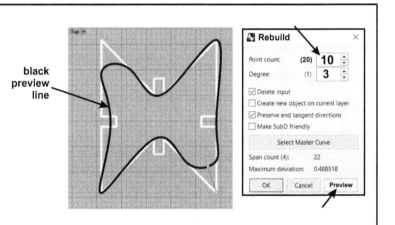

black preview line

Fig. 12

The **Rebuild Curve** dialog box explained

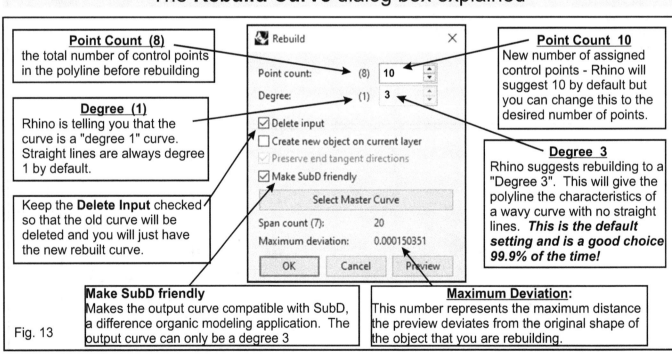

Point Count (8)
the total number of control points in the polyline before rebuilding

Degree (1)
Rhino is telling you that the curve is a "degree 1" curve. Straight lines are always degree 1 by default.

Keep the **Delete Input** checked so that the old curve will be deleted and you will just have the new rebuilt curve.

Point Count 10
New number of assigned control points - Rhino will suggest 10 by default but you can change this to the desired number of points.

Degree 3
Rhino suggests rebuilding to a "Degree 3". This will give the polyline the characteristics of a wavy curve with no straight lines. ***This is the default setting and is a good choice 99.9% of the time!***

Make SubD friendly
Makes the output curve compatible with SubD, a difference organic modeling application. The output curve can only be a degree 3

Maximum Deviation:
This number represents the maximum distance the preview deviates from the original shape of the object that you are rebuilding.

Fig. 13

- Change the number of points to **30** and click on the **Preview Button** again to update.

- Increasing the number of control points has given you much more detail and the resulting rebuilt curve will follow the general shape of the original polyline much more closely.

- **PROBLEM:** The preview line shows a shape that is <u>not symmetrical</u>!

- Click on the **Cancel** button to abort the command.

Fig. 14

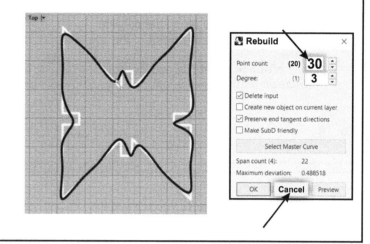

- *It is necessary to alter the geometry of the polyline so that it can be rebuilt into a symmetrical shape.*

- Select the polyline and click on the **Adjust closed curve seam** command as shown.

Adjust closed curve seam
command

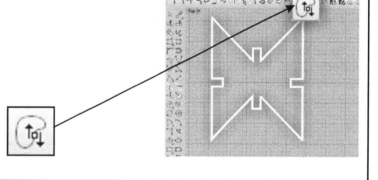

Fig. 15

- **Drag seam point to adjust. Press Enter when done** prompt:
  - Notice that at one angle, a point and an arrow will appear. This is the **"Curve Seam"**.
    - *Note: your curve seam may be at a different location - that does not matter.*
  - It is necessary to move this curve seam so that it is in a perfectly central location on the polyline.

Fig. 16

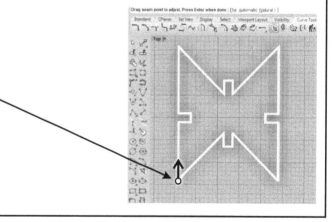

- Click to enable **Mid osnap.**

- Click and drag the point and arrow along the polyline as shown.
- While you are dragging, a little **OnCrv** tool-tip will appear.

Fig. 17

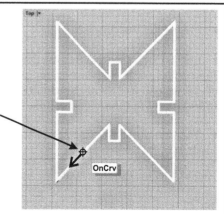

- Draw the cursor along the polyline until it snaps to the **Midpoint** of the line shown.
- **Left-click** to set this new *central location* for the curve seam.

Fig. 18

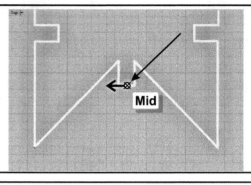

- After you have **left-clicked,** you will see the new location of the curve seam.

- The **curve seam** is now placed on the exact midpoint of the short horizontal line shown.

- Press **Enter** to end the command.

- **Save the file at this point as: polyline for butterfly.3dm. We will be using this polyline again for chapters further along in the book.**

Fig. 19

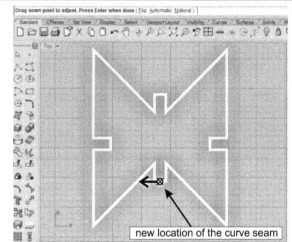

new location of the curve seam

- Select the polyline and click on the **Rebuild Cuve** command once again.

- Click on the **Preview** button in the **Rebuild Curve** dialog box.
  - **Notice that now the preview is symmetrical!**
  - Make sure that you assign the point count as **30.**
  - Click on the **OK** button in the **Rebuild Curve** dialog box.

Fig. 20

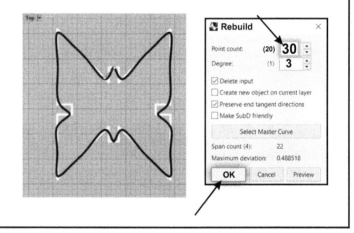

- The rebuilt curve is now symmetrical.

- Pre-select the polyline.

- **LEFT-CLICK** on the **Points On** command. The control points for the new single closed curve will be visible. Notice the symmetrical arrangement of the control points.

- You can press the **Esc** key to turn control points off.

LEFT CLICK for
Points On
command

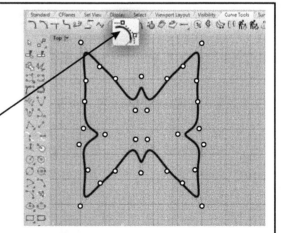

Fig. 21

- Window select the 2 control points shown.
  - For a selection window, click and drag from **❶** to **❷** , making sure that the window includes just the two points indicated.

- Press the **Delete** key on your keyboard to delete these points.

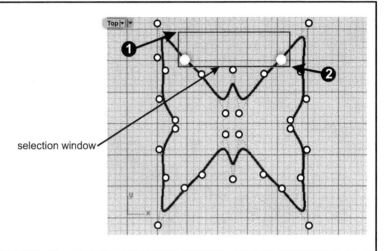

selection window

Fig. 22

- The shape of the wings has been simplified.

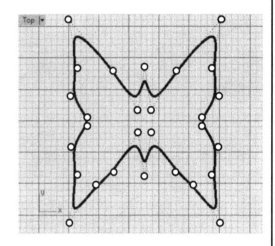

Fig. 23

- Start to click and drag control points to create the final butterfly shape.

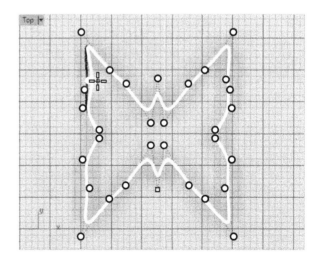

Fig. 24

- Making sure to use **ORTHO**, create 2 horizontal straight lines on the head and lower body of the butterfly as shown.

- You are going to add some control points to the head and lower body to allow for more design definition in these areas.

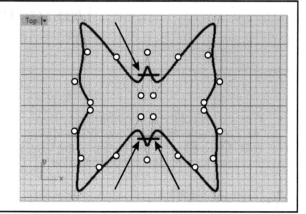

Fig. 25

- Enable **Intersection osnap**.

- Click on the **Insert Knot** command in the **Point Edit** toolbar flyout.

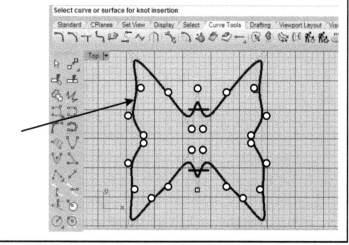

accesses the **Point Edit** toolbar flyout

Insert Knot command

Fig. 26

- **Select curve or surface for knot insertion** prompt:
    - Select the butterfly curve.
        - note: The butterfly curve will not turn yellow when selected but that is OK for this command.

Fig. 27

- **Point on curve to add knot. Press Enter when done** prompt:
    - **Zoom** in and **Pan** up to the head of the butterfly.
    - Snap to the **Intersection** shown and click to add a control point. ➊

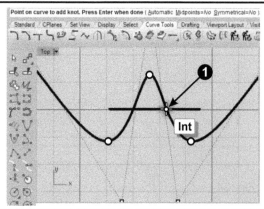

Fig. 28

- Click on the **Intersection** on the other side as shown to add another control point. **❷**

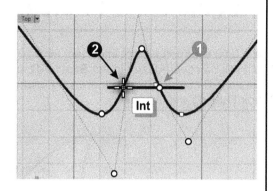

Fig. 29

- Pan to the bottom of the design to add 2 more control points as shown - **❸** & **❹**

- Press **Enter** to end the command.

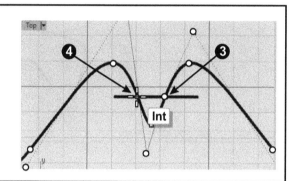

Fig. 30

- At the top and the bottom of the body of the butterfly, 2 control points have been added at each location.

- The two horizontal reference lines added in Fig. 25 can be deleted or hidden by selecting them and pressing the **Delete key**.

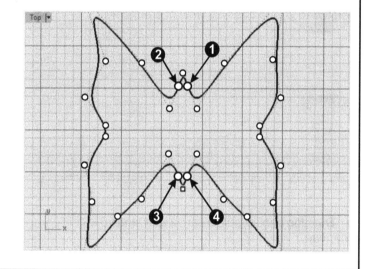

Fig. 31

- Point edit with your newly added control points and notice how much more flexibility you have to form the head and body of the butterfly.

- Save this file as **butterfly design.3dm** because you want the original **polyline for butterfly.3dm** file for a future chapter.

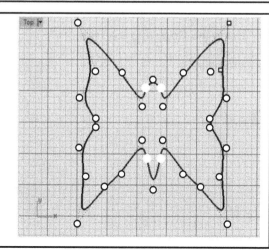

Fig. 32

Some Ways to Create a Butterfly Shape in this Exercise

- Total symmetry is not important for this exercise but will be covered later in the **Scale 1-D** and **Scale 2-D** commands which are very useful for point editing with symmetry.

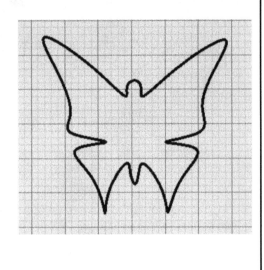

Fig. 33

- Many points on the right of the line were deleted to create this side view of a butterfly.

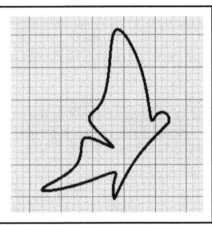

Fig. 34

- Deleting control points can create simplified shapes.

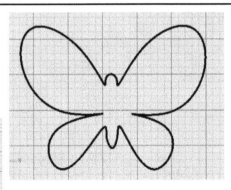

- Using the **Copy** and the **Trim** commands can open up many creative opportunities.

Fig. 35

Stone & Prong Layout
Creating with circles. Working with Layers.
Drawing the Stones

- Open Rhino and save the file as **stones & prongs.3dm.**

- **Curve Tools tabbed toolbar.**　〔Curve Tools〕

- Use the **Circle: center, radius** command to create a **10mm diameter** circle around "**0**" as shown.

Fig. 1

Circle: center, radius command

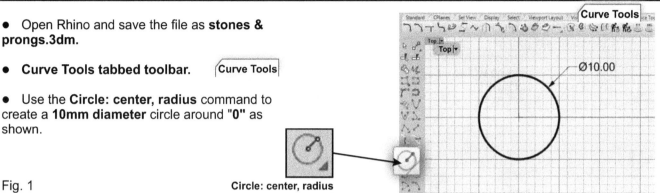

- Make sure that **Quad osnap** is enabled.

☑ Quad

- Click on the **Circle: diameter** command:
  - **Start of diameter** prompt:
    - Snap to the **Quad** point on the right side of the 10mm circle as shown.
    - Click to set location. **❶**

Fig. 2

Circle: diameter command

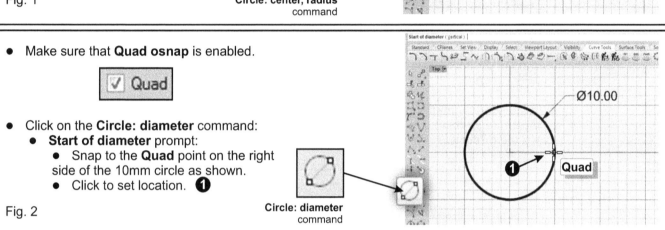

- **End of diameter** prompt:
  - Type a "**6**" in the **Command Line**.
  - Press **Enter.**

Fig. 3

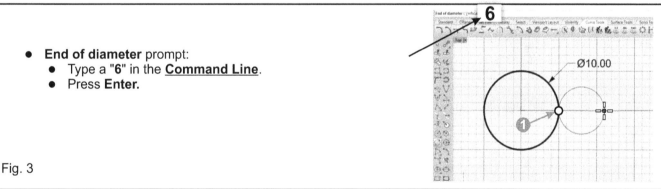

- Draw the cursor out to the right, using **ORTHO** to keep the diameter perfectly horizontal.

  - Click to set location of the end of the diameter. **❷**

- A new 6mm diameter circle will be created in contact with the 10mm circle.

Fig. 4

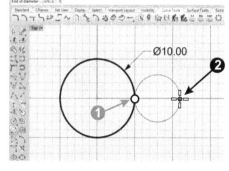

Setting the Inset Distance of the Prongs into the Stones
Offset Curve command

- Select the larger circle and click on the **Offset curve** command.
  - **Side to offset** prompt:
    - Draw the cursor into the inside of the circle to determine on which side of the line the offset will be created.

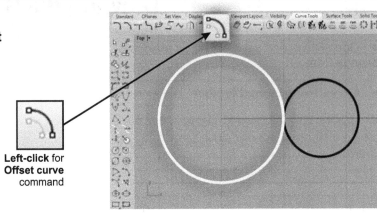

Left-click for **Offset curve** command

- Notice that a ***preview of the offset distance*** is now attached to the cursor, previewing the default 1mm offset distance (or the distance when the command was last used) which you will change.

    - ***Note: Make sure that the cursor is on the inside of the circle as this will decide what side of the curve the offset will be created.***

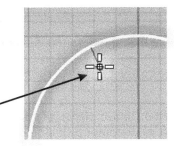

Fig. 5

Side to offset (Distance=*1* Corner=*Sharp* ThroughPoint Tolerance=*0.001* BothSides InCPlane=*Yes* Cap=*None*): **.5**

- **Side to offset** prompt:
  - Type **".5"** in the **Command Line** to set the offset distance.
  - Press **Enter.**
    - The offset distance preview will reflect the new designated offset distance of .5mm.

  - Click to set location.

click here

Fig. 6

- The large circle now has a smaller circle inside it at an offset distance of .5mm.

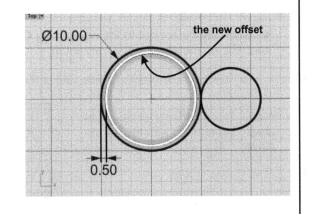

Ø10.00

the new offset

0.50

Fig. 7

- Select the smaller circle on the right and click on the **Offset curve** command again.
  - **Side to offset** prompt:
    - Type **".3"** in the **Command Line.**
    - Press **Enter.**
    - Click to set the location of the offset inside the selected circle.

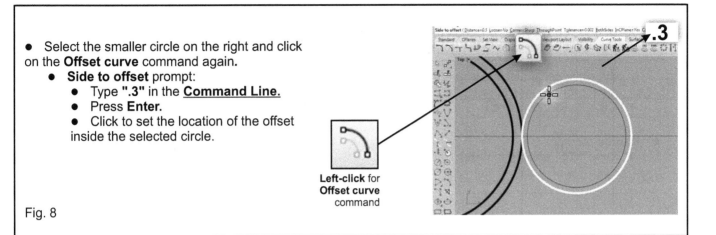

Left-click for
Offset curve
command

Fig. 8

- Both circles now have offsets that will guide the placement of prongs.
  - The offset for the larger circle is .5mm.
  - The offset for the smaller circle is .3mm.

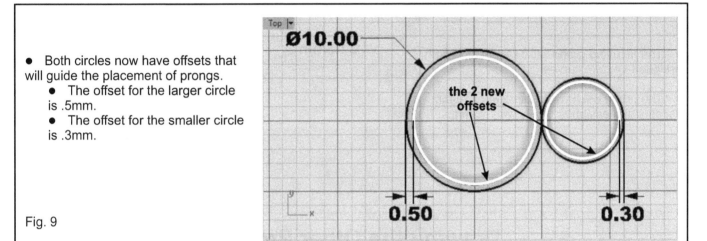

Fig. 9

Drawing the Shared Prong
Circle: Tangent, Tangent, Radius Command

- Click on the **Circle: tangent, tangent, radius** command.
  - **First tangent curve** prompt:
    - Draw the cursor over to one of the **inner circles** as shown.
    - Notice that a white constraint line appears where cursor touches the circle.
    - Click on the approximate location shown - *this will be one of the tangent curves.*❶

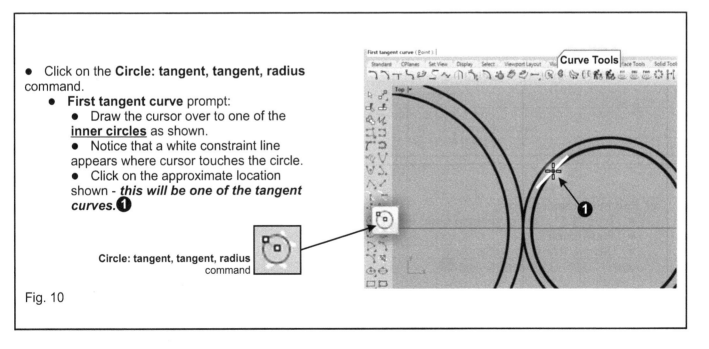

Circle: tangent, tangent, radius
command

Fig. 10

- **Second tangent curve or radius** prompt:
  - Draw the cursor over to the **inner circle** on the other side and notice the white constraint line where the cursor touches the inner circle.
  - Click to set location. ❷

- **Radius** prompt:
  - Type "**.75**" and press **Enter**.

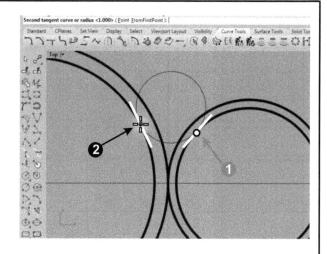

Fig. 11

- The resulting prong will be tangent to both assigned tangent curves.

- The prong will have a diameter of 1.5mm because the assigned radius was .75mm

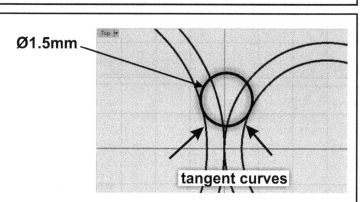

Fig. 12

Drawing the Other Prongs

- Click to activate **Quad osnap**.

  ☑ Quad

- Click on the **Circle: diameter** command.
  - **Start of diameter** prompt:
    - Snap to the upper quad point of the **inner** large circle as shown.
    - Click to set location. ❶

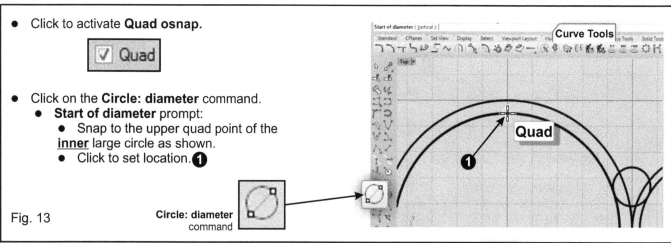

Circle: diameter command

Fig. 13

- **End of diameter** prompt:
  - Type "**1.5**" in the **Command Line**. ❷
  - Press **Enter**.
  - Using **ORTHO**, draw the cursor upward and click to set location. ❸

Fig. 14

- Select the outer smaller curve as shown and click on the **Offset Curve** command.
  - **Side to offset** prompt:
    - Type "**.5**" in the **Command Line**.
    - Press **Enter**.
    - Click to set location on the inside of the circle being offset.

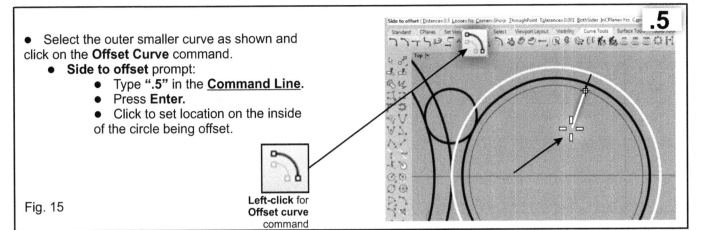

Left-click for
Offset curve
command

Fig. 15

- A new offset has been created on the inside of the small circle for the purpose of providing an offset distance for the last prong.

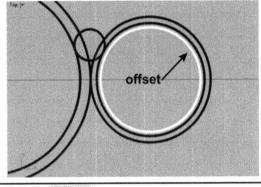

offset

Fig. 16

- Click on the **Circle: diameter** command once again.
  - **Start of diameter** prompt:
    - Snap to the **Quad** of the inner circle shown and click to set location. ❶
    - Type "**1.5**" in the **Command Line** and press **Enter.**

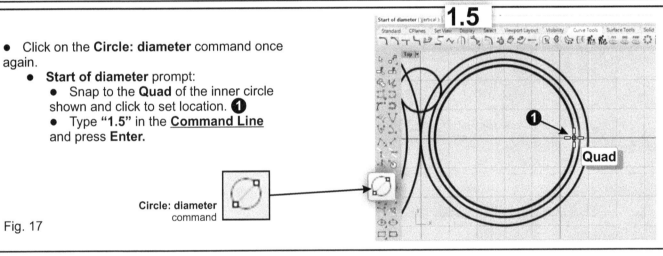

Circle: diameter
command

Quad

Fig. 17

- The diameter is constrained to 1.5mm.
  - Use **ORTHO** to make sure that the cursor is being drawn out in a perfectly horizontal direction so that the prong will be evenly placed along the X axis.
- Click to set location. ❷

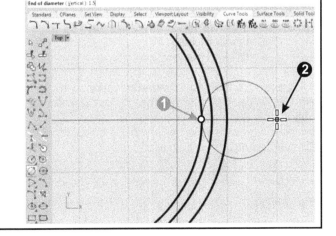

Fig. 18

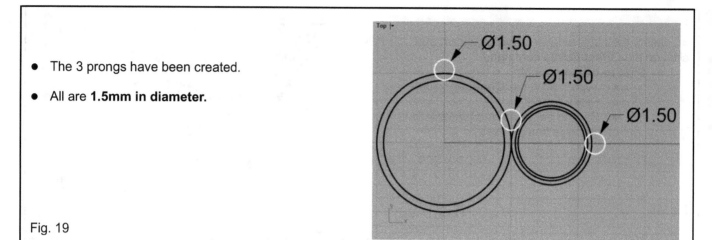

- The 3 prongs have been created.

- All are **1.5mm in diameter.**

Fig. 19

Drawing a Stone within a Square Frame

- Navigate your view to a clear area above the 3-stone drawing just created.

- Click on **Grid Snap**.

  Grid Snap

- Click on the **Circle: center, radius** command.
  - **Center of circle** prompt:
    - Click on the intersection of the Y axis (green color) and a major (darker) grid line as shown. **❶**

  Circle: center, radius
  command

Fig. 20

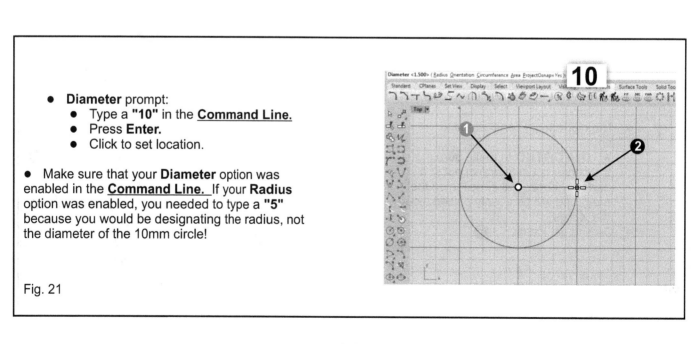

- **Diameter** prompt:
  - Type a **"10"** in the **Command Line.**
  - Press **Enter.**
  - Click to set location.

- Make sure that your **Diameter** option was enabled in the **Command Line.** If your **Radius** option was enabled, you needed to type a **"5"** because you would be designating the radius, not the diameter of the 10mm circle!

Fig. 21

- Use the **Polyline** command to draw an accurate 10mm x 10mm square to enclose the circle as shown, *drawing the polyline segments along the heavy grid lines.*

- Grid snap will make this an easy and accurate task.

Grid Snap

Fig. 22

Polyline command

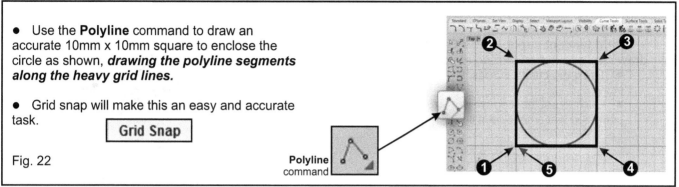

- **Offset** the circle to create an inner circle.
  - **Offset distance: .5mm**
  - **Diameter of new offset circle: 9m**

- **Clicl to toggle off Grid Snap.**

Grid Snap

Fig. 23

Left-click for
Offset curve
command

offset

0.50

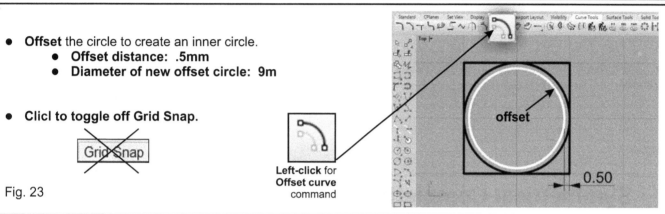

Drawing the Corner Prong
Circle: Tangent to 3 Curves Command

- Click on the **Circle: tangent to 3 curves** command in the **Circle** toolbar flyout.
  - **First tangent curve** prompt:
    - Draw the cursor over the curve shown.
    - A point and a white constraint line will appear when the cursor snaps to the line.
    - Click to assign this line as the first tangent curve.**❶**

accesses the **Circle** toolbar flyout

Fig. 24

Circle: tangent to 3 curves command

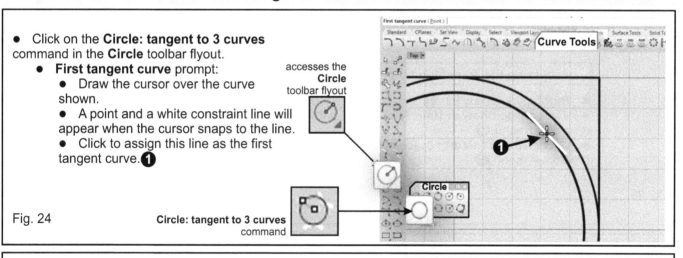

- **Second tangent curve or radius** prompt:
  - Draw the cursor over to the line shown.
  - A point and white constraint line will appear again.
  - Click to assign this line as the second tangent curve. **❷**

Fig. 25

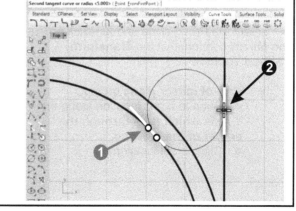

- **Third tangent curve. Press Enter to draw circle from first two points** prompt:
  - Draw the cursor across the line shown.
  - Click to set location when you see the point and white constraint line.❸

Fig. 26

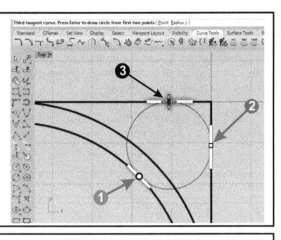

- The circle is accurately touching all 3 tangent curves.

Fig. 27

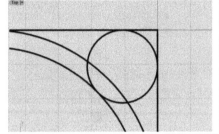

Symmetrical Completion of the Stone & Prong Layout
Mirror Command

- **Transform tabbed toolbar.**

- If the tab for this toolbar is not showing among the other tabs, follow these steps to access it:

> **accessing the Transform tabbed toolbar**
>
> - **Right-click** on any tab.❶
> - Click on the **Show or Hide Tabs** option in the drop down menu.❷
> - Click on the **Transform** option in the second drop-down menu.❸

Fig. 28

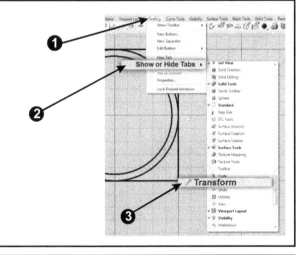

- Click to enable **Grid Snap.** | Grid Snap |

- Select the Prong circle and left-click on the **Mirror** command in the **Transform Tabbed Toolbar.**

  - **Start of mirror plane** prompt:
    - Snap to a grid location along the **Y Axis which runs through the center of the drawing.**
    - Click to set location.❶

left click for
Mirror
command

Fig. 29

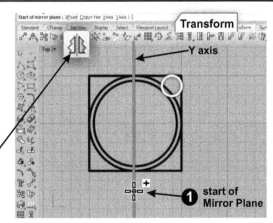

- **End of mirror plane** prompt:
  - Draw the cursor straight up **along the Y axis.**
  - Snap to a grid intersection on the Y axis.
  - Click as shown to assign location of the end of the mirror plane.❷

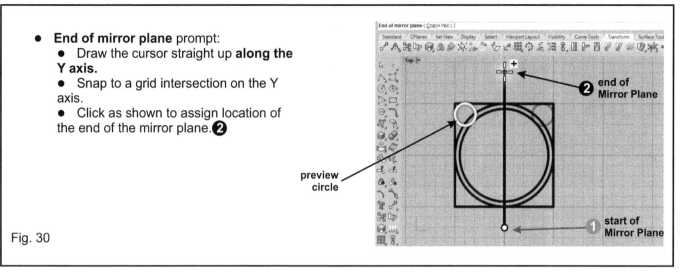

Fig. 30

- Click to enable **Center Osnap.**   ☑ Cen

Select the two prongs shown and left-click on the **Mirror** command again.

- **Start of mirror plane** prompt:
  - Snap to the center of the circles as shown.❶
  - Click to set location.

- **End of mirror plane** prompt:
  - Using **ORTHO,** draw the cursor out Ortho horizontally.
  - Click to set the **End of the mirror plane**. ❷

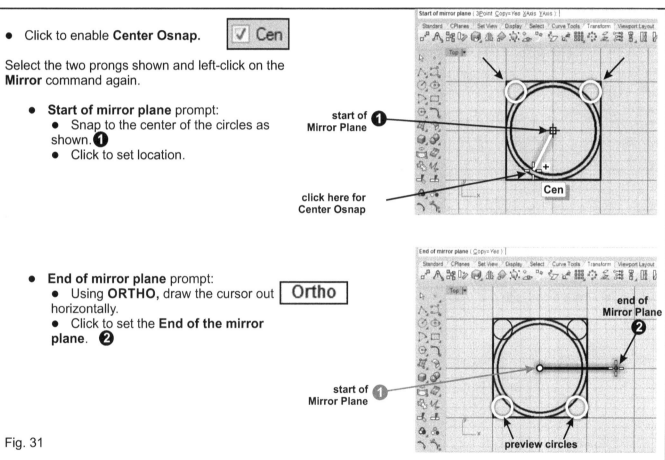

Fig. 31

- The **Mirror Planes** were both set so that they ran through the exact center of the drawing.

- All 4 prongs are now in place for a symmetrical drawing.

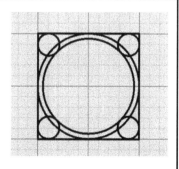

Fig. 32

- Navigate to the other drawing.

- Select the 2 prongs shown and click on the **Mirror** command.

  - **Start of mirror plane** prompt:
    - Type **"0"** in the <u>**Command Line.**</u>
    - Press **Enter.**

- The **Start of the Mirror Plane** will be located exactly at **"0", where the X and Y axes cross.** ❶

  - **End of mirror plane** prompt:
    - Using **Ortho**, draw the cursor out to the right. **Ortho**

    - Click to set the **End of Mirror Plane.** ❷

Fig. 33

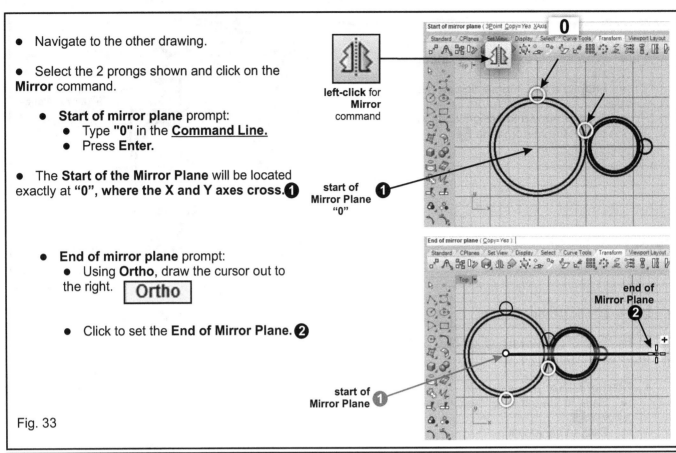

- Select the 3 prongs and the outer small circle shown and click on the **Mirror** command.

  - **Start of mirror plane** prompt:
    - Type **"0"** in the <u>**Command Line.**</u>
    - Press **Enter.** ❶

  - **End of mirror plane** prompt:
    - Using **ORTHO**, draw the cursor straight upward.
    - Click to set the **End of the Mirror Plane.** ❷

Fig. 34

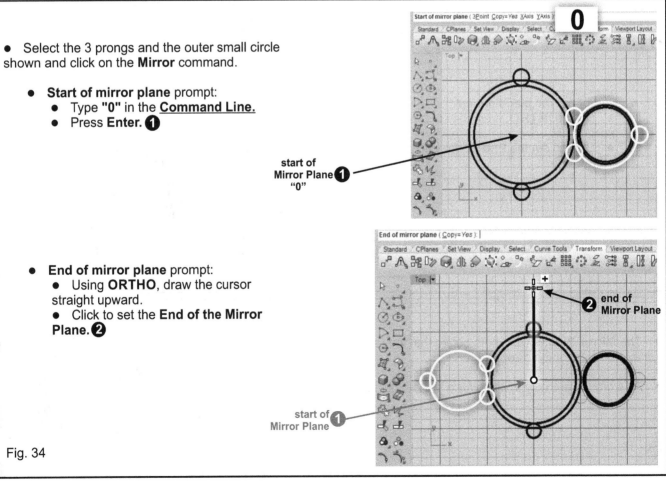

93

- A symmetrical drawing has been created as both mirror planes ran through the center of the drawing.

- ***note: Some of the inner circles were not mirrored over because they are no longer needed for the final drawing.***

- Notice that all of your lines are the same color. That is because they have all been created on the same **"Layer"**.

Fig. 35

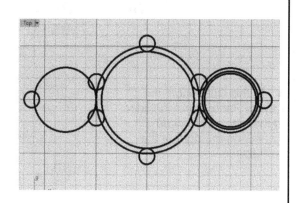

Organizing Your Work by Assigning Layers to Objects
Applying Layers to Stone & Prong Layout

- **Standard tabbed toolbar.**   ⌐ **Standard** |

- The **Tabbed Panels** are docked on the right of your workspace.

- Click on the **Layers tab** if another panel is showing its window. This will bring the Layers panel to the front as shown.

Fig. 36

94

- In this illustration, the Layers Panel is not included in the group of docked Panels on the right of the workspace.

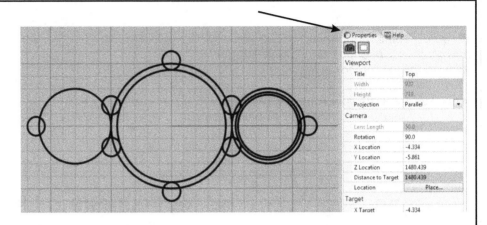

Fig. 37

- **Right-click** on any one of the **tabs** in the panel as shown. ❶

- A drop-down context menu will appear listing the various panels that are available for docking.

- Click on the **Layers** line as shown. ❷

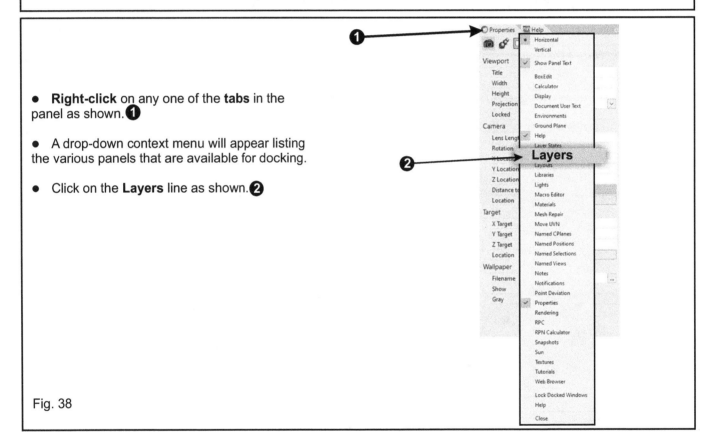

Fig. 38

- The **Layers** tab will now be added to the group as shown.

Fig. 39

If No Panels are Showing in the Workspace

- The **Panels** drop-down ❶ in the **Menu Bar** at the top of the workspace offers most of the available categories that can be included in the panels grouping.
- Click on the **Layers** category as shown. ❷

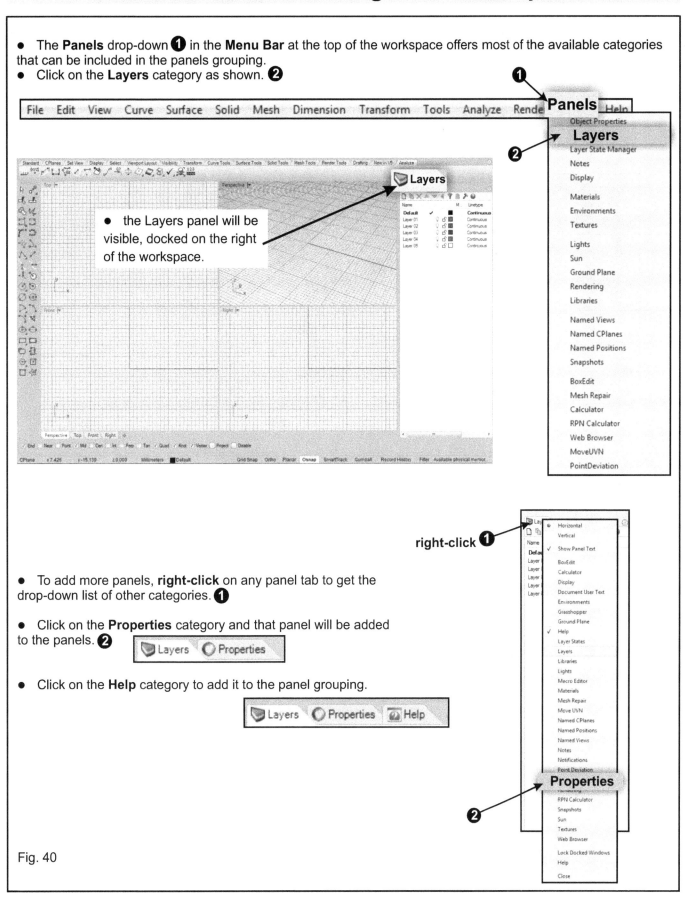

- the Layers panel will be visible, docked on the right of the workspace.

- To add more panels, **right-click** on any panel tab to get the drop-down list of other categories. ❶

- Click on the **Properties** category and that panel will be added to the panels. ❷

- Click on the **Help** category to add it to the panel grouping.

Fig. 40

- If your layers pane is "floating", drag it over to the right of the workspace to dock it.
- When it is ready to dock, a blue shadow will appear.
- Release your mouse button to complete the docking.

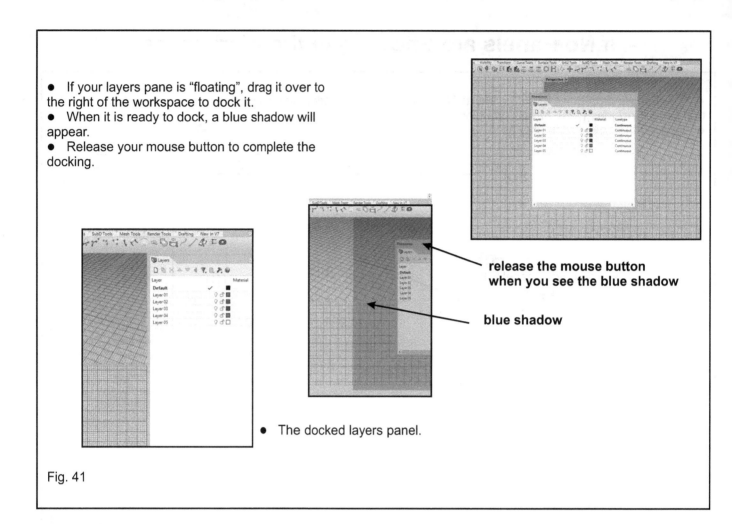

release the mouse button when you see the blue shadow

blue shadow

- The docked layers panel.

Fig. 41

The Layers Panel

- The list of layers that you see here is the default configuration.

- To read the full names of the tabs and layers, pull the panel ❶ and column headings ❷ out to widen it's visibility.

pull out layers panel ❶

pull out individual column headings

- Click to place a check mark in the **Default** layer as shown. ❸
    - This indicates that this is the **"Current"** layer. Anything that you create will be on the **Current** layer

Fig. 42

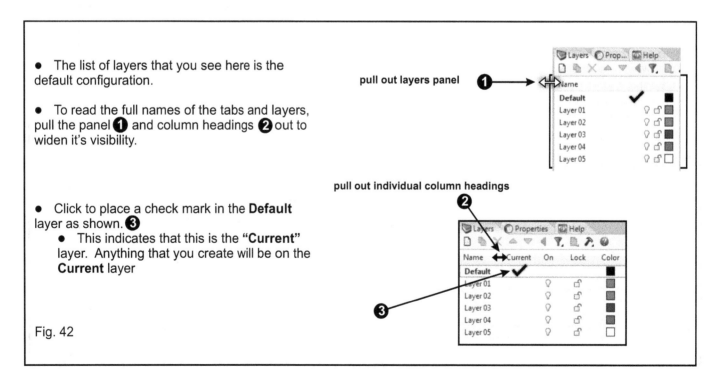

97

- **Right-click** on the **"Default"** layer. ❶
  - A drop-down context menu will appear.

- Click to select the **"Rename Layer"** option. ❷

right click
on layer name ❶

❷

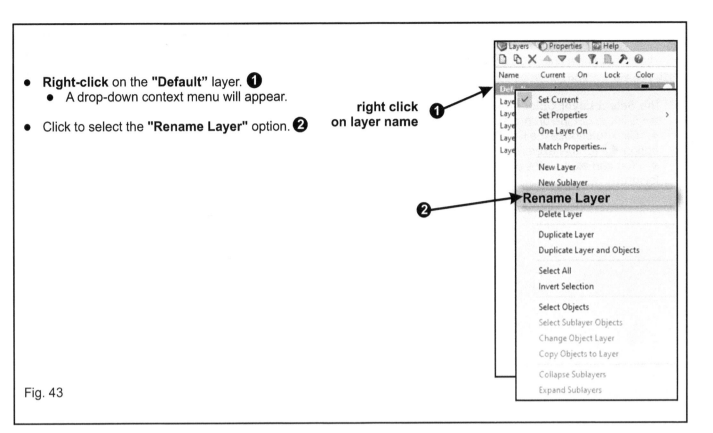

Fig. 43

- Rename the **default** layer **STONES**, as shown.

- This can also be done by hovering over the layer name until it goes into an Edit mode, like editing text in most computer apps.

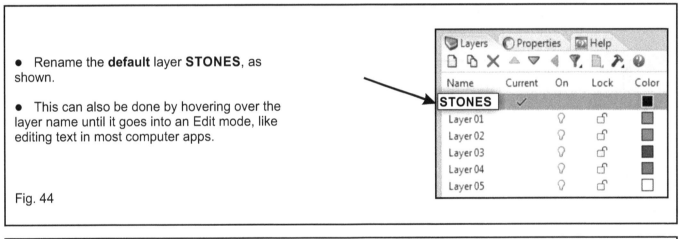

Fig. 44

- Rename layers as shown.
  - **STONES**
  - **construction lines**
  - **PRONGS**
  - **prong curves**

- Notice that some layer names are in upper case and some are in lower case.
  - This is a suggested way to organize the layers for quick and easy identification and selection.

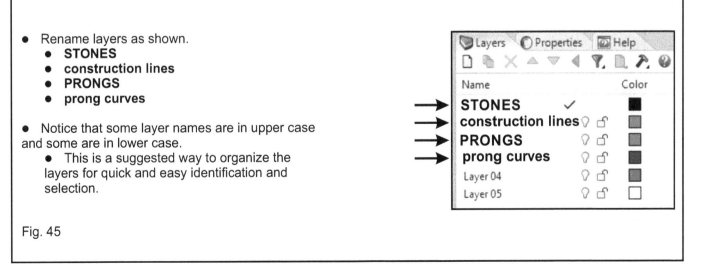

Fig. 45

- Click on the little color box **1** on the **PRONGS** layer line as shown.

- The **Select Layer Color** dialog box will open. **2**
  - Click to get the drop-down menu. **3**
  - Click to choose the **Custom Color List** option **4** for this exercise.
  - You can explore the other options at your leisure.

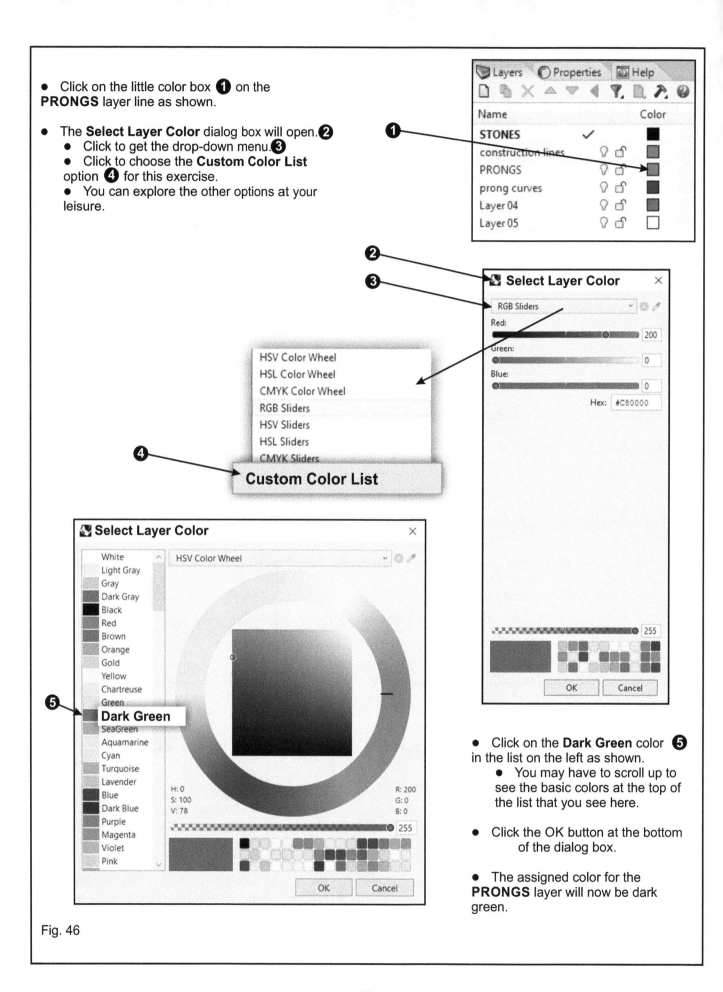

- Click on the **Dark Green** color **5** in the list on the left as shown.
  - You may have to scroll up to see the basic colors at the top of the list that you see here.

- Click the OK button at the bottom of the dialog box.

- The assigned color for the **PRONGS** layer will now be dark green.

Fig. 46

- Assign colors for all the layers:
  - **STONES:** **Black (already black)**
  - **construction lines:** **Red**
  - **PRONGS:** **Dark Green**
  - **prong curves:** **Brown**

- This color coding is a useful way to quickly and easily identify and select objects as you work.

Fig. 47

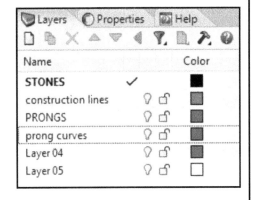

- Select all of the prong circles for both drawings as shown.

- **Right-click** on the **PRONGS** line as shown.

Fig. 48

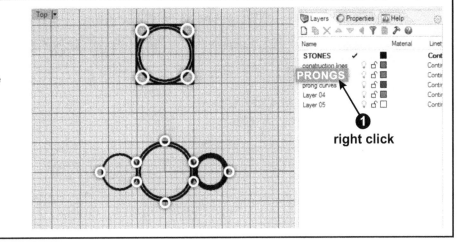

right click

➊

- A context drop-down menu will appear.

- Run the cursor down the list and click on the line that says **Change Object Layer.** ➋

Fig. 49

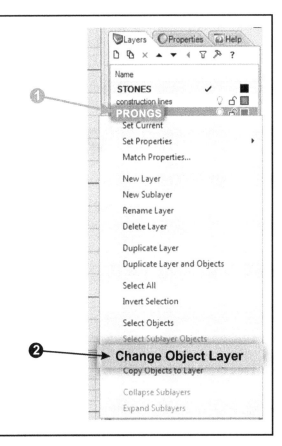

➋ → **Change Object Layer**

- Click away to de-select the prongs and notice that they are now green because they are now all on the **PRONGS** layer.

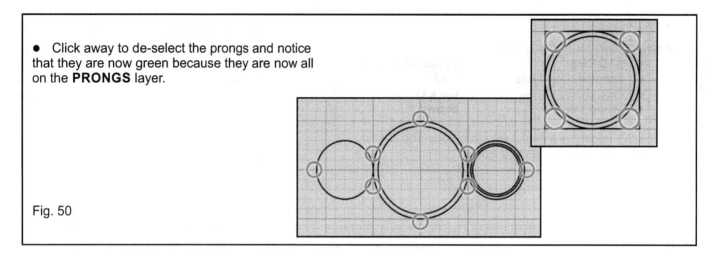

Fig. 50

Changing Layers using the Alternative Status Bar Method

- Select the 4 inner circles as shown.

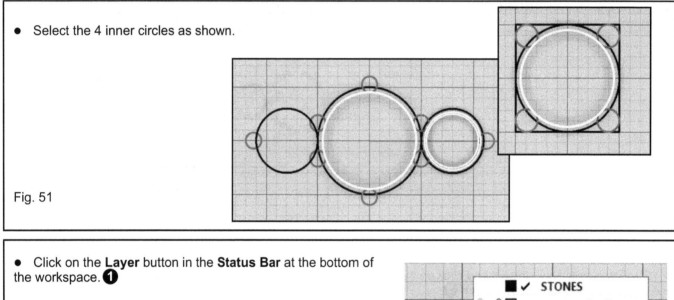

Fig. 51

- Click on the **Layer** button in the **Status Bar** at the bottom of the workspace. ❶

  - *[The button says **STONES** because that is the active layer at present. If an object from another layer is presently selected, the button will read the name of the layer of the selected object.]*

- A context pop-up menu will appear.

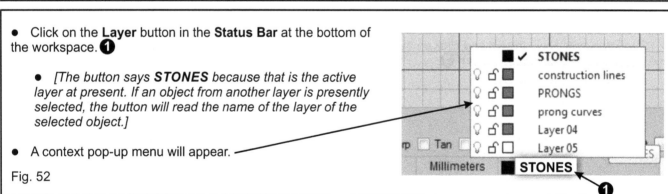

Fig. 52

Click on the **prong curves** line. ❷

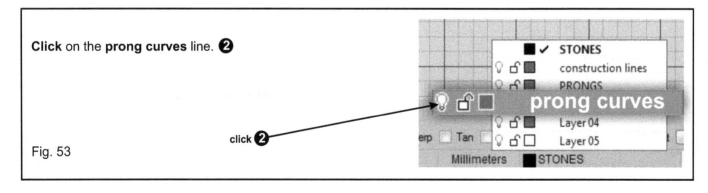

click ❷

Fig. 53

- Click away to de-select the inner circles.

- All of the inner circles are on the **prong curves layer** - note their **brown coloration.**

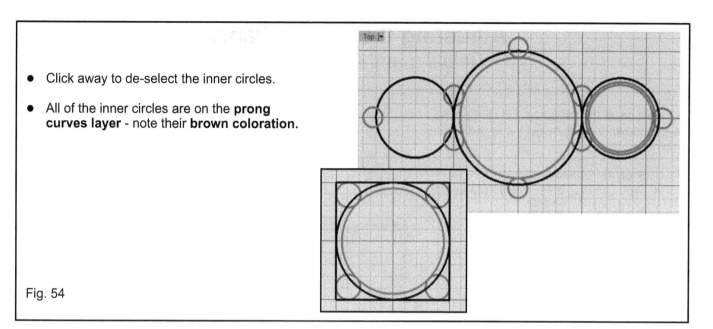

Fig. 54

- Select the square around the square setting and change it to the **construction lines** layer.

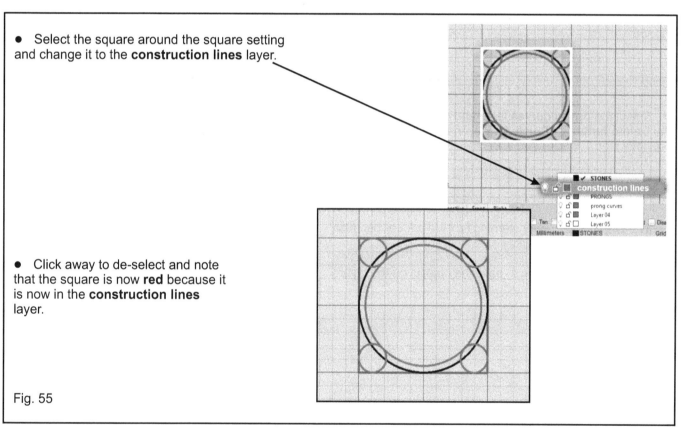

- Click away to de-select and note that the square is now **red** because it is now in the **construction lines** layer.

Fig. 55

102

Adjusting the Layers Panel
Deleting and Adding Layers

- Hold down the **Shift** key and click on the layers shown to multi-select these two unused layers.

- Click on the **Delete** button.
  - You can also press the **Delete key** on your keyboard.

- The selected layers will be deleted from the list.

Fig. 56

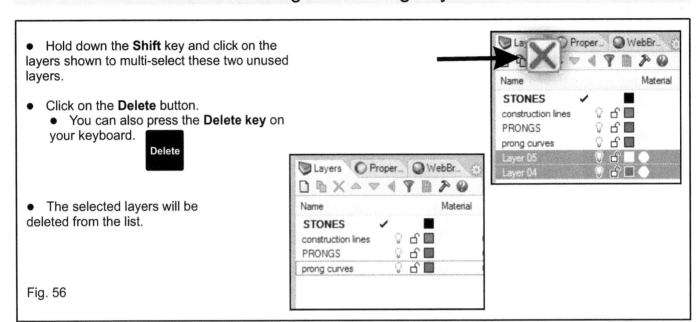

- Select the **prong curves** layer and click on the **Delete button** or **Delete Key** as in the previous step.

delete button

- The **Objects on Layer** warning box will appear because the selected layer has objects on it.

- Click on the **No button** to save the objects on the layer from being deleted.

Fig. 57

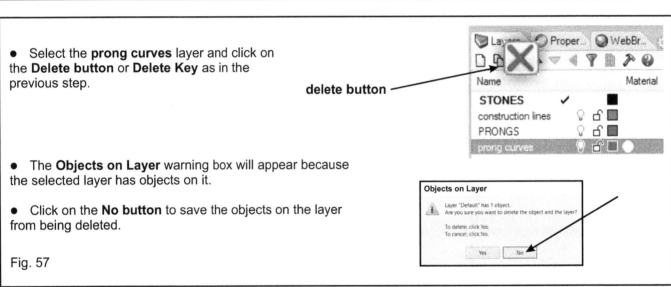

- Click on the **New Layer** command button.

New Layer
button

- A new layer will appear.

Fig. 58

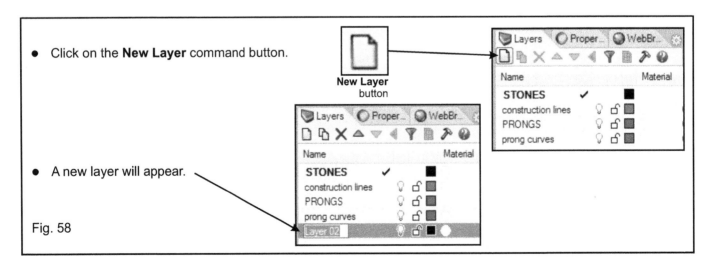

Moving Layers Up and Down in the Layers Panel List

- Select the new layer ❶ and click on the **Move Up** button. ❷

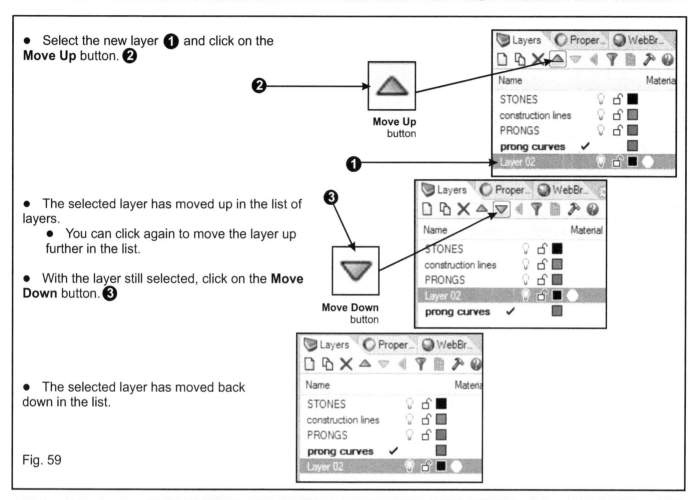

Move Up
button

- The selected layer has moved up in the list of layers.
  - You can click again to move the layer up further in the list.

- With the layer still selected, click on the **Move Down** button. ❸

Move Down
button

- The selected layer has moved back down in the list.

Fig. 59

Trimming For More Design Definition
Trim command

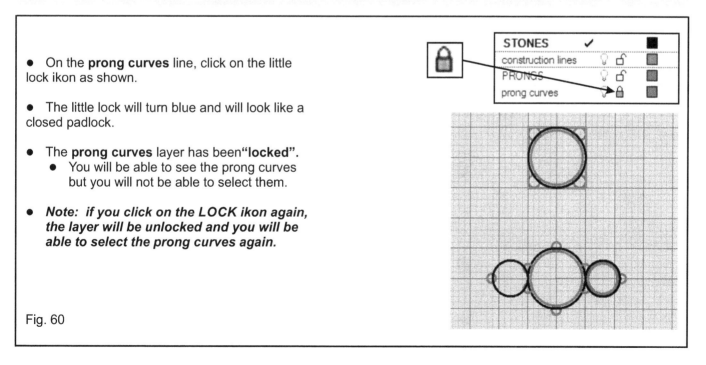

- On the **prong curves** line, click on the little lock ikon as shown.

- The little lock will turn blue and will look like a closed padlock.

- The **prong curves** layer has been **"locked"**.
  - You will be able to see the prong curves but you will not be able to select them.

- *Note: if you click on the LOCK ikon again, the layer will be unlocked and you will be able to select the prong curves again.*

Fig. 60

I On the **construction lines** layer, click on the little lightbulb icon.

I The little lightbulb will turn blue.

I The **construction lines** layer will be turned off and it's objects will be hidden from view.

I **Note: If you click on the LIGHTBULB icon again, the construction lines layer will be turned on again and the objects on that layer will be visible again.**

Fig. 61

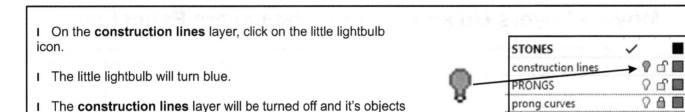

- **Curve Tools tabbed toolbar.** |Curve Tools|

- Left-click on the **Trim** command.

left-click for the
Trim
command

Fig. 62

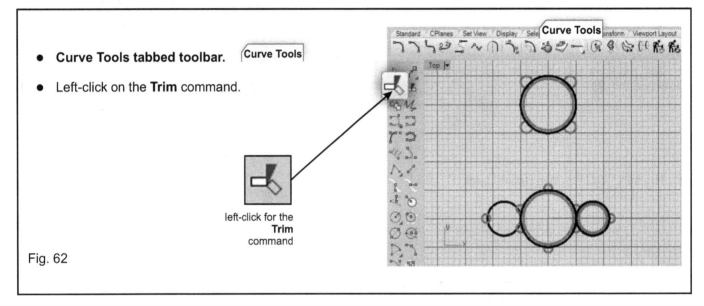

- **Select cutting objects** prompt:

Select cutting objects (ExtendLines=Yes ApparentIntersections=No):

- Click to access the **Layers pop-up menu** in the **Status Bar** as shown. ❶

- **Right-click** on the PRONGS layer❷
  - A drop-down context menu will appear.

right-click❷

- Click on the **Select Objects** option in the drop-down context menu as shown.❸

Fig. 63

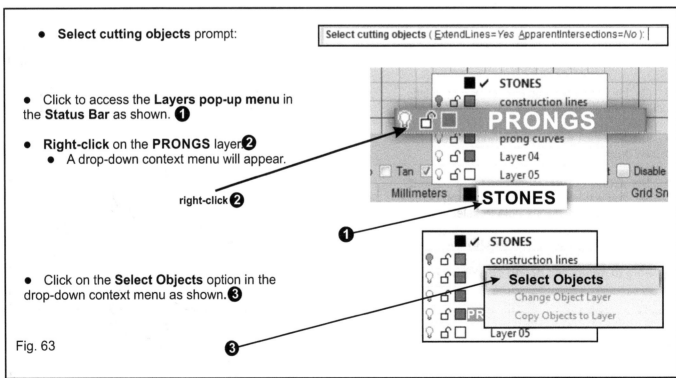

- All of the objects on the **PRONGS** layer will now be selected.

- Press **Enter** to tell Rhino that you have finished selecting the **cutting objects**.

Fig. 64

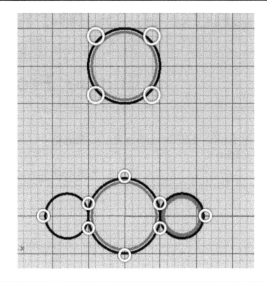

- **Select object to trim** prompt:
  - Click on the part of the circle curve that goes through the prong circle.

  - The line you clicked on has been trimmed to the boundaries of the designated cutting object which is the prong.

Fig. 65

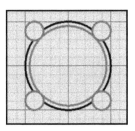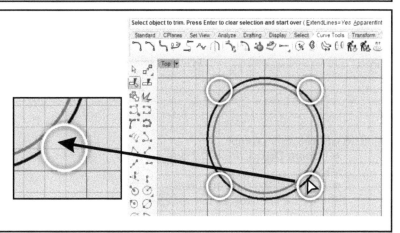

- Continue to trim out all of the prongs in the same way.

- Press **Enter** when you are finished trimming and the command will be ended.

Fig. 66

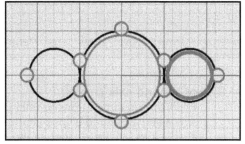

- Turn off the **prong curves** layer - it will now be both locked and turned off.

- View the finished drawings with all reference geometry turned off.

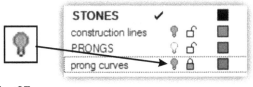

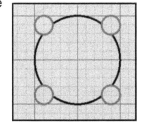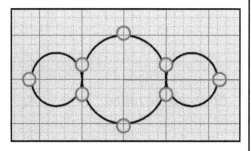

Fig. 67

Intro to Some More Basic 2-D Shapes
Ellipse, Rectangle, Polygon, Star

Ellipse: From Center - Freehand

- Open Rhino and save the file as **Basic Shapes.3dm**

- **Curve Tools tabbed toolbar.** ⌐Curve Tools⌐

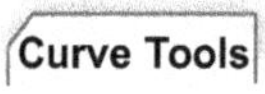

- Click on the **Ellipse: from center** command.

  - **Ellipse center** prompt:
    - Click on a location for the center of the ellipse. **1**

Ellipse: from center command

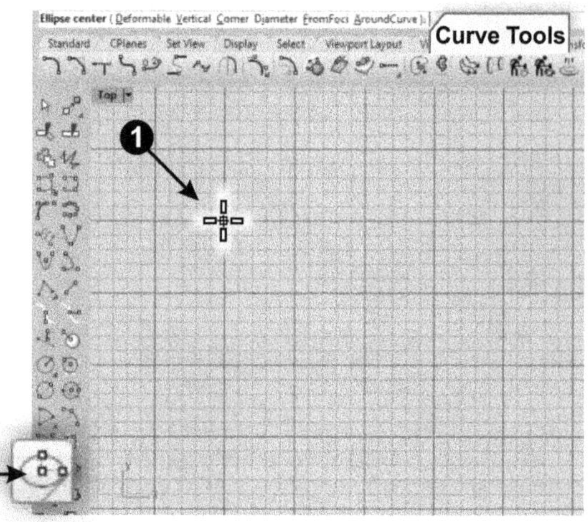

Fig. 1

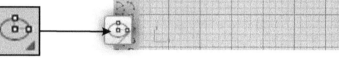

- **End of first axis** prompt:
  - Using **Ortho,** draw the cursor out as shown.
  - Click on the desired location for the end of the first axis as shown.**2**

Fig. 2

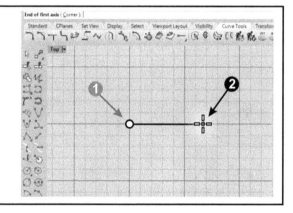

- **End of second axis** prompt:
  - Draw the cursor upward until you arrive at the desired ellipse shape.
  - Click to set the location of the second axis. **3**

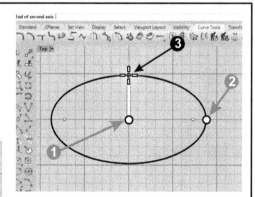

- The completed ellipse.

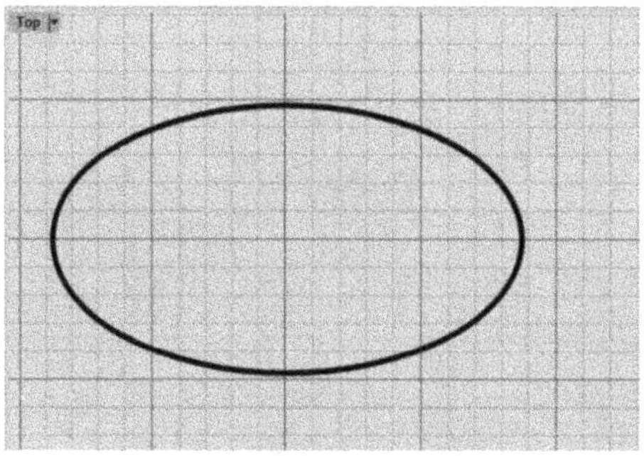

Fig. 3

107

Ellipse: Diameter - with Specified Dimensions

- **Curve Tools tabbed toolbar.** ⌐Curve Tools⌐

- Click on the **Ellipse: diameter** command.

  - **Start of first axis** prompt:
    - Click to set desired location. **❶**

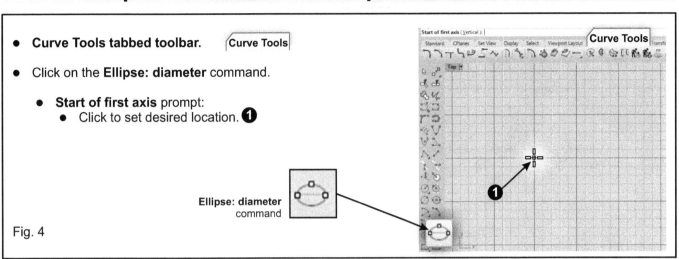

Ellipse: diameter
command

Fig. 4

- **End of first axis** prompt:
  - Type **"10"** in the **Command Line.**
- Fig. 5 — Press **Enter.**

End of first axis: **10**

- The length of the first axis is constrained to **10mm**.

- Click to set the desired location of the end of the first axis.
  - Notice that the cross hairs symbol that marks the actual end of the first axis. **❷**

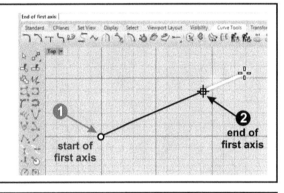

start of first axis

end of first axis

Fig. 6

- **End of second axis** prompt:
  - Type **"3"** in the **Command Line**.
- Fig. 7 — Press **Enter.**

End of second axis: **3**

- **End of second axis** prompt:
  - Click to set location. **❸**

- Dimensions have been added using the **Aligned Dimension** command *with control points turned on.*

- **Quad Osnap** was used to place the dimensions.

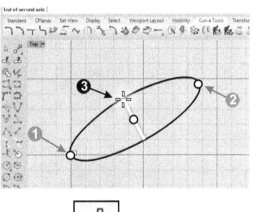

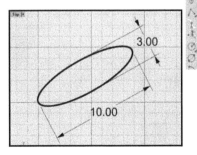

Aligned Dimension
command

Fig. 8

Rectangle: Corner to Corner - with Specified Dimensions

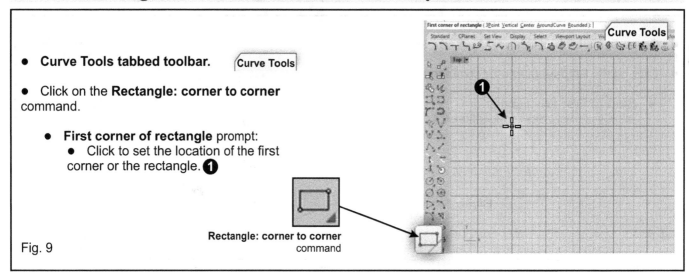

- **Curve Tools tabbed toolbar.** `Curve Tools`

- Click on the **Rectangle: corner to corner** command.

  - **First corner of rectangle** prompt:
    - Click to set the location of the first corner or the rectangle. ❶

Rectangle: corner to corner
command

Fig. 9

- **Other corner or length** prompt:
  - Type **"15"** in the <u>**Command Line.**</u>
  - Press **Enter.**

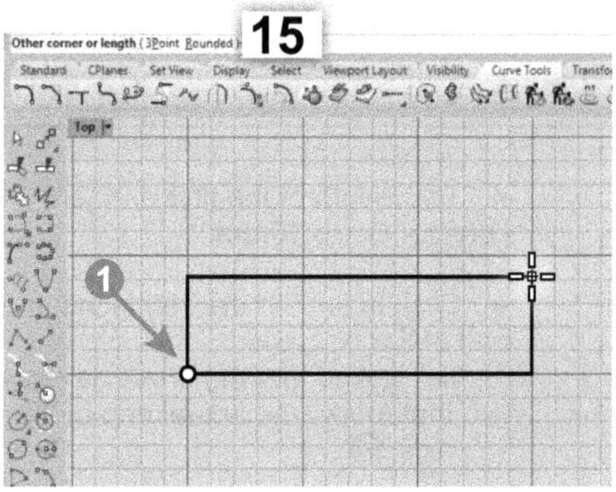

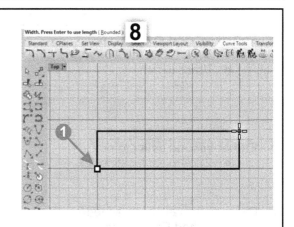

Fig. 10

- The horizontal length of the rectangle will be **15mm** in the **Xaxis** direction which always comes first.

- **Width. Press Enter to use length** prompt:
  - Type **"8"** in the <u>**Command Line.**</u>
  - Press **Enter.**

- *Note: If you had pressed **Enter**, instead of specifying a number, the width of the rectangle would **automatically be the same as the height**, creating a **square**, instead of a rectangle.*

Fig. 11

- The finished rectangle with the 8mm Width shown in the **Yaxis** direction.

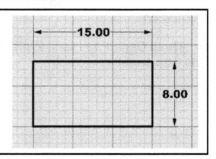

Fig. 12

Rectangle: Center, Corner

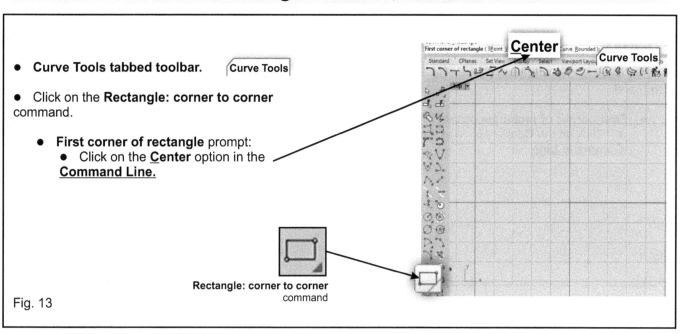

- **Curve Tools tabbed toolbar.** |Curve Tools|

- Click on the **Rectangle: corner to corner** command.

  - **First corner of rectangle** prompt:
    - Click on the **Center** option in the **Command Line.**

Rectangle: corner to corner
command

Fig. 13

- **Center of rectangle** prompt:
  - Then, type **"0"** in the **Command Line.**
  - Press **Enter.**

Center of rectangle (Rounded): **0**

- **Other corner or length** prompt:
  - Type **"20"**.
  - Press **Enter.**

Other corner or length (3Point Rounded): **20**

Fig. 14

- The rectangle is centered on **0**.

- The **horizontal length** along the **X axis** is constrained to **20mm**.

  - **Width. Press Enter to use length** prompt:
    - Type **"5"**.
    - Press **Enter.**

Width. Press Enter to use length (Rounded): **5**

center of
rectangle
"0"

Fig. 15

- The finished rectangle.

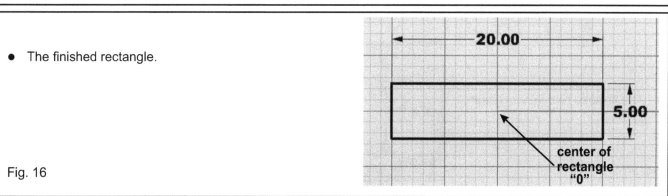

center of
rectangle
"0"

Fig. 16

Rectangle - Rounded Arc Corners

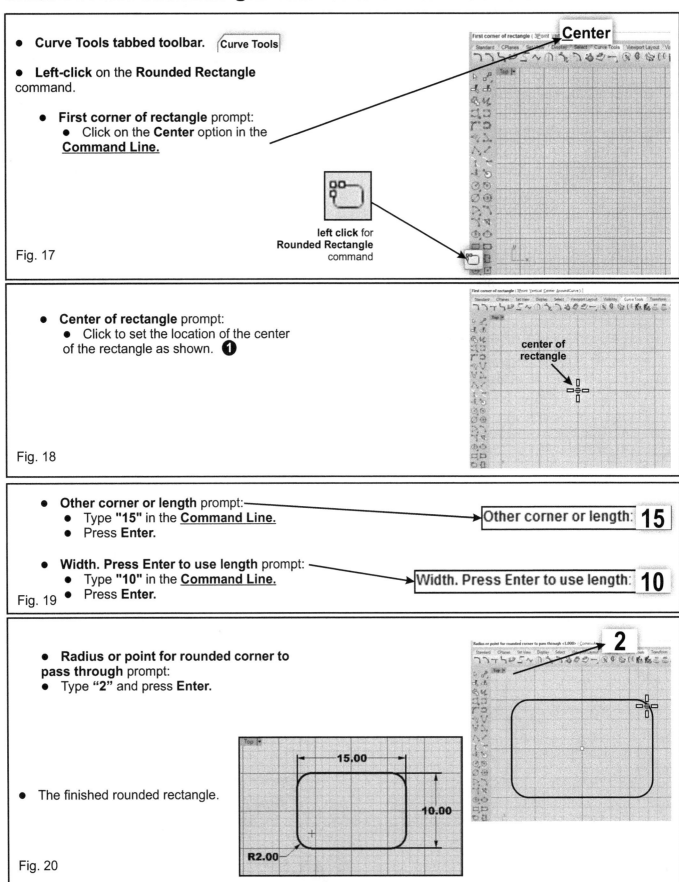

- **Curve Tools tabbed toolbar.** Curve Tools

- **Left-click** on the **Rounded Rectangle** command.

  - **First corner of rectangle** prompt:
    - Click on the **Center** option in the **Command Line.**

left click for
Rounded Rectangle
command

Fig. 17

- **Center of rectangle** prompt:
  - Click to set the location of the center of the rectangle as shown. ❶

center of
rectangle

Fig. 18

- **Other corner or length** prompt:
  - Type **"15"** in the **Command Line.**
  - Press **Enter.**

  Other corner or length: **15**

- **Width. Press Enter to use length** prompt:
  - Type **"10"** in the **Command Line.**
  - Press **Enter.**

  Width. Press Enter to use length: **10**

Fig. 19

- **Radius or point for rounded corner to pass through** prompt:
  - Type **"2"** and press **Enter.**

- The finished rounded rectangle.

  15.00

  10.00

  R2.00

Fig. 20

Rectangle - Rounded Conic Corners

- **Curve Tools tabbed toolbar.**

- **Right-click** on the same button for the **Rounded Rectangle: conic corners** command.

  - **First corner of rectangle** prompt:
    - Click on the desired location for the first corner of the rectangle. **❶**

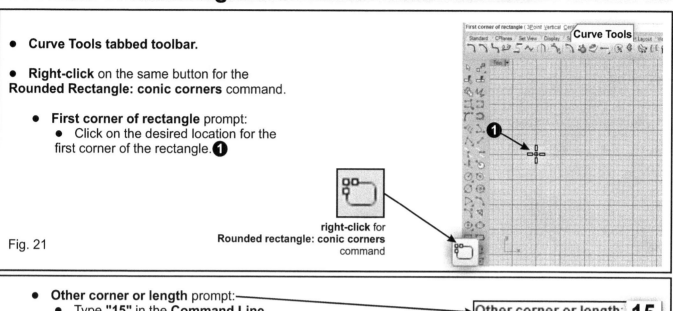

right-click for
Rounded rectangle: conic corners
command

Fig. 21

- **Other corner or length** prompt:
  - Type **"15"** in the **Command Line.**
  - Press **Enter.**

  → Other corner or length: **15**

- **Width. Press Enter to use length** prompt:
  - Type **"10"** in the **Command Line.**
  - Press **Enter.**

  → Width. Press Enter to use length: **10**

Fig. 22

- **Rho or point for conic corner to pass through** prompt:
  - Draw the cursor in and click when you have the desired rectangle. **❷**

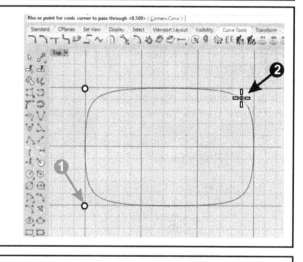

Fig. 23

- Note the difference between the finished **Conic rectangle** and the finished rectangle with **Arc corners.**

- Control points are turned on to see the difference in geometry.

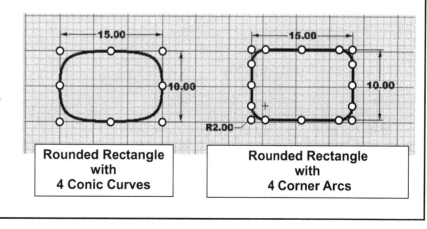

| Rounded Rectangle with 4 Conic Curves | Rounded Rectangle with 4 Corner Arcs |

Fig. 24

Polygon: center radius

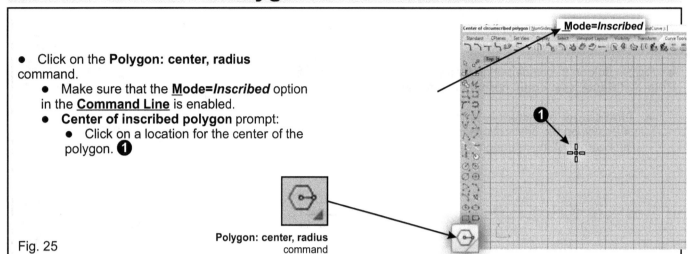

- Click on the **Polygon: center, radius** command.
  - Make sure that the **Mode=*Inscribed*** option in the **Command Line** is enabled.
  - **Center of inscribed polygon** prompt:
    - Click on a location for the center of the polygon. ❶

Polygon: center, radius
command

Fig. 25

- **Corner of polygon** prompt:
  - Click on the **(N**umSides=5) option in the **Command Line**.

- **Number of sides** prompt:
  - Type **"6"** in the **Command Line**
  - Press **Enter.**

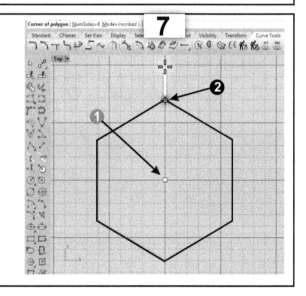

Fig. 26

- Notice that the cursor is pulling the polygon out by **one of its corners**.

- **Corner of polygon** prompt:
  - Use **Ortho** when pulling the polygon up to keep it straight.
  - Type **"7"** to set the radius of the polygon.
  - Press **Enter**.

- **Corner of polygon** prompt:
  - Notice the white constraint line that is constraining the radius of the polygon to **7mm**. ❷
  - Click to finish the polygon command.

Fig. 27

- The finished **6-sided polygon**.

- Note that the **"7"** that you entered fixed the distance between the **Center** of the polygon and **one of its corners** as shown by the dimension.
  - The dimension was placed with the use of **Center osnap** and **End osnap**.

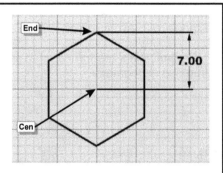

Fig. 28

Circumscribed Polygon: center, radius

- Click on the **Circumscribed polygon: center, radius** command in the **Polygon** toolbar flyout as shown.
  - Make sure that the **Mode=Circumscribed** option in the **Command Line** is enabled.
  - **Center of circumscribed polygon** prompt:
    - Click on desired location for the center of the polygon. **❶**

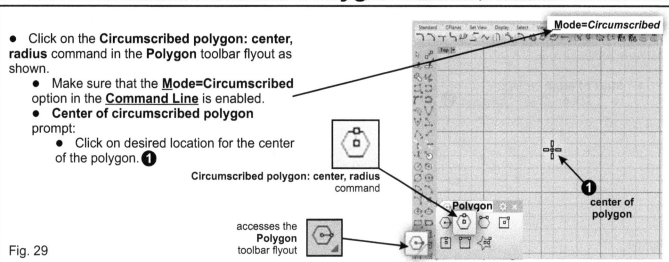

Circumscribed polygon: center, radius command

accesses the **Polygon** toolbar flyout

Fig. 29

- **Midpoint of polygon edge** prompt:
  - Click on the number of sides option in the **Command Line.**

- **Number of sides** prompt:
  - Type **"8"** in the **Command Line.**
  - Press **Enter.**

Fig. 30

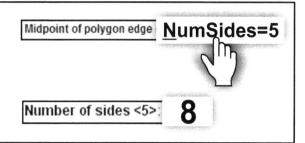

- Notice that the cursor is pulling the polygon out by the **midpoint of one of its edges.**

- **Midpoint of polygon edge** prompt:
  - Notice the 8 sides of the polygon as you draw the cursor up.

  - Type **"10"** in the **Command Line** to set the radius of the polygon.
  - Press **Enter.**

  - Draw the cursor straight up using **Ortho.**
  - Click to set location. **❷**

Fig. 31

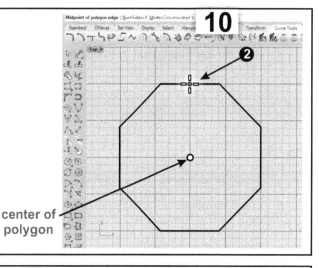

center of polygon

- The finished polygon.

- The radius dimension measures the distance between the **Center** of the polygon and the **Midpoint of the Edge.**

Fig. 32

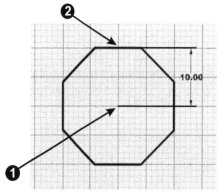

114

Polygon: Edge

- Click on the **Polygon: edge** command in the **Polygon** toolbar flyout.

  - **Start of edge** prompt:
    - Click on desired location. ❶

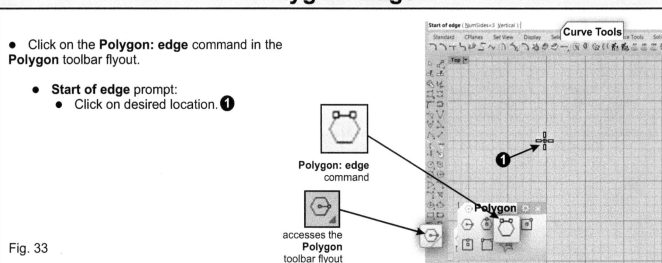

Polygon: edge
command

accesses the
Polygon
toolbar flyout

Fig. 33

- **End of edge** prompt:
  - Click on the **NumSides=8** option in the **Command Line.**

- **Number of sides** prompt:
  - Type **"6"** in the **Command Line.**
  - Press **Enter.**

Fig. 34

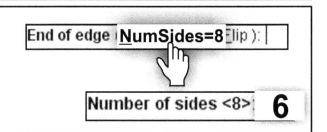

- The polygon now has **6 sides.**

- Click on the **Flip** option in the **Command Line.**

Fig. 35

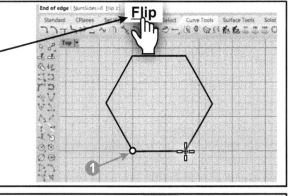

- The orientation of the polygon has been "flipped" so it is now pointed downward.

- **End of edge** prompt:
  - Type **"5"** in the **Command Line.**
  - Press **Enter.**

- **End of edge** prompt:
  - The length of the edge is now **constrained to the designated 5mm**.
  - Click to set the location of the end of edge. ❷

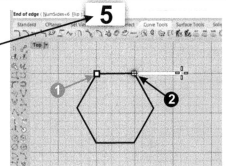

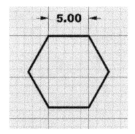

- The finished polygon with **5mm edges.**

Fig. 36

Star - Default Star Shape

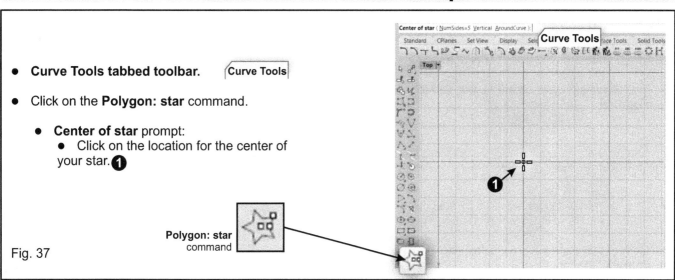

- **Curve Tools tabbed toolbar.** [Curve Tools]

- Click on the **Polygon: star** command.

    - **Center of star** prompt:
        - Click on the location for the center of your star.**❶**

Polygon: star command

Fig. 37

- **Corner of star** prompt:
    - The star will probably have the default number of 5 "sides" as you can see from the options line in the **Command Line.** Keep this default number of sides.
    - To set the **radius of the star,** type **"5"** in the **Command Line.**

Fig. 38
    - Press **Enter.**

Corner of star (NumSides=5): **5**

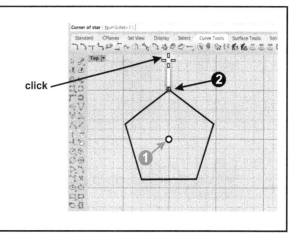

- The distance between the Center of the star ❶ and the point has been set to **5mm.** **❷**

- Click to set location.
- In this illustration, **Ortho** has been used to keep the star in line with the grid.

click

Fig. 39

- Move the cursor inward toward the center of the star and see a preview of the star taking shape.

    - **Second star radius. Press Enter for automatic** prompt:
        - You can click anywhere to get your desired star shape but, in this exercise, **press Enter** for the default star shape.

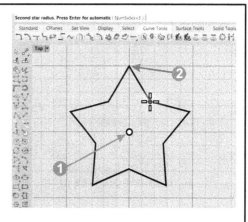

Fig. 40

- The star will take a default, or **"automatic"** shape.

- This is the shape of the most commonly designed stars that you see everywhere.

- The Dimension was created using **Center** and **End osnaps**.

Fig. 41

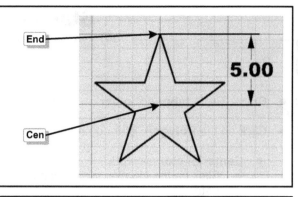

- See the variations you can get by specifying different numbers of sides when creating the star.

- Both of these stars were made using the **"automatic"** option used above.

Fig. 42

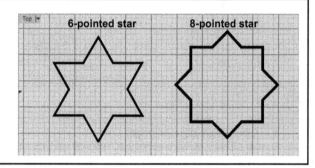

Star with Specified Radii

- **Curve Tools tabbed toolbar.** Curve Tools

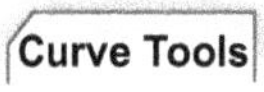

- For reference, create two circles with the same center point. Note the diameter dimensions of **5mm and 15mm.**

- Click on the **Polygon: star** command.

Fig. 43

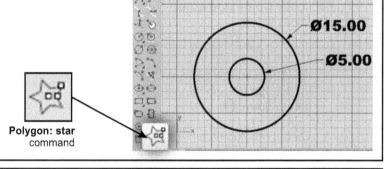

Polygon: star
command

- **Center of star** prompt:
    - Use **Center osnap** to snap to the center of the inner star.
    - Click to set location for the center of the star. **1**

Fig. 44

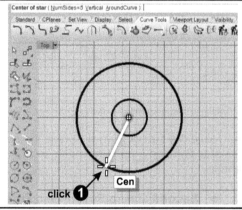

- **Corner of star** prompt:

    - Click on the **NumSides=5** option in the **Command Line.**
    - **Number of sides** prompt:
        - Type **"15"** and press **Enter.**

Fig. 45

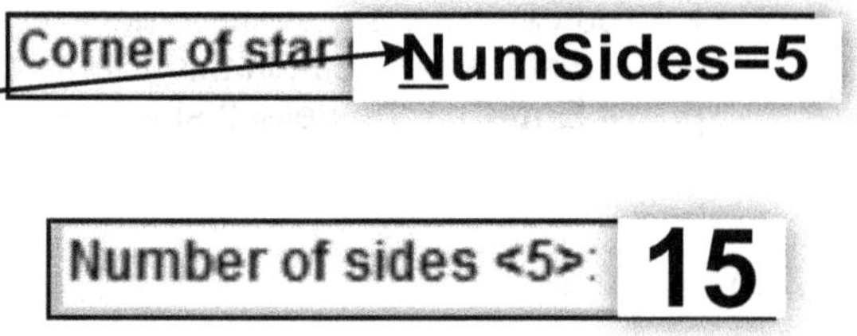

Corner of star ➔ **NumSides=5**

Number of sides <5>: **15**

- **Corner of star** prompt:
  - Draw the cursor up to the **quad** of the larger outer circle .
  - Click to set location. ❷

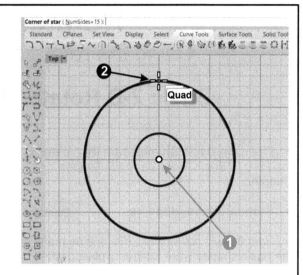

Fig. 46

- **Second star radius** prompt:
  - Draw the cursor down and snap to the upper quad point of the small inner circle.
  - Click to set location. ❸

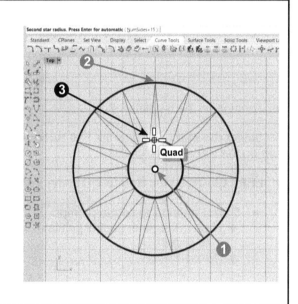

Fig. 47

- Hide or Delete the circles.

- You don't have to have circles to snap to. This exercise used circles to illustrate how the star is constructed, specifying inner and outer radii.

- This star has 15 "sides".

- Save this file as **basic shapes.3dm.**

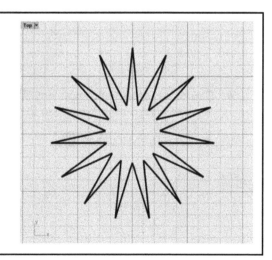

Fig. 48

118

Rotate 2-D Command
Using the rotate command for 2-D drawings.

Basic 2-D Rotate: Freehand Rotating by Eye

- Open the **Basic Shapes.3dm** file created in the *Intro to Some More Basic 2D Shapes* Chapter..

- **Standard tabbed toolbar.**   Standard

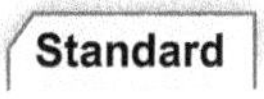

- Your file will not look like this one as many of the basic shapes were arbitrarily placed when creating this file.

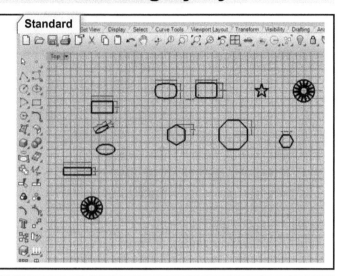

Fig. 1

- Zoom in on the 5-pointed star.

- **Select the star** and press the **F10 Hotkey** to turn on the star's control points.   F10

- **LEFT CLICK** on the **Rotate 2-D** command.

  - **Select objects to rotate** prompt:
    - Select the outer control points of the star as shown.
    - Press **Enter.**

LEFT CLICK for **Rotate 2-D** command

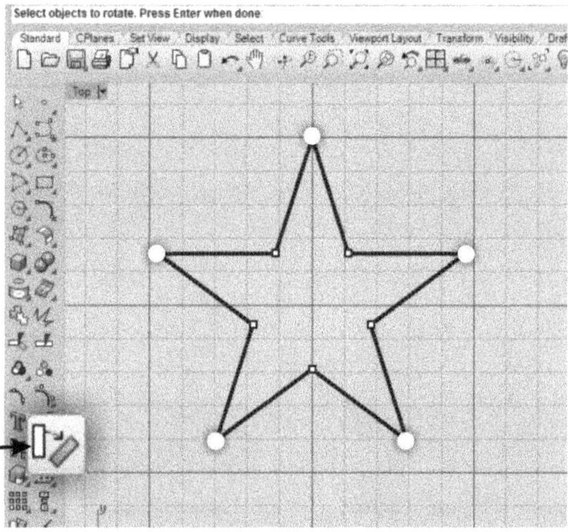

Fig. 2

- **Center of rotation** prompt:
  - Use **Cen osnap** to snap to the center of the star.
  - Click to set location. ❶

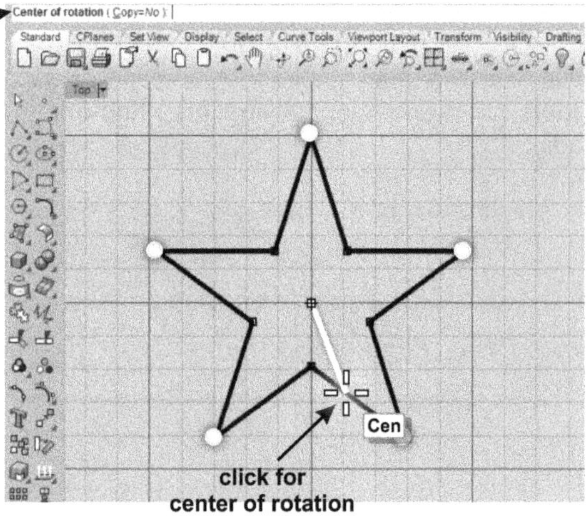

click for center of rotation

Fig. 3

- **Angle or first reference point** prompt:
  - As you draw the cursor out, you will see a **black preview line** that represents the radius of the rotation. You will also see a white circle that represents the **arc of rotation.**
  - Click to set a first reference point as shown. This is done at random in this illustration. ❶

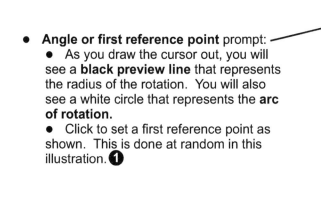
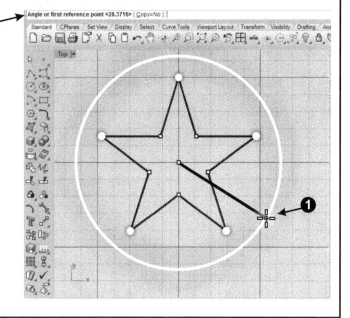

Fig. 4

- **Second reference point** prompt:
  - Notice that the white circle has changed to a black circle.
  - As you draw the cursor around, the angle of rotation is previewed.
  - Also, notice the preview of the new star shape and the thin lines showing its original shape.
  - Click to set the **Second reference point.** ❸

Fig. 5

- The finished revolve.

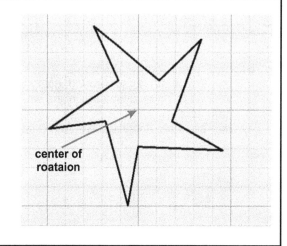

Fig. 6

Basic 2-D Rotate: Using Osnap for Reference Points

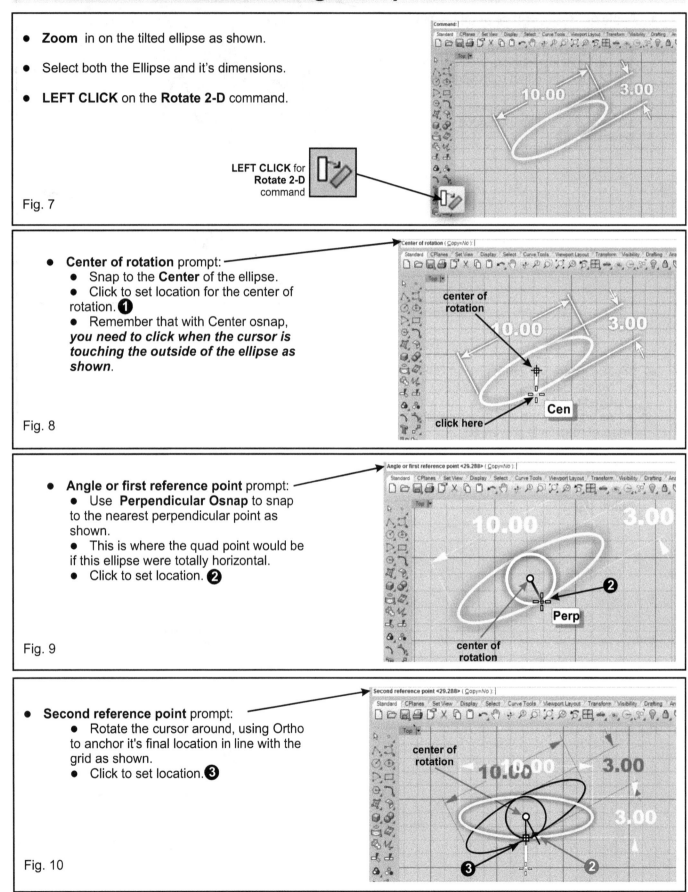

- **Zoom** in on the tilted ellipse as shown.

- Select both the Ellipse and it's dimensions.

- **LEFT CLICK** on the **Rotate 2-D** command.

LEFT CLICK for
Rotate 2-D
command

Fig. 7

- **Center of rotation** prompt:
  - Snap to the **Center** of the ellipse.
  - Click to set location for the center of rotation. ❶
  - Remember that with Center osnap, *you need to click when the cursor is touching the outside of the ellipse as shown*.

center of rotation

Cen

click here

Fig. 8

- **Angle or first reference point** prompt:
  - Use **Perpendicular Osnap** to snap to the nearest perpendicular point as shown.
  - This is where the quad point would be if this ellipse were totally horizontal.
  - Click to set location. ❷

❷

Perp

center of rotation

Fig. 9

- **Second reference point** prompt:
  - Rotate the cursor around, using Ortho to anchor it's final location in line with the grid as shown.
  - Click to set location. ❸

center of rotation

❸   ❷

Fig. 10

- The finished revolve.

- The ellipse is perfectly horizontal.

- Notice that the orientation of the dimension extension lines and text have been updated in their new position.

Fig. 11

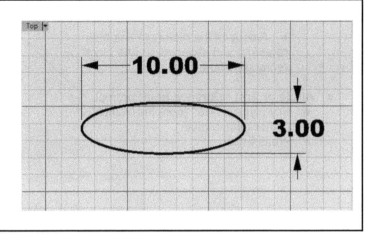

Basic 2-D Rotate: Using Specified Rotation Angles

- When specifying an angle of rotation, note that when you are rotating clockwise, you need to put a "minus" sign in front of the number of the angle when you are typing it.
  - Example: **-45**

Fig. 12

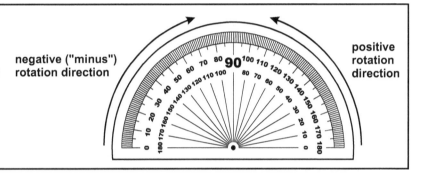

- Zoom in on the **15 x 8 Rectangle.**

- Click the **Copy=No** option in the **Command Line.** The option will be toggled to **Copy=Yes**.

  - **Center of rotation** prompt:
    - Use **Center osnap** to snap to the center of the rectangle.
    - Click to set location

Fig. 13

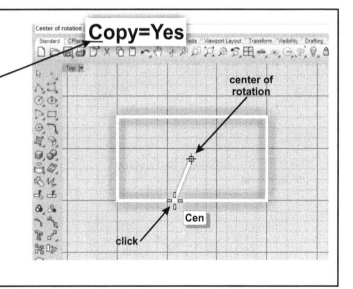

- **Angle or first reference point** prompt:
  - Type **"45"** in the **Command Line.**
  - Press **Enter.**

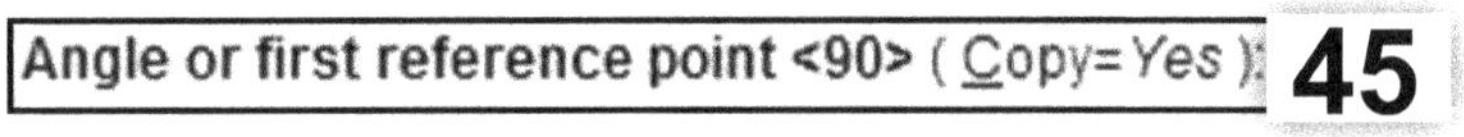

Angle or first reference point <90> (Copy=Yes) **45**

Fig. 14

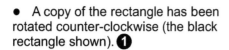

- A copy of the rectangle has been rotated counter-clockwise (the black rectangle shown). **❶**

- **Angle or first reference point** prompt:
  - Now, type a **"-45"** (note the "minus" sign before the number).
  - Press **Enter.**

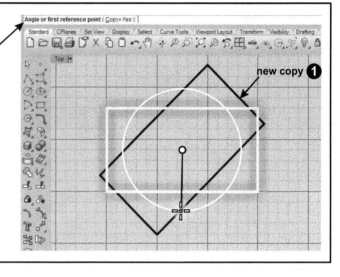

Fig. 15

- A new rectangle has been created, rotated in the other direction as shown. **❷**

- You can make as many copies as you wish. You can also switch to freehand placement at any time within the command.

- Press **Enter** to end the command.

- The completed rotation has created 2 copies.

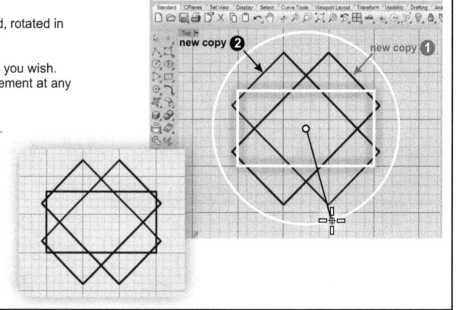

Fig. 16

- Use the Trim command to try some design concepts.

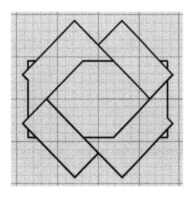

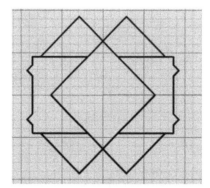

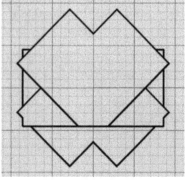

Fig. 17

Technical Drawing - Simple Pearl Ring
Drawing with Circles

- Open Rhino and save the file as **pearl ring technical drawing.3dm.**

- As with all technical drawings, you will be working in the **Top Viewport.**
  - Maximize the top viewport for optimal visibility.
  - Note: In this book, the top viewport is not maximized due to page space considerations.

Drawing the Front View of the Ring Shank

- Create the layers shown.

- Click to place the check mark on the **TECH LINES** layer line.

- The check mark means that this layer is "Current". *Anything you create now will be on this layer.*

Fig. 1

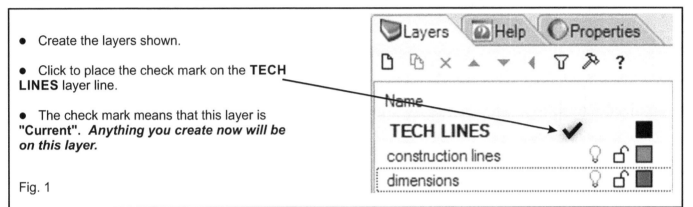

- **Curve Tools tabbed toolbar.** [Curve Tools]

- Use the **Circle: center, radius** command to create a circle.
  - **Center of circle: 0**
  - **Circle Diameter: 17.35mm**

Fig. 2

Circle: Center, Radius
command

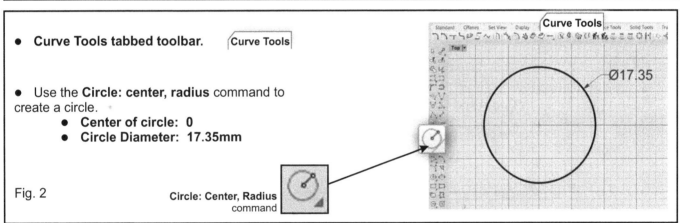

Ø17.35

- Select the circle ❶ and click on the **Offset curve** command.
  - **Side to offset** prompt:
    - Type **"2"** in the **Command Line.** ❷
    - Make sure the cursor is on the outside of the circle.
    - Press **Enter.**
    - This will assign a thickness of 2mm to the ring band in this Front view elevation.

LEFT CLICK for
Offset Curve
command

Fig. 3

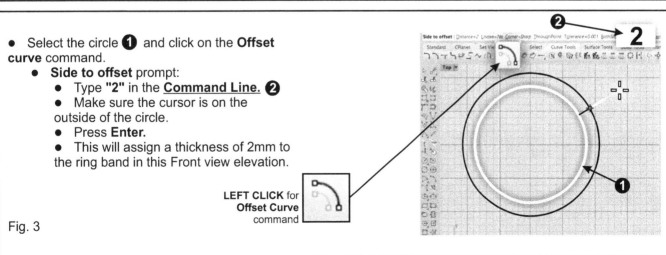

- The new offset has been completed to show the 2mm thickness of the shank as seen from the front.

Fig. 4

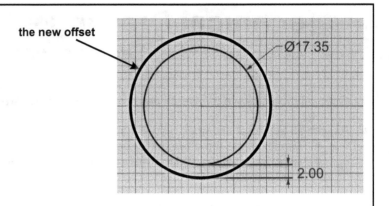

the new offset

Ø17.35

2.00

Adding the Pearls to the Front View of the Shank

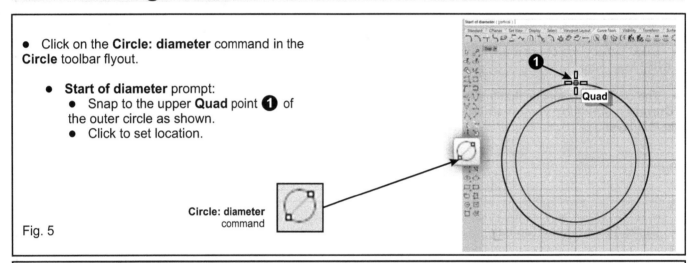

- Click on the **Circle: diameter** command in the **Circle** toolbar flyout.

  - **Start of diameter** prompt:
    - Snap to the upper **Quad** point ❶ of the outer circle as shown.
    - Click to set location.

Circle: diameter command

Fig. 5

Quad

- **End of diameter** prompt:
  - Type **"5"** in the <u>Command Line.</u> ❷
  - Press **Enter.**
  - *This will assign a <u>5mm diameter</u> to the center pearl on the top of the band.*

Fig. 6

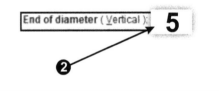

End of diameter (Vertical): **5**

❷

- **End of diameter** prompt:
  - Use **Ortho** and draw the cursor straight up for a vertical diameter. ❸
  - The diameter of the pearl is constrained to 5mm.
  - Click to set location.

- A 5mm pearl has been created on the top of the ring band.

Fig. 7

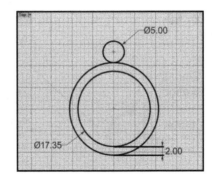

Ø5.00

Ø17.35

2.00

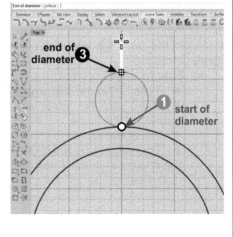

end of diameter ❸

start of diameter ❶

- Click on the **Circle: tangent, tangent, radius** command.

  - **First tangent curve** prompt:
    - Move the cursor until it snaps to the circle as shown. ❶ (see the white constraint line.)
    - Click to set location.

Circle: tangent, tangent, radius command

Fig. 8

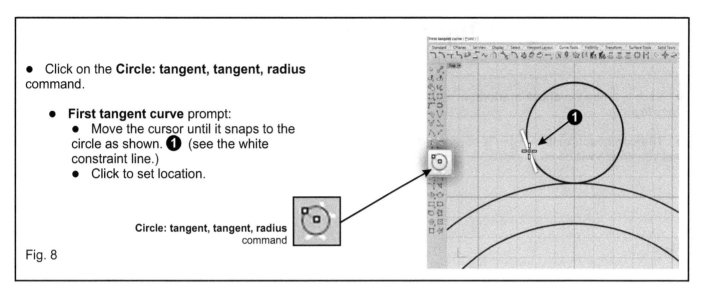

- **Second tangent curve or radius** prompt:
  - Draw the cursor down until it snaps to the large circle as shown. ❷ (See the white constraint line.)
  - Click to set location.
- **Radius** prompt:
  - Type **"2"** in the **Command Line** ❸ and press **Enter.**

Fig. 9

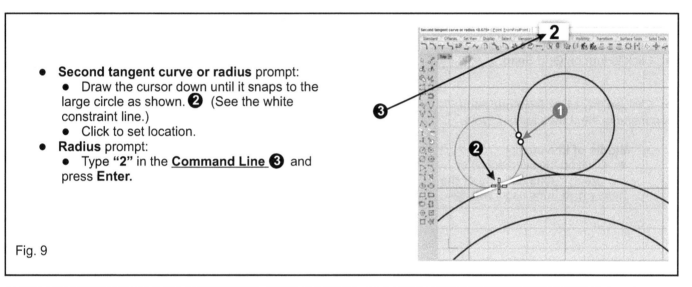

- The new circle will be constrained to a **4mm diameter.**
- The new circle is tangent to both the large pearl and the ring band.

Ø4.00 Ø5.00

- Use the same technique to add a **3mm** pearl as shown.
  - The **radius** will be **"1.5".**

Ø5.00 Ø4.00 Ø3.00

Fig. 10

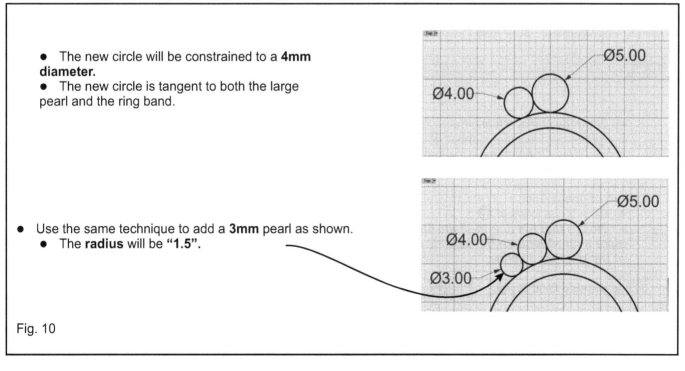

- Click to move the **check mark** down to the **construction lines** layer.

- The **construction lines** layer is now current. Anything that you create will be on this layer.

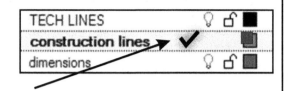

Fig. 11

- Click to turn on **Grid Snap**.

- Click on the **Line: from midpoint** command in the **Lines** toolbar flyout.

  - **Middle of line** prompt:
    - Click on the intersection of the **green Y axis** and **one of the heavy grid lines** as shown. ❶

accesses the **Lines** toolbar lfyout

Line: from midpoint command

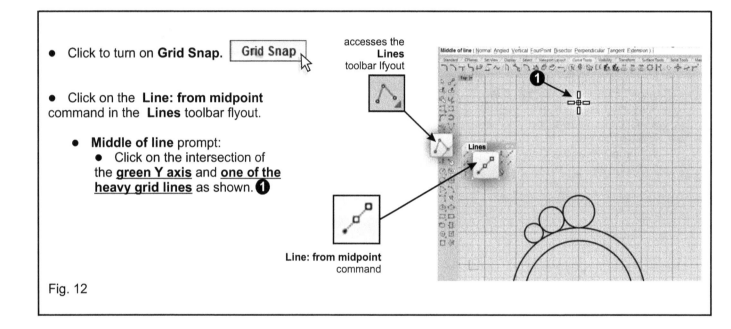

Fig. 12

  - Draw the cursor out and notice that the line generates from the midpoint ❶ as shown. *Use **Ortho** as extra insurance that this line will be perfectly horizontal.*

- **End of line** prompt:
  - Click to set location. ❷
  - *Notice that the length of the line is quite a bit wider than the outside diameter of the ring band below.*

- Click to **Disable Grid Snap**.

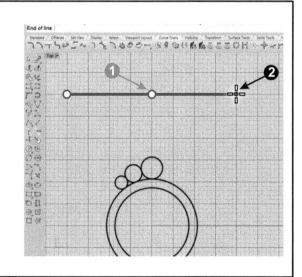

Fig. 13

- Click on the **Line** command.

  - **Start of line** prompt:
    - Snap to the **Quad ❶** on the left of the outer circle as shown.
    - Click to set location.

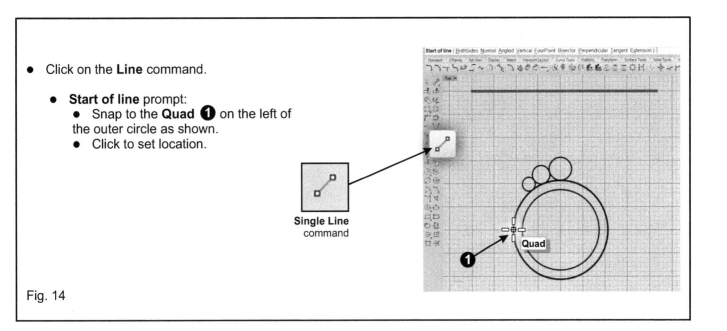

Single Line
command

Quad

❶

Fig. 14

- **End of line** prompt:

  - Draw the cursor up, using **ORTHO** for accuracy.

  - Click to set location when the line is high enough to cross the horizontal line as shown. ❷

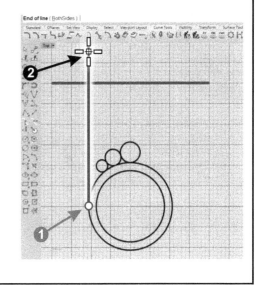

❷

❶

Fig. 15

- **Transform tabbed toolbar.** ⌐Transform⌐

- Select the perpendicular line and the two outer circles as shown.

- Click on the **Mirror** command.

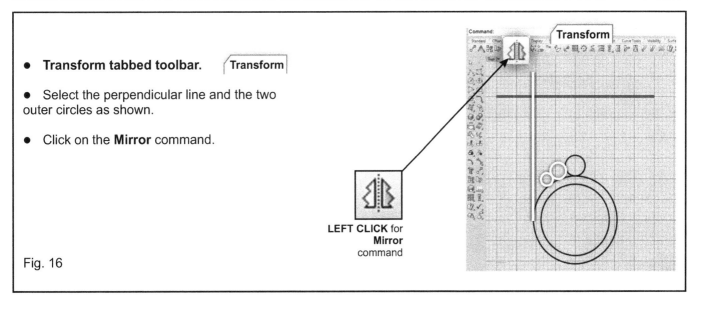

LEFT CLICK for
Mirror
command

Fig. 16

- **Start of mirror plane** prompt:
  - Type **"0"**.
  - Press **Enter**.

Fig. 17

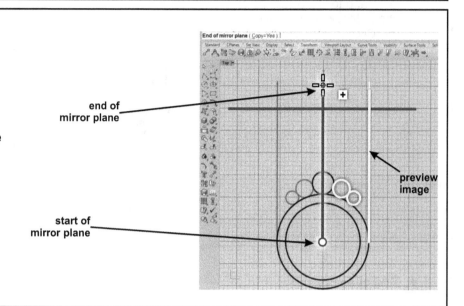

Start of mirror plane (3Point Copy=Yes XAxis YAxis) **0**

- **End of mirror plane** prompt:
  - Using **Ortho** draw the cursor straight up.
    - A preview image of a mirrored copy will appear as shown.
  - Click to set the **End of the mirror plane.**

- **The selected objects are now mirrored over to the other side of the ring.**

Fig. 18

end of mirror plane

preview image

start of mirror plane

- Create a center line for the ring.
  - Start of line: **"0"** ❶
  - End of line: perpendicular to first point. ❷ **Use ORTHO!**

Fig. 19

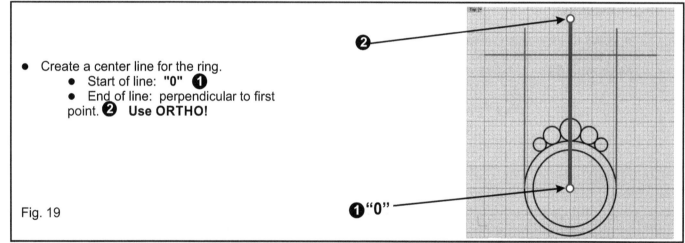

❷

❶ **"0"**

- **Curve tools tabbed toolbar.** ⌐Curve Tools⌐

- Select the horizontal construction line.

- Click on the **Offset Curve** command.

LEFT CLICK for **Offset Curve** command

Fig. 20

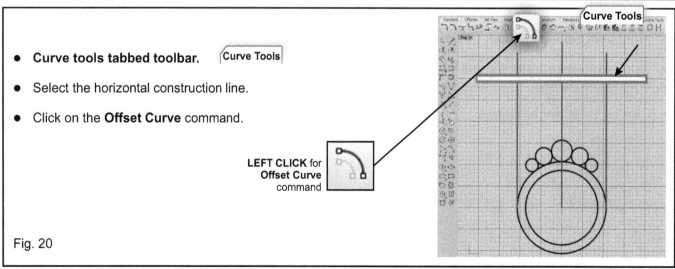

Curve Tools

- **Side to offset** prompt:
  - Click to toggle on the **BothSides** option in the **Command Line.**

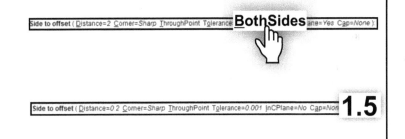

- **Side to offset** prompt:
  - Type **"1.5** in the **Command Line.**
  - Press **Enter.**

Side to offset (Distance=0 2 Corner=Sharp ThroughPoint Tolerance=0.001 InCPlane=No Cap=Non **1.5**

Fig. 21

- *Notice the preview:*
  - *The offset will be on **both sides** of the assigned line.*
  - *The distance is constrained to **1.5mm** offset for each side.*

  - Click to set location.

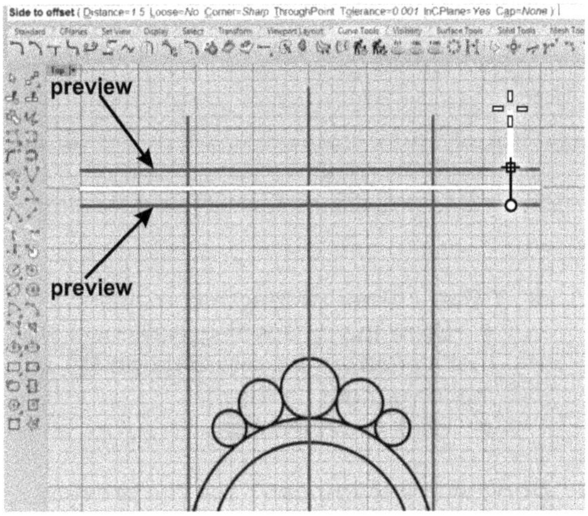

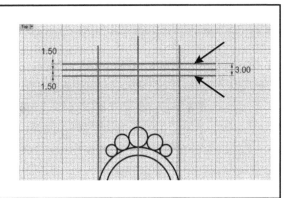

Fig. 22

- Two offsets have been created that are parallel to the middle, original, line.

- In the Top View, the thickness of the ring shank will be **3mm.**

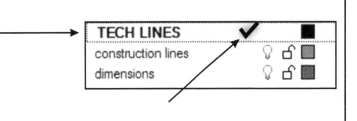

Fig. 23

- Click to put the check mark on the **TECH LINES** layer.
  - **TECH LINES** layer is now current.

TECH LINES	✓	■
construction lines	♀ ♂	■
dimensions	♀ ♂	■

Fig. 24

- Click on the **Rectangle: corner to corner** command.

  - **First corner of rectangle** prompt:
    - Snap to the **Intersection** ❶ of the two construction lines shown on the upper left.
    - Click to set location.

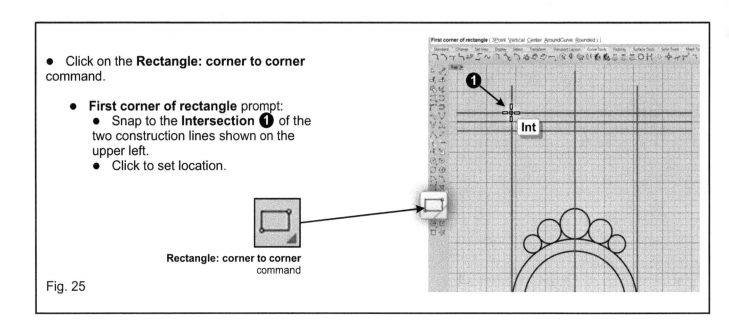

Rectangle: corner to corner
command

Fig. 25

  - **Other corner or length** command:
    - Draw the cursor diagonally over so that it snaps to the **intersection** ❷ at the lower right as shown.
    - Click to set location.

  - ***Don't worry if you can't see the preview line of the rectangle. The red construction lines may be hiding it.***

Fig. 26

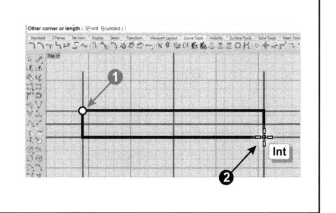

- If you turn off the **construction lines** layer, you can see the rectangle you have just created.

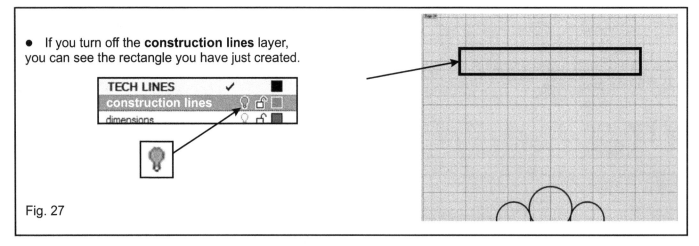

Fig. 27

- Click to make the **construction lines** layer current and it will ***automatically turn on again and become visible.***

Fig. 28

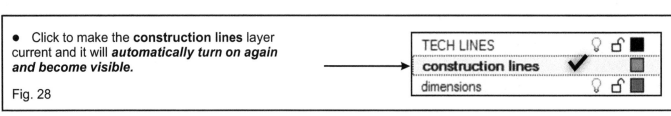

- Click on the **Line** command.

  - **Start of line** prompt:
    - Click on the **quad** of the inner circle as shown. ❶

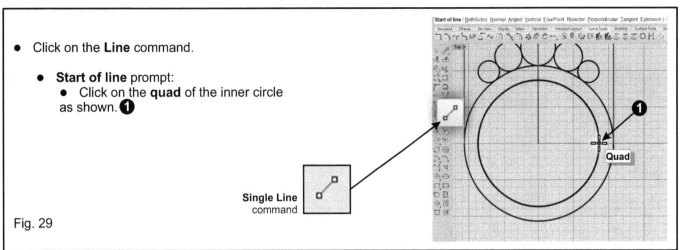

Single Line command

Fig. 29

- **End of line** prompt:
  - Using **ORTHO,** draw the cursor up and click to set a perpendicular line that crosses the 3 horizontal lines as shown.
  - Click to set the end of the line. ❷

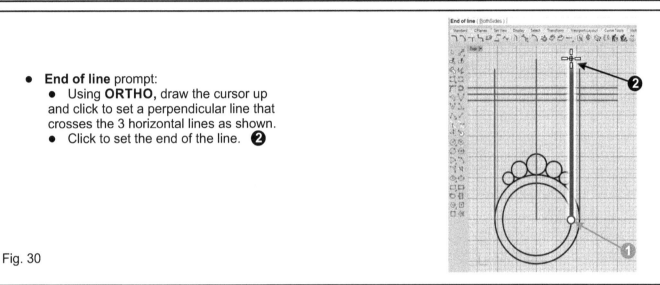

Fig. 30

- Click to put the check mark on the **TECH LINES** layer.
  - **TECH LINES** layer is now current.

Fig. 31

TECH LINES	✔	■
construction lines	💡 🔓	▩
dimensions	💡 🔓	■

- Click on the **Ellipse: diameter** command:

  - **Start of first axis** prompt:
    - Snap to the **intersection** shown.
    - Click to set location. ❶

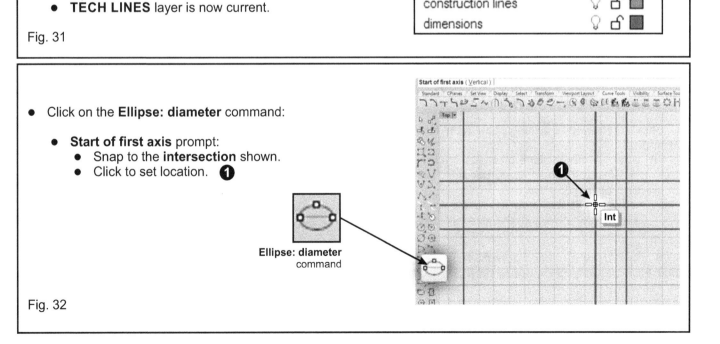

Ellipse: diameter command

Fig. 32

132

- **End of first axis** prompt:
  - Draw the cursor over and snap to the **intersection** shown.
  - Click to set location. ❷

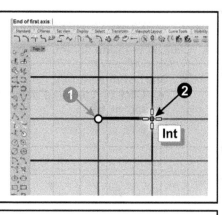

Fig. 33

- **End of second axis** prompt:
  - Draw the cursor up and snap to the **Intersection to the right.**
  - The **end of the second axis** will be placed in line with the intersection as shown.
  - Click to set location. ❸

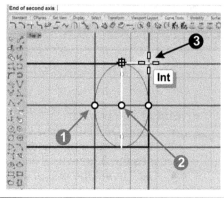

Fig. 34

- Click on the light bulb to turn off the **construction lines** layer.

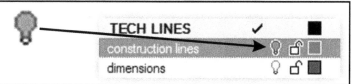

Fig. 35

- The ellipse that you have just made is a cross-section of the ring shank.

  - ***The cross-section is oval, not round***, *because the* ***2mm width*** *of the shank in the front view is different the* ***3mm width*** *in the top view.*

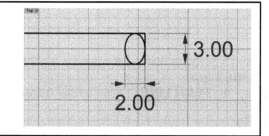

Fig. 36

- **Transform tabbed toolbar.** ⌐Transform⌐

- Select the new oval ❶ and click on the **Mirror command.**
  - **Start of Mirror plane** prompt:
    - Type **"0"** and press **Enter.** ❷
  - **End of Mirror plane:**
    - Using **Ortho,** draw the cursor up and click to set the end of the mirror plane. ❸

- *A new ellipse has been mirrored over from the other side of the ring.*

LEFT CLICK for **Mirror** command

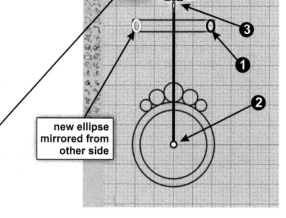

Fig. 37

133

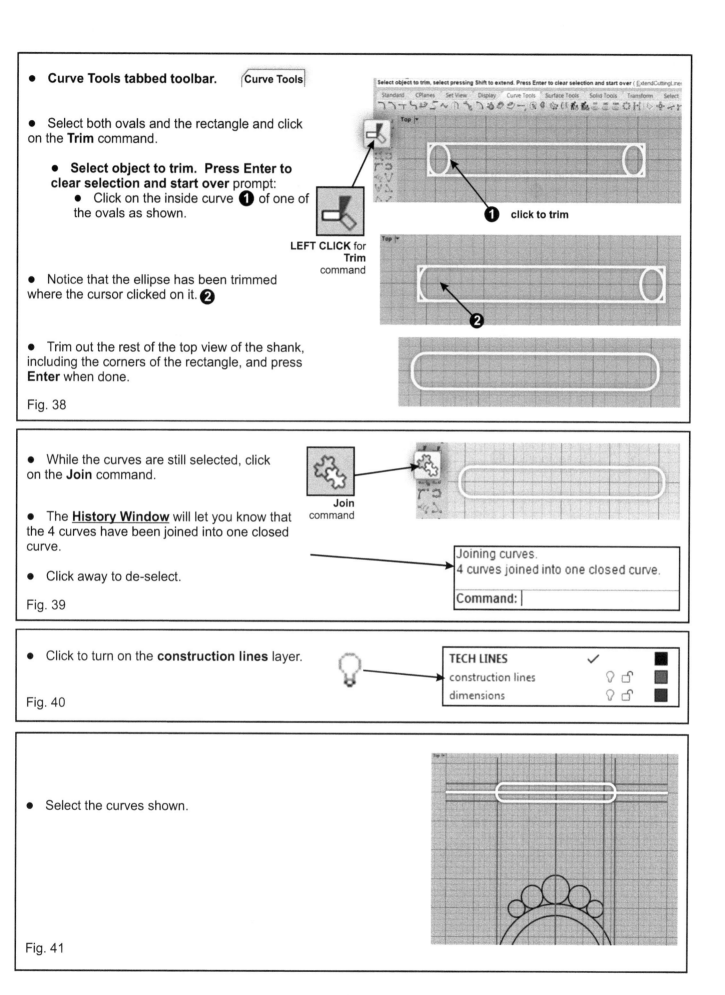

- **Curve Tools tabbed toolbar.** [Curve Tools]

- Select both ovals and the rectangle and click on the **Trim** command.

  - **Select object to trim. Press Enter to clear selection and start over** prompt:
    - Click on the inside curve ❶ of one of the ovals as shown.

  LEFT CLICK for **Trim** command

- Notice that the ellipse has been trimmed where the cursor clicked on it. ❷

- Trim out the rest of the top view of the shank, including the corners of the rectangle, and press **Enter** when done.

Fig. 38

❶ click to trim

- While the curves are still selected, click on the **Join** command.

  Join command

- The **History Window** will let you know that the 4 curves have been joined into one closed curve.

- Click away to de-select.

Fig. 39

Joining curves.
4 curves joined into one closed curve.

Command: |

- Click to turn on the **construction lines** layer.

Fig. 40

TECH LINES ✓
construction lines 🔆 🔓
dimensions 🔆 🔓

- Select the curves shown.

Fig. 41

- **Transform tabbed toolbar.** `Transform`

- Left-click on the **Rotate 2D** command in the **Transform tabbed toolbar.**

  - **Center of rotation** prompt:
    - Type **"0"** in the **Command Line**
    - Press **Enter.** ❶

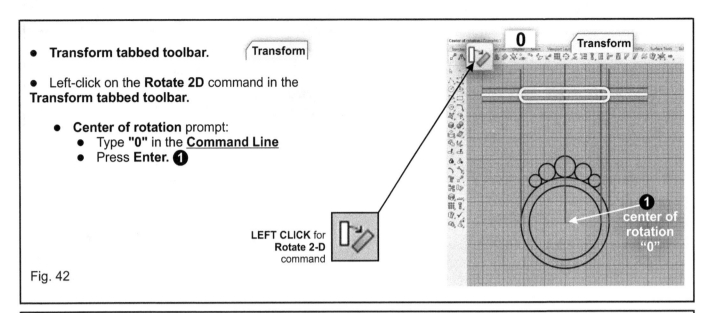

LEFT CLICK for
Rotate 2-D
command

Fig. 42

- **Angle or first reference point** prompt:
  - Click to toggle to the **Copy=Yes** option ❷ in the **Command Line.**
  - Using **ORTHO,** draw the cursor straight up as shown.
  - Click to set location. ❸

- **Second reference point** prompt:
  - Draw the cursor around to the side shown and, using **Ortho**, click to set the location ❹ of the copy that you are making.
  - Press **Enter** to end the command.

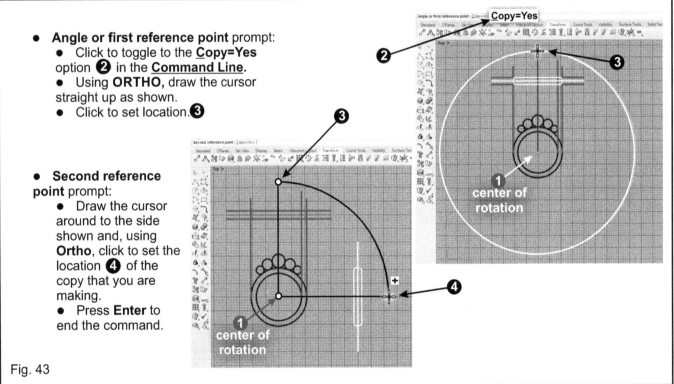

Fig. 43

- Click away to de-select if necessary.

  - *You have rotated to create a copy of the top view of the ring to create a side view for this basic ring shank.*

    - For better visibility for the **TECH LINES**, refer to the next chapter, **Draw Order Commands.**

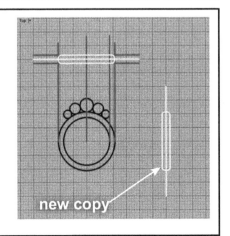

new copy

Fig. 44

Adding the Pearls to the Top and Side Views of the Band

- Make sure that **Center** and **Perpendicular** **osnaps** are enabled.

☑ Cen   ☑ Perp

- Select the large pearl circle and click on the **Copy** command.
  - **Point to copy from** prompt:
    - Snap to the **Center ❶** of the selected pearl as shown.
    - Click to set location.

LEFT CLICK for **Copy** command

Fig. 45

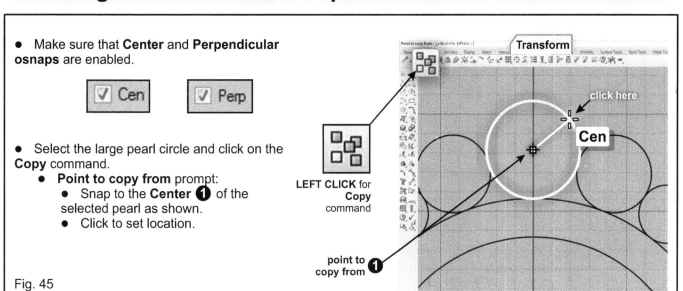

- **Point to copy to** prompt:
  - Drag the selected circle up and snap to the **Perpendicular ❷** point on the horizontal center line of the Top View as shown. **Intersection osnap** will also work here.
  - Click to set location.

- The new copy is exactly vertical to the original circle.

Fig. 46

new copy

- **Point to copy to** prompt:
  - For the next copy, draw the cursor over to the right and snap to the **Perpendicular ❸** point on the vertical center line of the Side View.
  - Click to set location.
  - Press **Enter** to end the command.

new copy

closeup view

Fig. 47

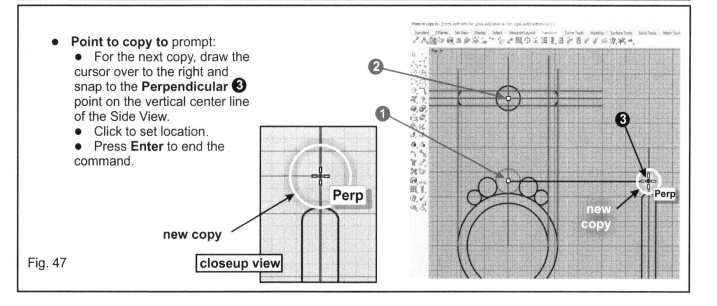

- Select the next pearl down and click on the **Copy** command.

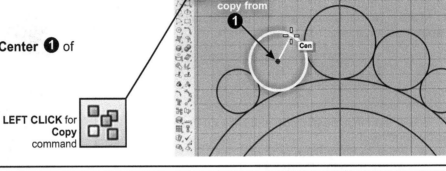

  - **Point to copy from** prompt:
    - Like before, snap to the **Center** ❶ of the circle.
    - Click to set location.

LEFT CLICK for
Copy
command

Fig. 48

- **Point to copy to** prompt:
  - Draw the cursor up and snap to the point on the center line ❷ of the Top View that is exactly **Perpendicular** to the point from which you are copying.
  - Click to set location.

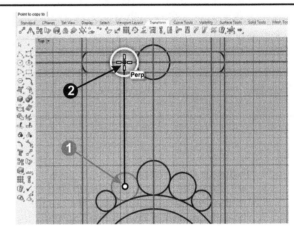

Fig. 49

- **Point to copy to** prompt:
  - Like before, draw the cursor over to the right and snap to the point that is **Perpendicular** to the point copied from.
  - Click to set location. ❸
  - Press **Enter** to end the command.

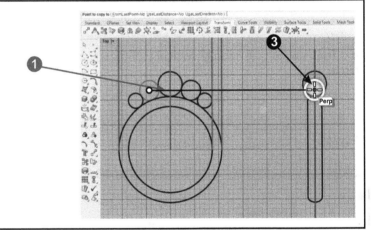

Fig. 50

- Two of the pearls have been placed on the top and side views.

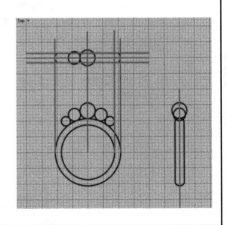

Fig. 51

- Use the same technique to set the copies of the smallest pearl on the Top and Side views.

- Zoom in close to place the small pearl on the perpendicular point on the side view!

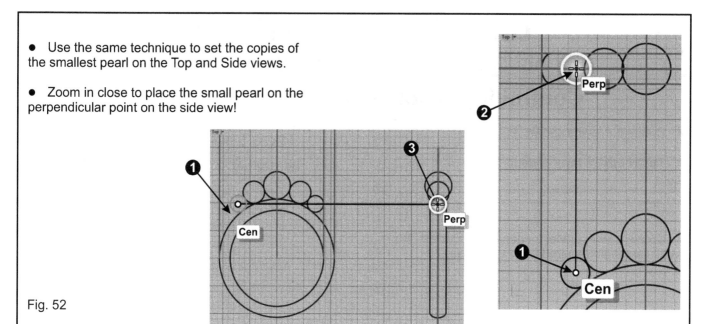

Fig. 52

- **Mirror** the side pearls in the top elevation over to the other side of the ring.
    - **Start of mirror plane: "0" ❶**
    - Using **Ortho,** draw the cursor up and click on the Y Axis ❷ to set the direction of the mirror plane.

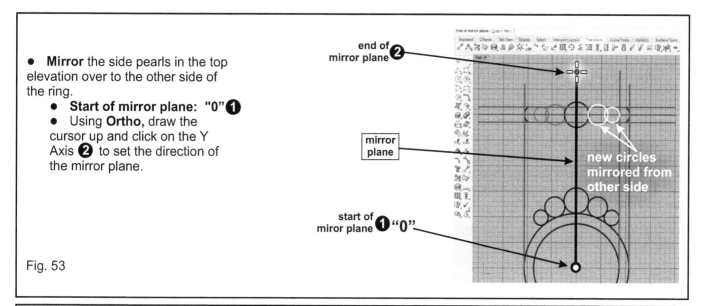

Fig. 53

- Use the **Trim** command to trim out the pearls for final design definition as shown.

- Save the file as **pearl ring technical drawing.3dm.**
- This drawing will be used in the chapter on printing technical drawings.

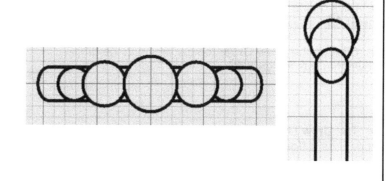

Fig. 54

Draw Order Commands
Controlling Display of Overlapping Objects

Controlling Display of Overlapping Lines

- Create the layers shown.

- **TECH LINES** layer current.

Fig. 1

| TECH LINES | ✓ | ■ |
| ref geo | ♀ 🔓 | ☐ |

- Create some parallel (or non-parallel) lines. No particular length required for this exercise.

ref geo   ✓   ■

- Create some lines that overlap the lines you just created as shown.

new lines

- Notice that the new lines overlap the previous ones, giving the appearance that they are "in front" of the original lines.

WHITE line seems to pass in front of the BLACK line

Fig. 2

- **RIGHT-CLICK** on any tab. ❶

- Click on the **Show Toolbar** option in the drop-down menu. ❷

- Click on the **Draw Order** toolbar option in the drop-down that lists toolbars. ❸

- The **Draw Order** toolbar will appear as a *floating toolbar.*

- *note: you can also add this as a tabbed toolbar if you want.*

Fig. 3

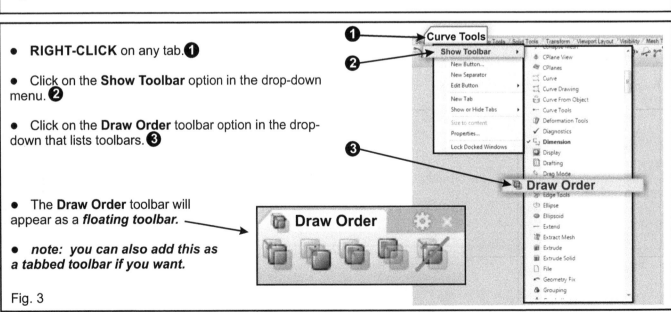

- Select all of the original dark lines that you created first.

- Click on the **Display order: bring to front** button in the **Draw Order** toolbar.

Display order: bring to front
command

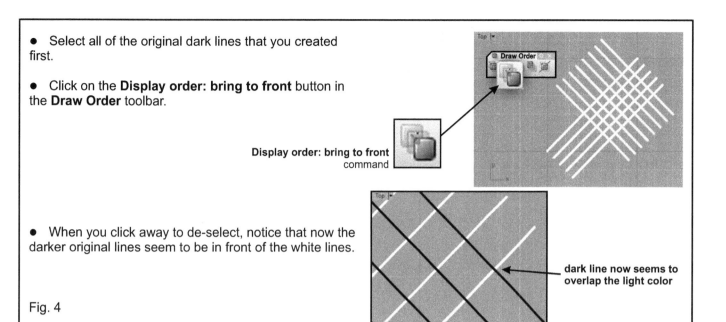

- When you click away to de-select, notice that now the darker original lines seem to be in front of the white lines.

dark line now seems to
overlap the light color

Fig. 4

- **Important note: This is about the change of display only. No objects get actually moved in this command!**

- The selected object has been created in the **Simple Pearl Ring Technical Drawing** with the use of construction lines that are a warmer color than the selected object which is black. Also, they were created first, before the selected object.

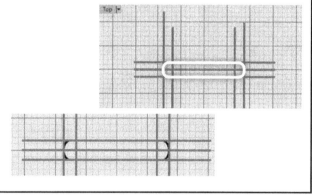

- Click away to de-select and notice that this object is almost completely hidden from view by the overlapping construction lines.

Fig. 5

- Select all of the overlapping construction lines and click on the **Display order: send to back** command

Display order: send to back
command

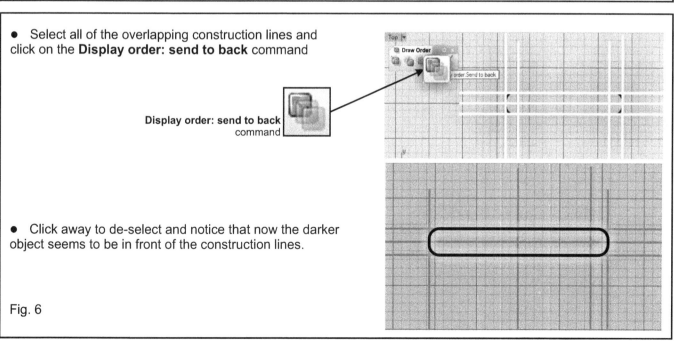

- Click away to de-select and notice that now the darker object seems to be in front of the construction lines.

Fig. 6

1-D and 2-D Scaling
Scaling Elements in Drawings and Layouts

Create Objects for Scaling

- Create the squares and circles shown.
  - **squares: 10mm sides**
  - **circles: 6mm diameter**
  - **lge circle: Ø10mm**

  - Use **Grid Snap** to quickly create these simple objects.

  Grid Snap

- Click to toggle off Grid Snap when you are finished drawing these objects.

  Grid Snap

Fig. 1

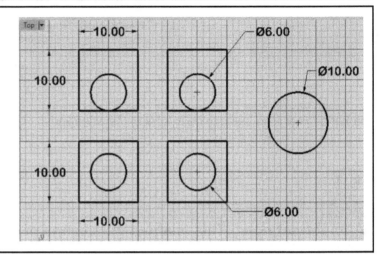

Scale 1-D Command - 1-Dimensional Scaling

- **Standard tabbed toolbar.**   Standard

- Zoom in on the square in the upper left corner.

- Click on the **Scale 1-D** command in the **Scale** toolbar flyout.

accesses the **Scale** toolbar flyout

Fig. 2   **Scale 1-D** command

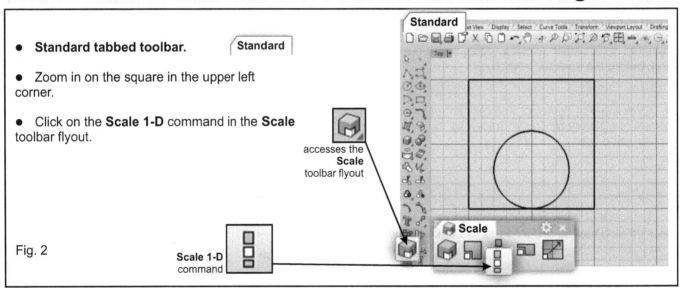

- **Select objects to scale** prompt:
  - Select the circle and press **Enter.**

Fig. 3

- **Base point**. **Press Enter for automatic** prompt:
  - Snap to the **Mid** point of the bottom of the square. ❶
    - *[Note: **Intersection** or **Quad** osnap will also work here.]*
  - Click to set location.

Fig. 4

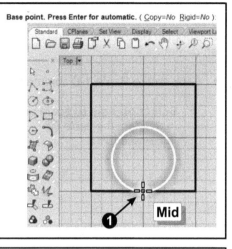

- **Scale factor or first reference point** prompt:
  - Drag the cursor up to the top of the circle and snap to the top **Quad** point. ❷
  - Click to set location.

Fig. 5

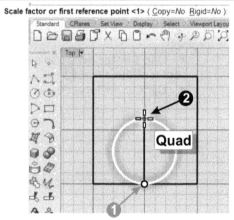

- **Second reference point** prompt:
  - Snap to the **Mid** point of the top of the square as shown. ❸
  - Click to set location.

Fig. 6

- The circle has been scaled in 1 direction from the base point to form an elongated shape.

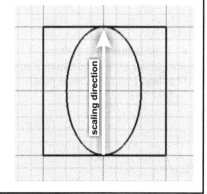

Fig. 7

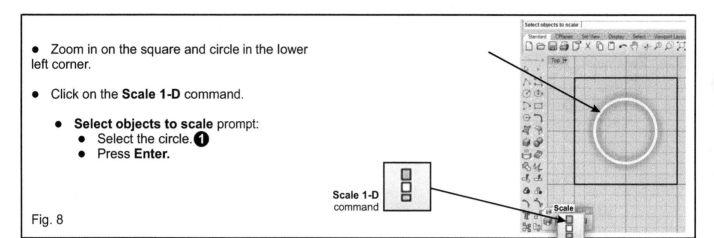

- Zoom in on the square and circle in the lower left corner.

- Click on the **Scale 1-D** command.

  - **Select objects to scale** prompt:
    - Select the circle. ❶
    - Press **Enter.**

Scale 1-D command

Fig. 8

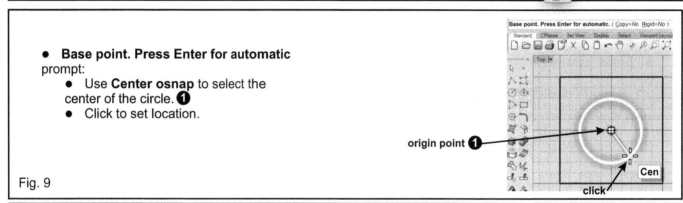

- **Base point. Press Enter for automatic** prompt:
  - Use **Center osnap** to select the center of the circle. ❶
  - Click to set location.

origin point ❶

Fig. 9

- **Scale factor or first reference point** prompt:
  - Draw the cursor up to snap to the top **Quad** of the circle. ❷
  - Click to set location.

Fig. 10

- **Second reference point** prompt:
  - Draw the cursor up to the **Mid** point at the top line of the square. ❸
  - Click to set location.

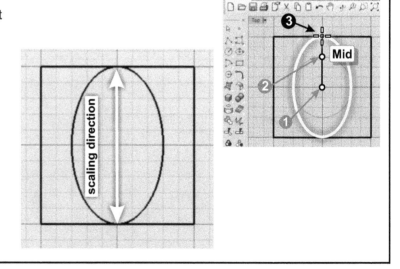

scaling direction

- The **Scale 1-D** command has created an elongated shape because it scaled in only one direction from the base point.

Fig. 11

Scale 2-D Command - 2-Dimensional Scaling

- Zoom out so that you can see the two sets of squares and circles in the top row.

- Click on the **Scale 2-D** command in the **Scale** toolbar flyout.

Scale 2-D command

accesses the **Scale** toolbar flyout

Fig. 12

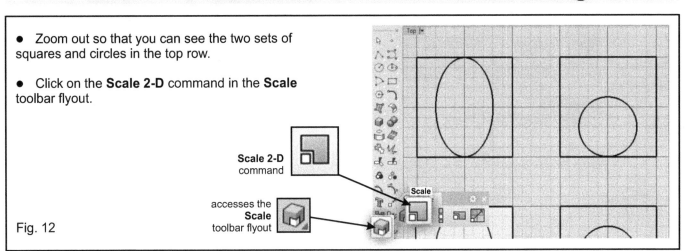

- **Select objects to scale** prompt:
  - Select the circle shown and press **Enter.**

Fig. 13

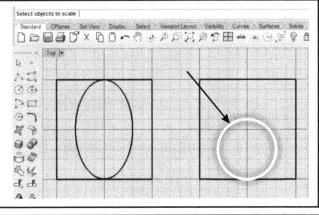

- **Base point** prompt:
  - Snap to the lower **Mid** point of the square.
    - *[Notice that, because **Quad** osnap is also enabled, both snaps show up in the cursor tooltip.]*
  - Click to set location. ❶

Fig. 14

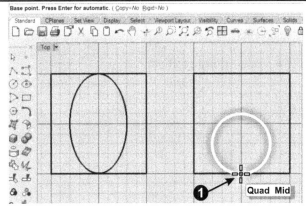

- **Scale factor or first reference point** prompt:
  - Draw the cursor up to the top **Quad** point of the circle.❷
  - Click to set location.

Fig. 15

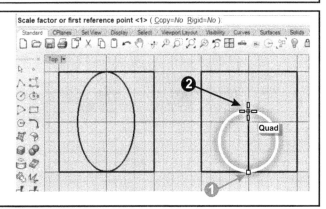

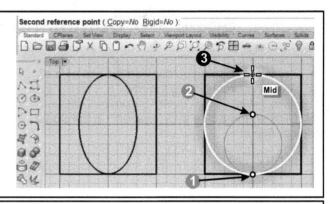

- **Second reference point** prompt:
  - Draw the cursor up to the top of the square and snap to the **Midpoint** of the top line.❸
  - Click to set location.

Fig. 16

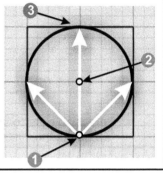

- The scaled circle fills the surrounding square and is still a circle.

- Scale 2-D has scaled the circle *in all directions* from the **Base Point.** ❶

Fig. 17

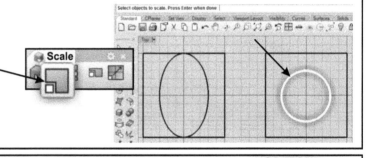

- Pan downward so that you can see the two lower squares and circles.

- Click on the **Scale 2-D** command again.

  - **Select objects to scale** prompt:
    - Select the circle shown and press **Enter.**

Fig. 18

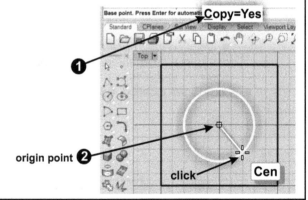

- **Base point** prompt:
  - Click to toggle to the **Copy=Yes** option in the **Command Line.**❶
  - Use **Center osnap** to snap to the center of the circle. ❷
  - Click to set location.

Fig. 19

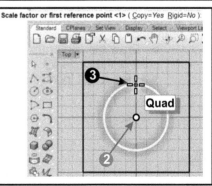

- **Scale factor or first reference point** prompt:
  - Draw the cursor up to snap to the upper **Quad** point of the circle. ❸
  - Click to set location.

Fig. 20

145

- **Second reference point** prompt:
  - Draw the cursor up and snap to the **Midpoint** of the top line of the square. **④**
  - Click to set location.

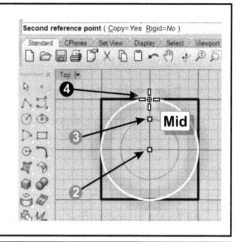

Fig. 21

- **Second reference point** prompt:
  - Press **Enter** to end the command.

    - *Note: You can continue to click in different locations to make more copies if you wish. Press **Enter** to end the command.*

Fig. 22

- The original circle and the scaled **Copy**.

- With the base point in the center of the circle, the **Scale 2-D** command scaled the circle out from its center point.

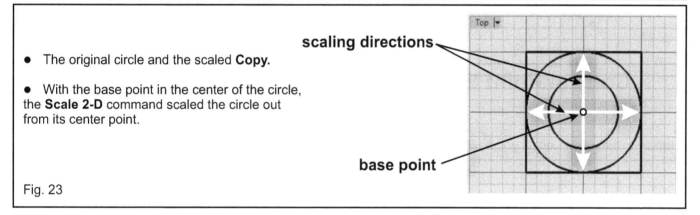

Fig. 23

Specifying a Scale Factor
Scaling by Percentage

- Zoom in on the single **Ø10mm** circle on the right.

- Click on the **Scale 2-D** command.

  - **Select objects to scale** prompt:
    - Select the circle and press **Enter.**

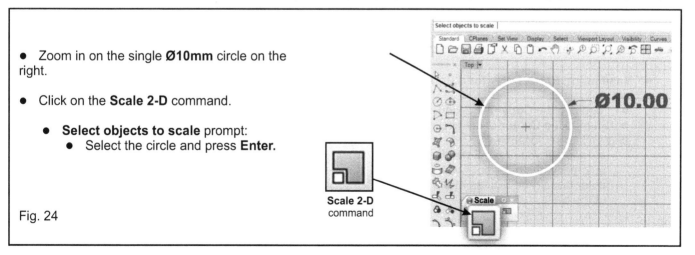

Scale 2-D
command

Fig. 24

- Click to toggle to the **Copy=Yes** option in the **Command Line**.

- **Base point. Press Enter for automatic** prompt:
  - Snap to the **Center** of the circle.
  - Click to set location.

Fig. 25

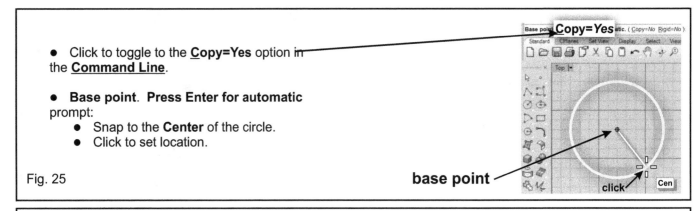

base point

click

Cen

- **Scale factor or first reference point** prompt:
  - Type **"1.5"** in the **Command Line** and press **Enter.**

Fig. 26

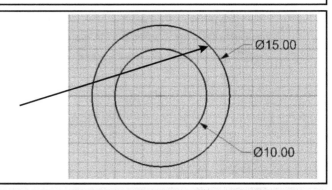

Scale factor or first reference point <1.000>(Copy=Yes): **1.5**

- The circle has been scaled up by a factor of **1.5 (150%)**

Fig. 27

Ø15.00

Ø10.00

Control Point Editing with Scale 1-D and Scale 2-D

- **Pre-select** the circle and then press the **F10 Hotkey** to turn on its control points. **F10**

- Click on the **Scale 1-D** command.

  - **Select objects to scale** prompt:
    - Select the two control points shown.
    - Press **Enter.**

Fig. 28

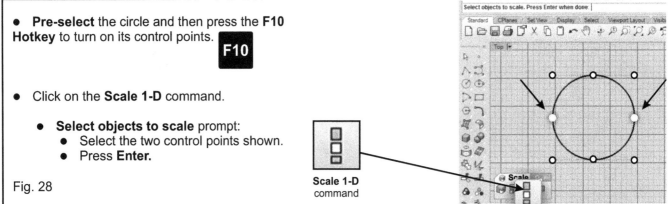

Scale 1-D
command

- **Base point. Press Enter for automatic** prompt:
  - Toggle to the **Copy=No** option.
  - Snap to the **Center** of the circle and click to set location. **❶**
    - note: if you press **Enter** for automatic, the base point will automatically be located at the center of the circle.

Fig. 29

Copy=No

base point ❶

click

Cen

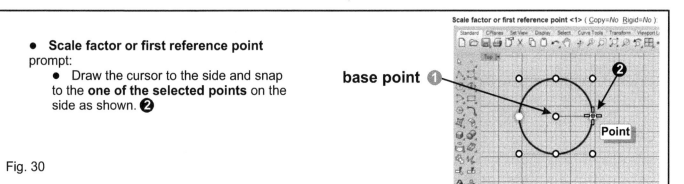

- **Scale factor or first reference point** prompt:
  - Draw the cursor to the side and snap to the **one of the selected points** on the side as shown. ❷

Fig. 30

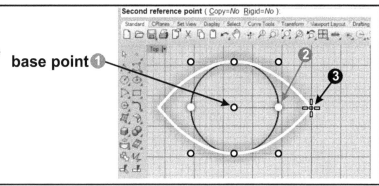

- **Second reference point** prompt:
  - Draw the cursor out further and notice that a preview appears, showing the scaling of the two control points outward and the way the circle is changing.
  - Click when your preview shows the shape you want. ❸

Fig. 31

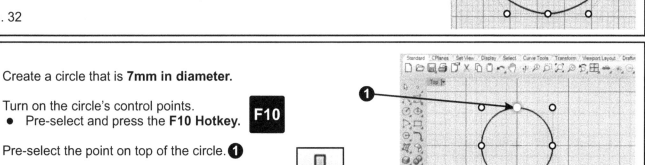

- Two points have been scaled out in one horizontal direction to create the finished shape.

- Turn off control points by pressing the **Esc Key** twice, once to de-select selected points and the second time to turn off the control points.

Esc

Fig. 32

- Create a circle that is **7mm in diameter.**

- Turn on the circle's control points.
  - Pre-select and press the **F10 Hotkey.** **F10**

- Pre-select the point on top of the circle. ❶

- Click on the **Scale 1-D** command:

Scale 1-D command

Fig. 33

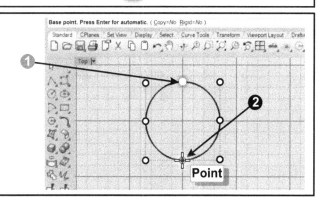

- **Base point. Press Enter for** automatic prompt:
  - Snap to the **Point** on the bottom of the circle. ❷
  - Click to set location.

Fig. 34

- **Scale factor or first reference point**
  prompt:
    - Snap to the selected point ❸ on the top of the circle..
    - Click to set location.

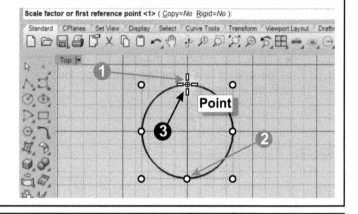

Fig. 35

- **Second reference point** prompt:
    - Type **"10"** in the **Command Line.**
    - Press **Enter.**

Fig. 36

Second reference point (Copy=*No* Rigid=*No* **10**

- The selected point has been scaled upward to a distance that is **10mm** away from the base point at the bottom of the circle.

- Press the **Esc key** a couple of times to turn off control points.

    `Esc`

- A drawing of a **7mm x 10mm pear shaped stone** has been created.

Fig. 37

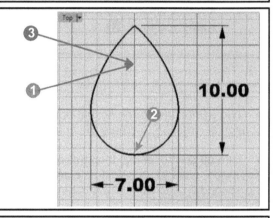

- Create another circle **and turn on its control points.** Diameter dimension does not matter.

    `F10`

- Pre-select the **4 outer control points** shown.

- Click on the **Scale 1-D** command.

    - **Base Point. Press Enter for automatic** prompt:
        - Snap to the **Point ❶** at the bottom of the circle.
        - Click to set location.

Fig. 38

Scale 1-D command

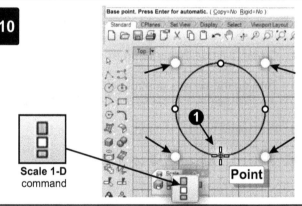

- **Scale factor or first reference point**
  prompt:
    - Draw the cursor to the right and snap to the lower right point shown. ❷
    - Click to set location.

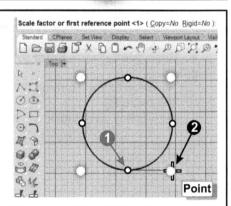

Fig. 39

149

- **Second reference point** prompt:
  - Draw the cursor over to the right until the preview line shows you the shape you want.
  - Click to set location. ❸

Fig. 40

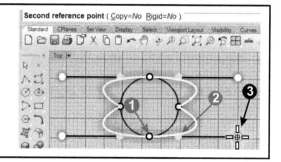

- The finished shape shows how the **base point** can also be above or below the object being edited, as long as it is at the middle of your object as shown.

Fig. 41

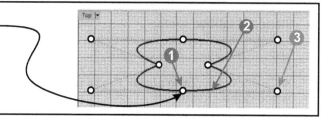

- Undo the last scale or create another circle.

- Pre-select the circle and press the **F10 Hotkey** to turn on control points.

F10

- Click on the **Scale 2-D** command.

  - **Base point. Press Enter for automatic** prompt:
    - Snap to the **Center** of the circle. ❶
    - Click to set location.

Scale 2-D command

Fig. 42

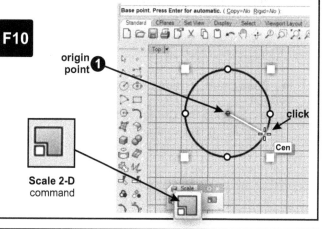

- **Scale factor or first reference point** prompt:
  - You can draw the cursor out and click on a random, unspecified location as shown. ❷

Fig. 43

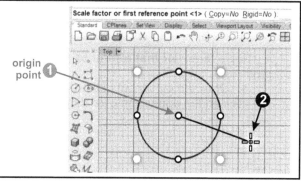

- **Second reference point** prompt:
  - Draw the cursor out until the preview curve shows the shape you want.
  - Click to set.

- The selected control points have been evenly scaled out as shown.

Fig. 44

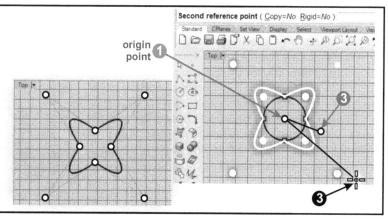

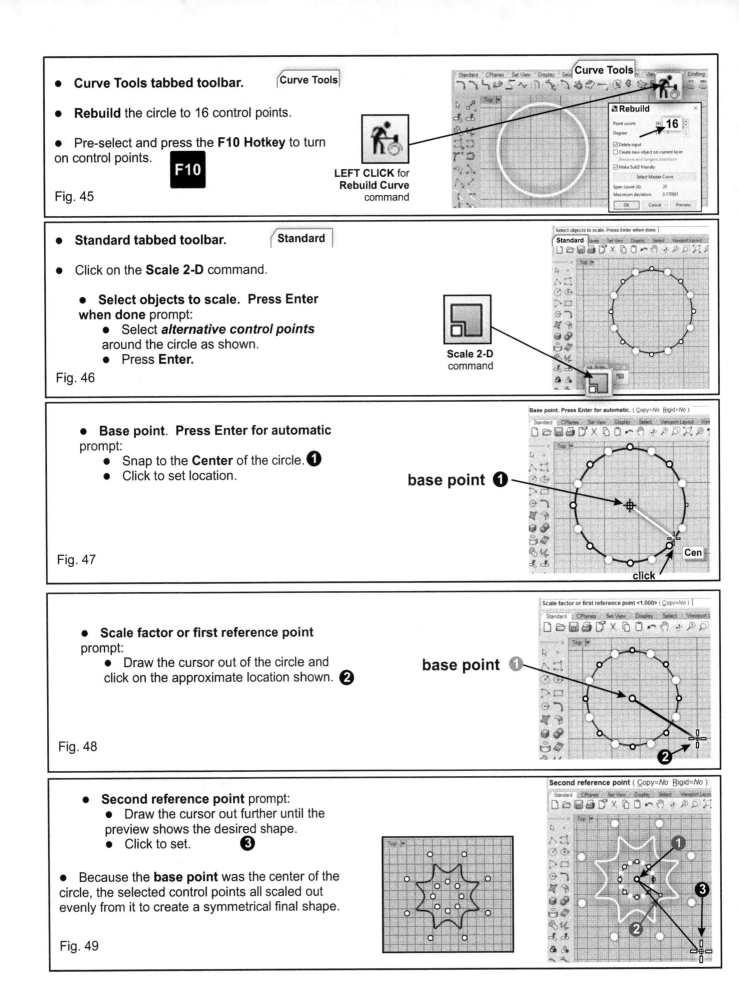

- **Curve Tools tabbed toolbar.** Curve Tools

- **Rebuild** the circle to 16 control points.

- Pre-select and press the **F10 Hotkey** to turn on control points. **F10**

Fig. 45

LEFT CLICK for
Rebuild Curve
command

- **Standard tabbed toolbar.** Standard

- Click on the **Scale 2-D** command.

  - **Select objects to scale. Press Enter when done** prompt:
    - Select *alternative control points* around the circle as shown.
    - Press **Enter.**

Fig. 46

Scale 2-D
command

- **Base point. Press Enter for automatic** prompt:
  - Snap to the **Center** of the circle. ❶
  - Click to set location.

Fig. 47

base point ❶

Cen

click

- **Scale factor or first reference point** prompt:
  - Draw the cursor out of the circle and click on the approximate location shown. ❷

Fig. 48

base point ❶

❷

- **Second reference point** prompt:
  - Draw the cursor out further until the preview shows the desired shape.
  - Click to set. ❸

- Because the **base point** was the center of the circle, the selected control points all scaled out evenly from it to create a symmetrical final shape.

Fig. 49

- In this example, **Scale 2-D** is creating a different shape because the **base point** is on the bottom of the circle as shown.

Fig. 50

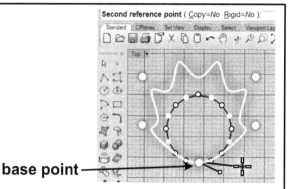

base point

Control Point Editing the Butterfly with Scale Commands

- Open the file **polyline for butterfly.3dm** original drawing and create a line down the middle of the drawing, **snapping to mid points** for accuracy.

- Turn on Control Points by selecting the polyline and pressing the **F10 hotkey.**

Fig. 51

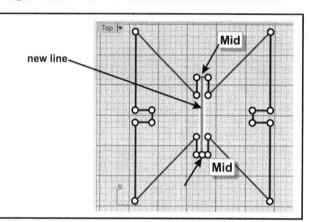

new line

- Click on the **Scale 2-D** command.

  - **Select objects to scale. Press Enter when done** prompt:
    - Select the two control points at the top as shown.
    - Press **Enter.**

Fig. 52

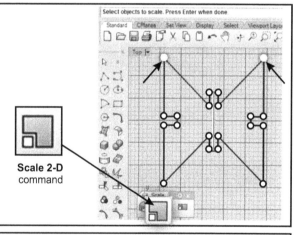

Scale 2-D command

- **Base point** prompt:
  - Snap to the **Mid point** on the center line just created.❶

Fig. 53

base point ❶

152

- **Scale factor or first reference point** prompt:
  - Using **ORTHO** for symmetry, draw the cursor out to the side. ❷
  - Click to set location.

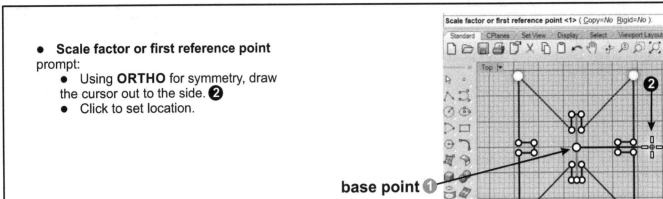

base point ❶

Fig. 54

- **Second reference point** prompt:
  - Draw the cursor out further.
  - The selected control points will scale outward and upward, **scaling from the base point in a symmetrical arrangement.**
  - Click when the preview shows approximately as shown. ❸

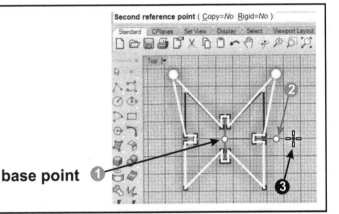

base point ❶

Fig. 55

- The newly edited shape of the polyline is still symmetrical.

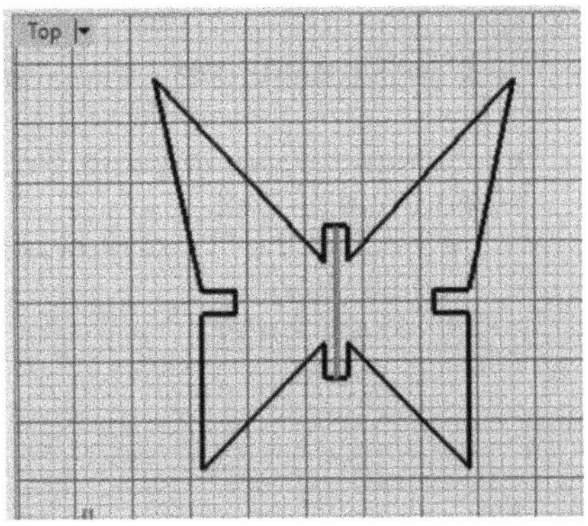

Fig. 56

- Select the two lower control points as shown.

- Click on the **Scale 1-D** command as shown.

  - **Base point** prompt:
    - Snap to the **Mid point** on the center line. ❶
    - Click to set location.

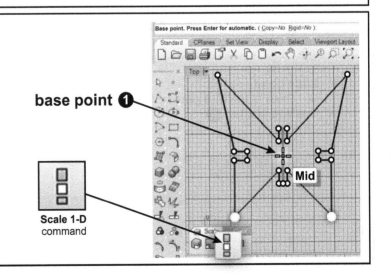

base point ❶

Scale 1-D
command

Fig. 57

153

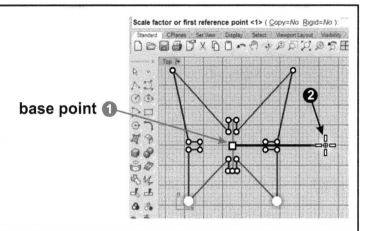

- **Scale factor or first reference point**
prompt:
  - Using **ortho** for symmetry, draw the cursor outward.
  - Click in the approximate location shown. **②**

Fig. 58

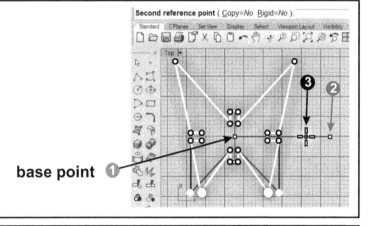

- **Second reference point** prompt:
  - Draw the cursor inward.
  - Click to set location when the desired shape is created. **③**

- Press the **Esc** key a couple of times to turn off control points.

Fig. 59

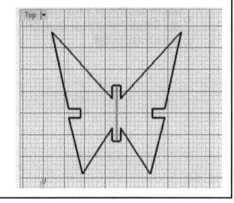

- **Scale 2-D** and **Scale 1-D** have created a rough symmetrical butterfly shape.

Fig. 60

- **Rebuild** the polyline to 30 control points.

- ***Don't forget to adjust the closed curve seam (<u>Adjust Closed Curve Seam</u> command in the <u>Curve Tools tabbed toolbar</u>) so that you get an even and symmetrical distribution of control points!***
  - ***[ref: Figs. 11-20 - in previous chapter, From a Polyline to a Butterfly.]***

- Turn on Control Points by pre-selecting and pressing the **F10 Hotkey**.

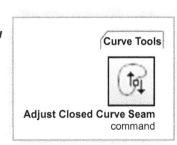

Curve Tools

Adjust Closed Curve Seam
command

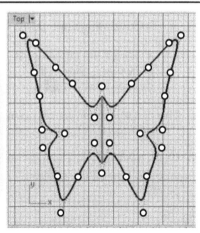

Fig. 61

- Select the two control points shown.

- Click on the **Scale 1-D** command.

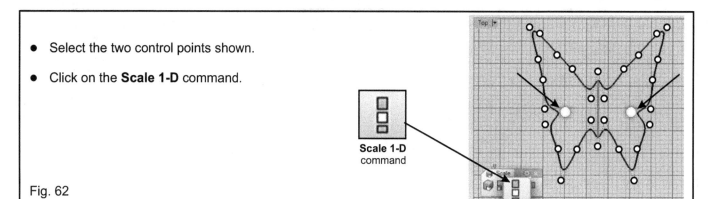

Scale 1-D
command

Fig. 62

- **Base point. Press Enter for** automatic prompt:
    - Snap to a point on the center line and click to set location. **❶**

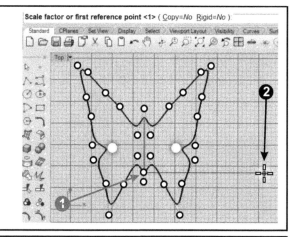

base point **❶**

Fig. 63

- **Scale factor or first reference** prompt:
    - Draw the cursor outward and click to set location. **❷**

Fig. 64

- **Second reference point** prompt:
    - Draw the cursor in as shown and click in the desired location. **❸**

- The result is symmetrical point editing.

- Press the **Esc** key a couple of times to turn off the control points.

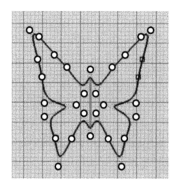
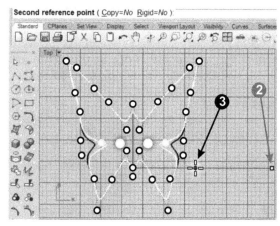

Fig. 65

155

Freeform Curves
Control Point Curves, Interpolate Point Curves

Control Point Curves

- **Curve Tools tabbed toolbar.** `Curve Tools`

- **Left-click** on the **Control point curve** command.

  - **Start of curve** prompt:
    - Click on the desired location of the start of the curve. ❶

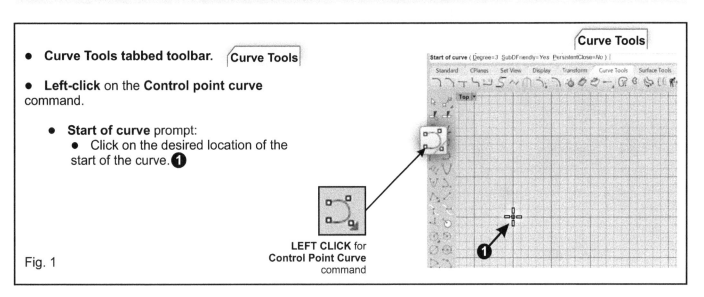

LEFT CLICK for
Control Point Curve
command

Fig. 1

- **Next point** prompt:
  - Click on the next point of your curve. ❷

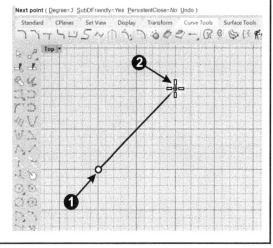

Fig. 2

- **Next point. Press Enter when done** prompt:
  - Notice that when you draw the cursor away to locate the third point, the curve draws away from the second control point.

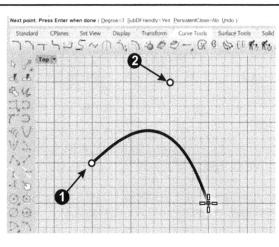

Fig. 3

- Click in desired locations to continue creating the curve and you will see how the curve is controlled by the points but does not pass through them. ❸ ❹ ❺ ❻ ❼

- Click on the **<u>Undo</u>** option in the **Command Line** as shown.

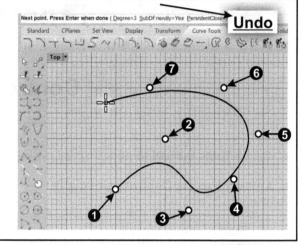

Fig. 4

- The last point ❼ will disappear.
- You can click the **<u>Undo</u>** option repeatedly to cancel previous locations in the order in which they were created.

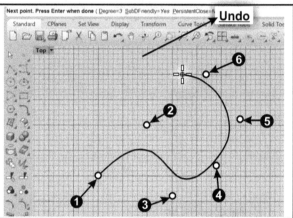

Fig. 5

- Click to continue the line a couple of additional times ❼ ❽ until your curve comes around near to the start point.

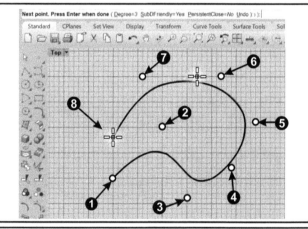

Fig. 6

- As you draw the cursor over the start point of the curve, it will automatically snap to the **Point** of the start of the curve. ❶

- *The curve will deform itself to become a totally smooth curve.*

- *Notice how it pulls away from its own start point to achieve this.*

- Click to set the last point and the command will end because you have created a *closed curve*.

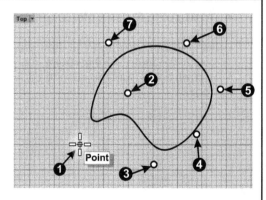

Fig. 7

Interpolate Point Curve with an End Kink

- **Curve Tools tabbed toolbar.** Curve Tools

- **Left-click** on the **Curve: Interpolate points** command.
  - **Pick point** prompt:
    - In the **Command Line**, click to toggle from **SubDFriendly=Yes** to **SubDFriendly=No.**
      - **SubD** is a Rhino module that uses kink free curves when modeling organic objects.

  - Left click on the location for the start of your curve.❶

Fig. 8

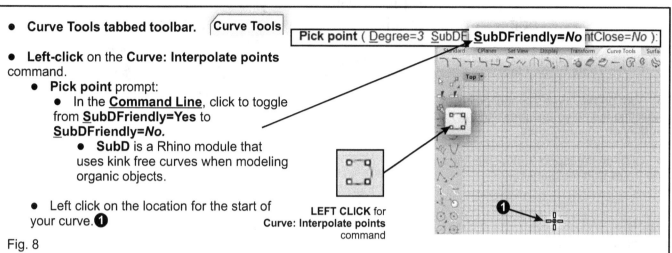

Pick point (Degree=3 SubD SubDFriendly=No ntClose=No):

LEFT CLICK for
Curve: Interpolate points
command

- As you continue to click to make more points to form your curve, notice that the curve continues to pass through the points where you clicked. ❷ ❸ ❹ ❺ ❻

  - *This is the major difference between the Curve: Interpolate points command and the Control point curve command.*

- In the **Command Line,** click on the **Sharp=No** option to toggle it to **Sharp=Yes.**

Fig. 9

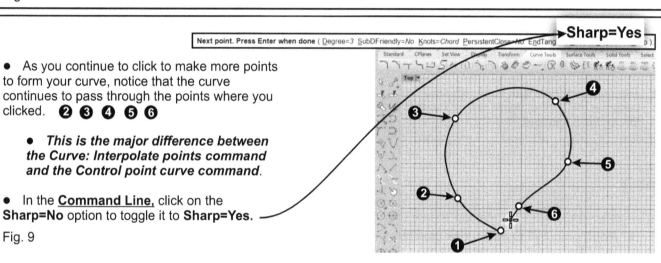

Next point. Press Enter when done (Degree=3 SubDFriendly=No Knots=Chord PersistentClose=No EndTang → **Sharp=Yes**

- Draw your cursor over the first point.
  - The cursor will automatically snap to the **Point** at this location to make a closed curve.
- Click on this location. ❶

- The point where the beginning and end of the curve meet is a kink, rather than a smooth join.

- This is because you toggled on the **Sharp=Yes** option.
- The **Sharp** option can also be used with **Control Point Curves.**

Fig. 10

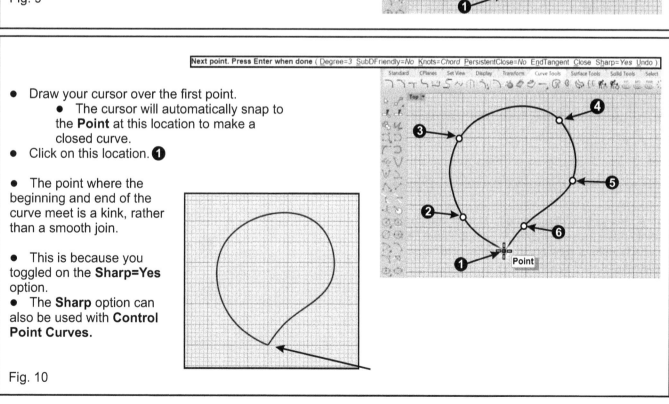

Next point. Press Enter when done (Degree=3 SubDFriendly=No Knots=Chord PersistentClose=No EndTangent Close Sharp=Yes Undo)

Adding a Kink to a Curve
Addition of a Kink will enable you to point
edit sharp corners into the design of your drawing.

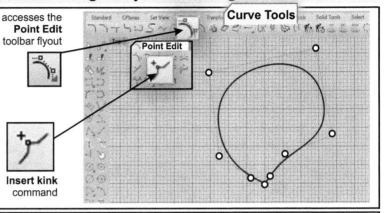

- **Curve Tools tabbed toolbar.** Curve Tools

- Turn on the curve's control points by selecting the curve and pressing the **F10 hotkey** on your keyboard.

- Click on the **Insert kink** command in the **Point Edit** toolbar flyout.

accesses the **Point Edit** toolbar flyout

Insert kink command

Fig. 11

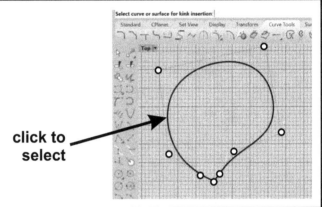

- **Select curve or surface for kink insertion** prompt:
  - Select the curve as shown.

- The curve will not "light up" when selected because the control points are on but that is OK in this command.

click to select

Fig. 12

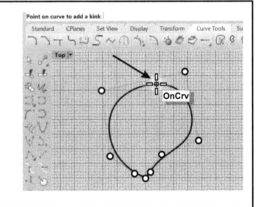

- **Point on curve to add a kink** prompt:
  - Click on a location near the top of the curve as shown.

- Notice that during this command, an **On Crv** tooltip shows when the cursor is in contact with the curve.

  - Press **Enter** to end the command.

Fig. 13

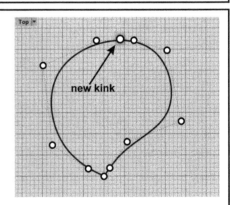

- A new kink will be created. Notice that control points have moved slightly around the new kink and a couple of new control points have been added right next to the new kink.

- Note: The curve is now a Polycurve and can be exploded into 2 segments.

- You can insert as many kinks as you wish.

new kink

Fig. 14

- **Move** or **Drag** the new kink to change the design.

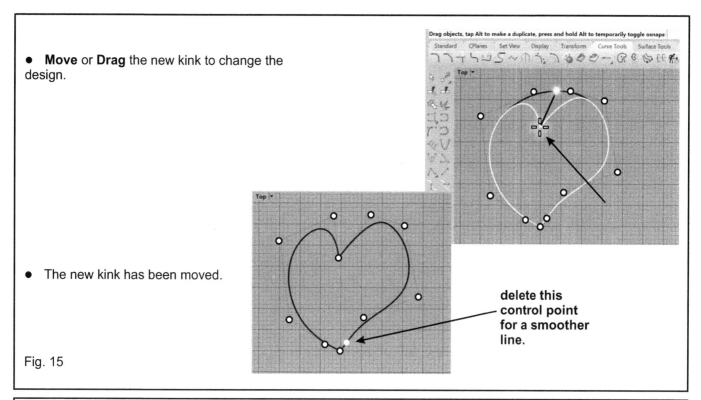

- The new kink has been moved.

delete this control point for a smoother line.

Fig. 15

- Refine your design with further control point manipulation.

- Notice that deleting one of the control points has resulted in a smoother line at the bottom of the heart..

- Save this file as **freeform heart.3dm.** We will be using this file again for an **Array Along Curve** exercise.

Fig. 16

Open Freeform Curves

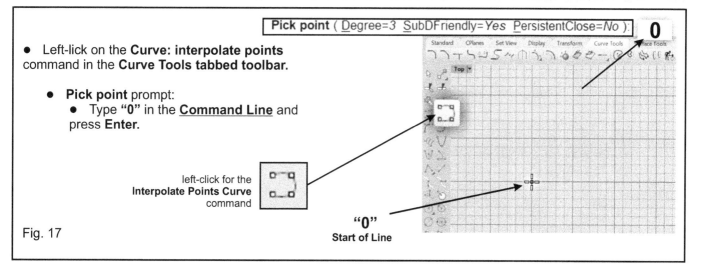

- Left-lick on the **Curve: interpolate points** command in the **Curve Tools tabbed toolbar.**

  - **Pick point** prompt:
    - Type **"0"** in the **Command Line** and press **Enter.**

left-click for the
Interpolate Points Curve
command

"0"
Start of Line

Fig. 17

- **Next point. Press enter when done** prompt:
  - Click a few times to create a rough S shaped curve.
  - After you have clicked enough points to make the S shape, press **Enter** to finish the curve.

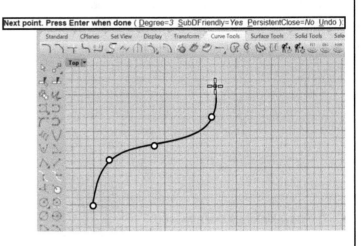

- The curve will be completed, stopping at the last point you clicked.

- *You have created an **open curve**, instead of the closed curve that you created in previous exercises.*

Fig. 18

- Left-click on the **Curve: interpolate points** command in the **Curve Tools tabbed toolbar**.

  - **Pick point** prompt:
    - Snap to the **End** of the previous curve as shown.
    - Click to set location.

  left-click for the
  Interpolate Points Curve
  command

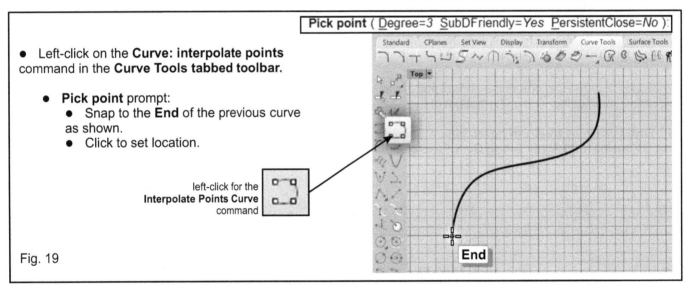

Fig. 19

- **Next point. Press Enter when done** prompt:
  - After a few clicks, snap to the other **End** of the line.
  - Press **Enter** to finish the line and end the command.

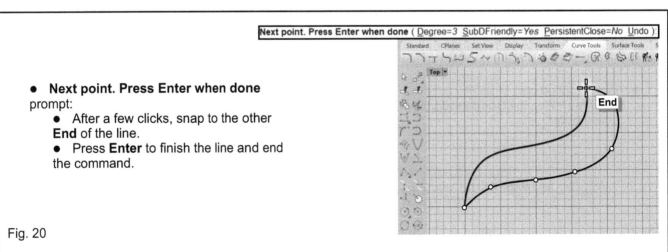

Fig. 20

Join & Explode Commands

Joining the Two Curves to Create a Single Closed Curve

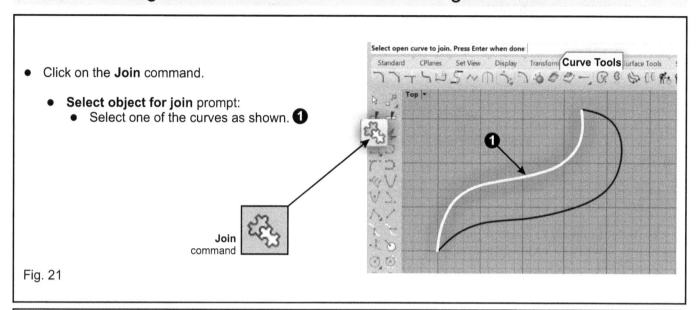

- Click on the **Join** command.

  - **Select object for join** prompt:
    - Select one of the curves as shown. ❶

Join command

Fig. 21

- **Select curve to join. Press Enter when done** prompt:
  - Select the other curve. ❷

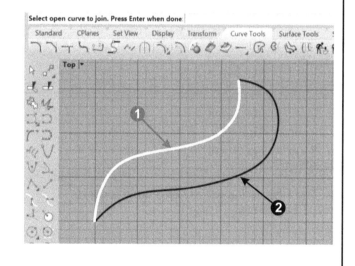

Fig. 22

- The curves will automatically de-select because they are now a closed curve.

- The **History line** will tell you that **2 curves have been joined into one** <u>closed curve (or "closed polyline")</u>
  - *You can not join another curve to a closed curve or closed polyline.*

- **This is a closed polyline because the Join command was applied to two curves that were touching at both end points.**
  - *If the curves were not touching at both ends. the curve will still be an open polyline.*

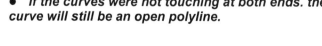

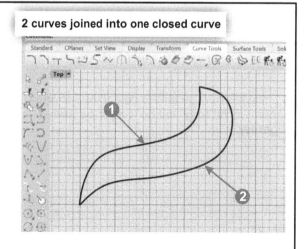

Fig. 23

Exploding the Closed Curve Back Into 2 Segments

- **Left-click** on the **Explode** button.

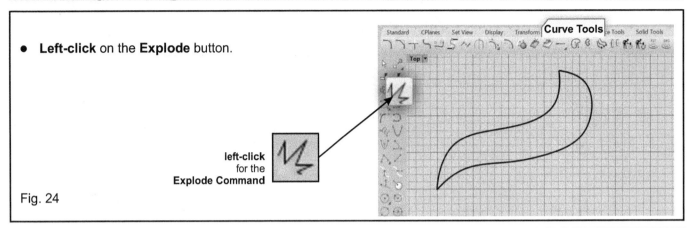

left-click
for the
Explode Command

Fig. 24

- **Select objects to explode** prompt:
  - Click to select the closed curve shown.
  - Press **Enter.**

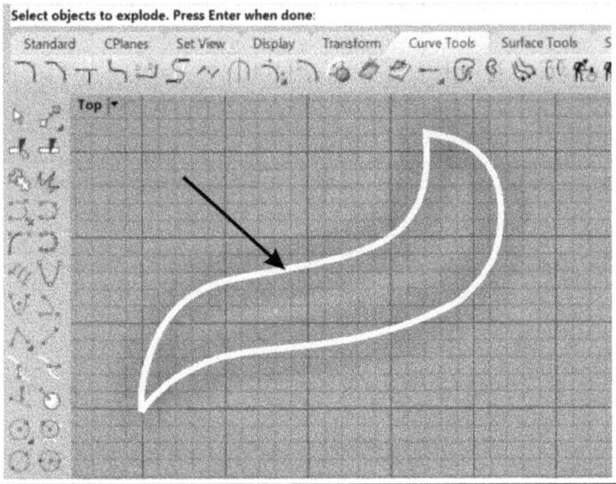

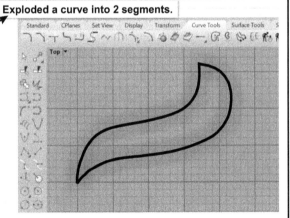

Fig. 25

- If the curves do not de-select, click away to de-select.

- The History line will say **Exploded a curve into 2 segments.**

Exploded a curve into 2 segments.

Fig. 26

- You will now be able to select the two lines separately as *they will no longer be joined together.*

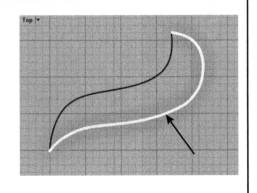

Fig. 27

Picture Plane Command
Placing and Scaling a Design Image in Rhino
Tracing with Freeform Curves

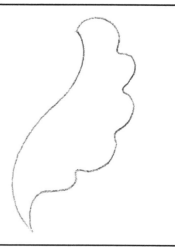

- This is the image that will be used in this chapter that will deal with bringing an image, **leaf scan for bitmap trace,** into the Rhino workspace and tracing it using Rhino's drawing tools.

- It is included in the file library that you can download from the www.rhinoforjewelry.com website.

Fig. 1

- **Surface Tools tabbed toolbar.** Surface Tools

- **Left-click** on the **Picture Plane** command as shown.

Picture Plane
command

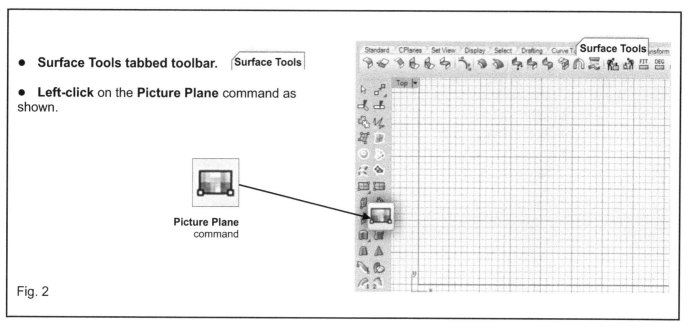

Fig. 2

- The **Open Bitmap** dialog box will open.

- Navigate to the folder in your computer that contains the downloaded texture and Emap files and select **leaf scan for bitmap trace** as shown.❶

- Click on the **Open** button. ❷

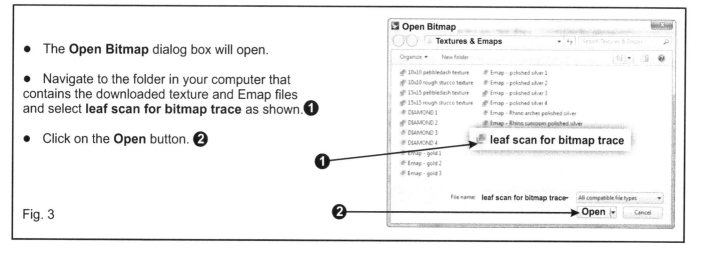

Fig. 3

- **First corner of picture** prompt:
  - Click somewhere in the lower left of the viewport as shown. **1**

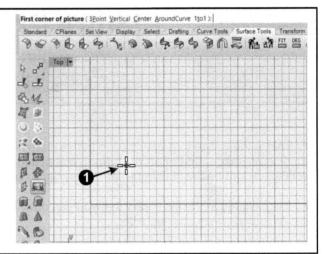

Fig. 4

- **Other corner or length** prompt:
  - Drag the cursor upward at a diagonal across the viewport as shown.
  - A preview of the shape of the image will form as you drag the cursor.
  - By default, the picture plane will be placed in line with the grid.

Fig. 5

- **Left click** on the opposite corner to set location. **2**

- *note: this image will be scaled to the desired size later in this exercise.*

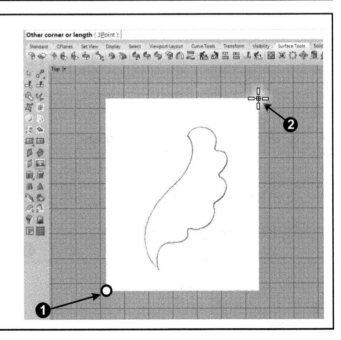

Fig. 6

Making the Image more Transparent
Transparency can make the image easier to trace.

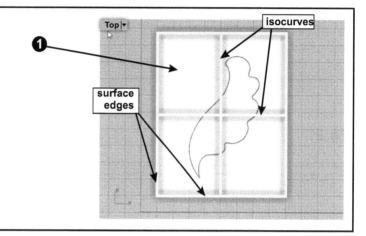

- The sketch that you have placed on the Rhino workspace is a bitmap image that has been "mapped" to a "surface". This will be referred to as the "picture plane".
- Click to select the picture plane surface. **1**
  - The rectangular border lines are the **edges of the surface.**
  - The lines that cross the middle of the surface are called **isocurves** and are a feature of all surfaces, displaying direction and other geometry.

Fig. 7

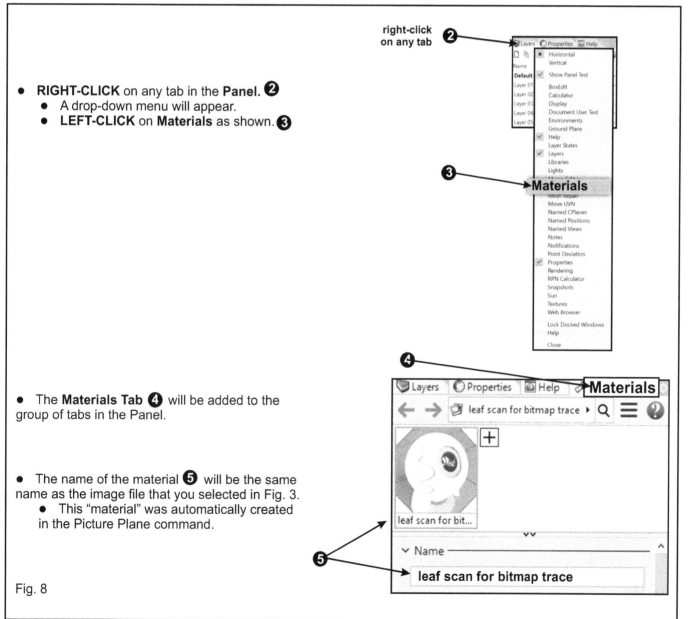

- **RIGHT-CLICK** on any tab in the **Panel. 2**
  - A drop-down menu will appear.
  - **LEFT-CLICK** on **Materials** as shown. **3**

- The **Materials Tab 4** will be added to the group of tabs in the Panel.

- The name of the material **5** will be the same name as the image file that you selected in Fig. 3.
  - This "material" was automatically created in the Picture Plane command.

Fig. 8

166

- Double-click on the title of the assigned material **1** to open the Materials window.

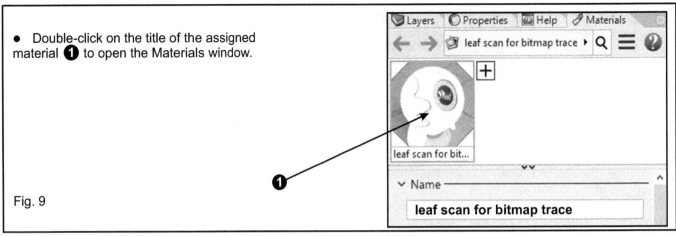

Fig. 9

- The Materials window will open up, displaying the properties of the selected picture surface.

- Click and drag the little triangle on the **Transparency slider** until the percentage of transparency reads about 34%.

Transparency: 0   △ **34%**   100

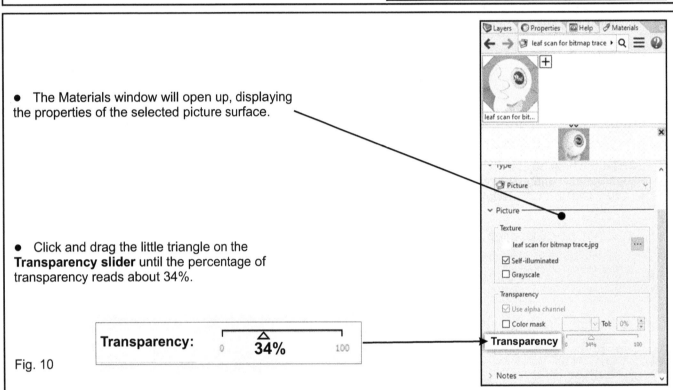

Fig. 10

- the **Picture Plane** image is now transparent which can make it easier to trace.

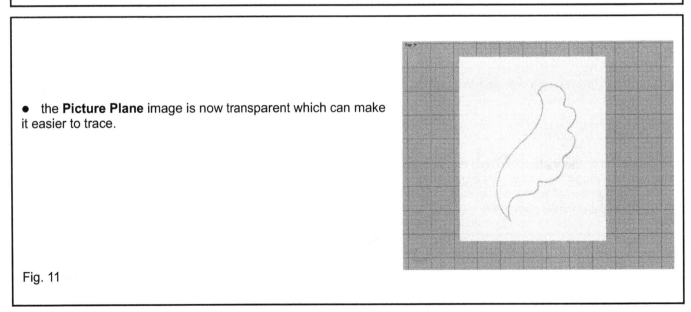

Fig. 11

Tracing the Picture Plane Image
Using a Freeform Curve Command to Trace the Design

- **Standard tabbed toolbar.** ⟨Standard⟩

- Select the picture plane surface and **left click** on the **Lock** command as shown.
  - This "locks" the picture plane so that you can not select it but you can still see it for the tracing that follows.

*[Note: To **Unlock**, just **RIGHT-CLICK** on the **Lock** command button and the surface will be unlocked once again.]*

LEFT-CLICK for
Lock
commaned

Fig. 12

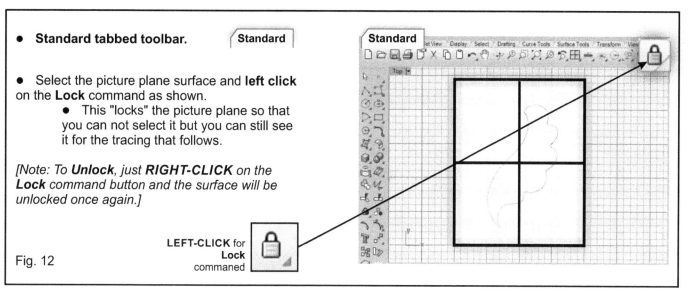

- **Curve Tools tabbed toolbar.** ⟨Curve Tools⟩

- **LEFT CLICK** on the **Curve: interpolate points** command.

LEFT CLICK for
Curve: interpolate points
command

Fig. 13

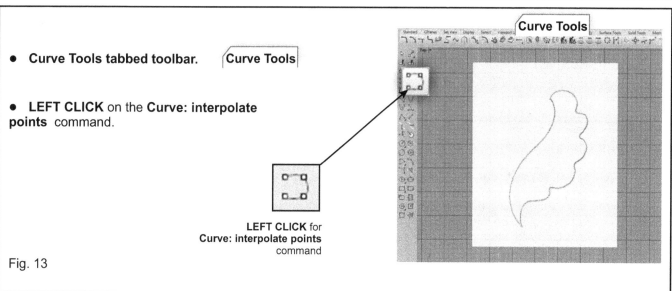

- **Pick point** prompt:
  - **Left click** on the bottom tip of the leaf to start the tracing, locating this point by eye. ❶

Fig. 14

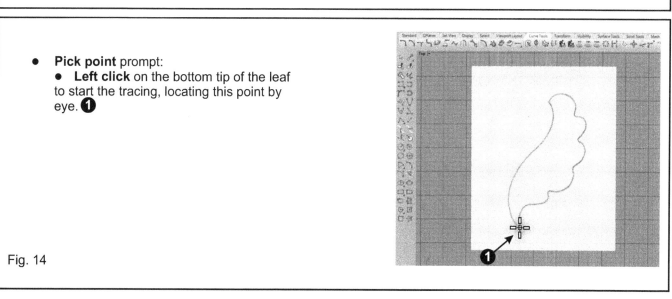

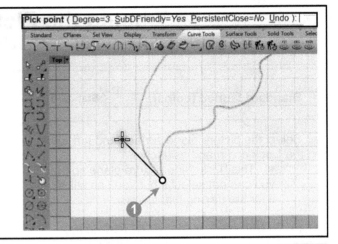

- **Pick point** prompt:
  - As you draw the cursor outward, notice the "rubber band" effect.

Fig. 15

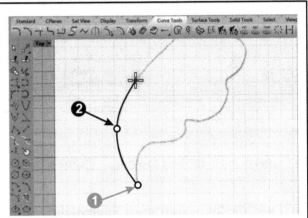

- **Left click** on the approximate location shown. **2**

- **Pick point. Press Enter when done** prompt:
  - Draw the cursor further along the line.
  - Notice the "rubber band" preview line as it curves along the leaf design.

Fig. 16

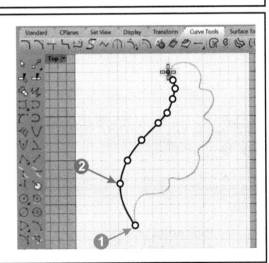

- **Pick point: Press Enter when done** prompt:
  - Keep clicking along the line until you arrive at the top of the leaf.
  - Press **Enter** to end the command.

- *Note: click as few times as possible for a smoother line.*

Fig. 17

- View the finished curve.

Fig. 18

- **Select** the curve you just created and **LEFT CLICK** on the **Show Curve Edit Points** command as shown.

- **Edit points** will appear along the curve.

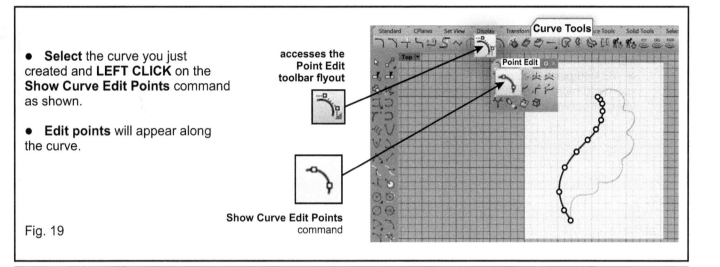

accesses the
Point Edit
toolbar flyout

Show Curve Edit Points
command

Fig. 19

- **Move** or **Drag** Edit Points to refine the line you just created.
- You also select the **Delete** points by pressing the **Delete key.**

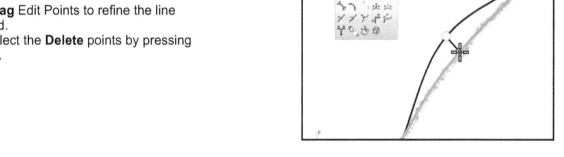

Fig. 20

- You can **Window Select** more than one point at a time and then **Drag** or **Move** them together.

- When you finished editing, press the **Esc** key or **right-click** on the **Edit points on** button to turn off the Edit points.

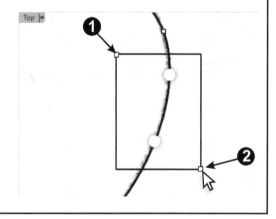

Fig. 21

- **Left click** on the **Curve: interpolate points** command again.

  - **Pick point** prompt:
    - **LEFT CLICK** on the end of the curve you just created.
    - Use **End osnap** to make sure that the new curve will start exactly at the endpoint of the existing curve.

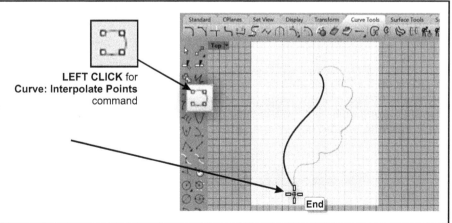

LEFT CLICK for
Curve: Interpolate Points
command

Fig. 22

170

- **Pick point. Press Enter when done** prompt:
    - As you place Edit points, notice how you need more of them to trace lines with sharper curves/more detail.

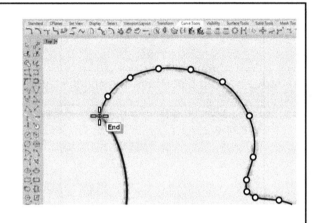

Fig. 23

- **Pick point. Press Enter when done** prompt:
    - Snap to the endpoint of the top of the previous line and click to set the last **Edit point** for the curve.
    - Press **Enter** to end the command.

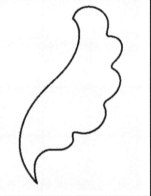

Fig. 24

- The second curve has been created.

- The first and second curves touch each other at both ends and can be later joined together to make them a single **Closed Curve** after point editing.

Fig. 25

- Point Edit to refine the curves.

- You can use either **Edit Points** or **Control Points.**

- Click on the little **Disable** box on the status bar at the bottom of the workspace to disable osnap, making editing of the line easier. *Click on it again to enable object snap later.*

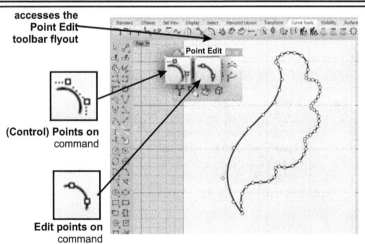

accesses the
Point Edit
toolbar flyout

Point Edit

(Control) Points on
command

Edit points on
command

Fig. 26

171

- **Left-click** on the **Join** command.

  - **Select curve to join. Curves, surfaces and polysurfaces must be open. Press Enter when done** prompt:
    - Select one of the curves as shown. **❶**

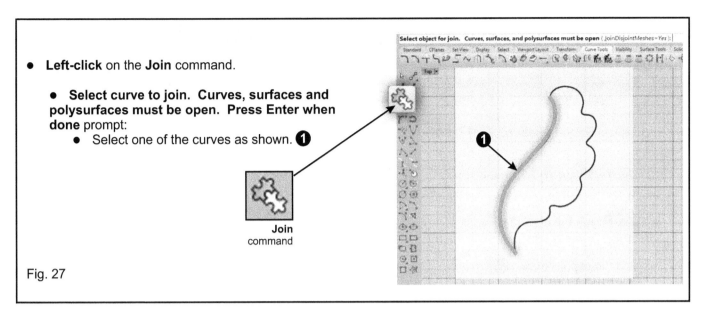

Join
command

Fig. 27

- **Select curve to join. Press Enter when done** prompt:
  - Select the other curve.
  - Both curves will be de-selected.

- The command is ended. ***You can not join any more curves to a closed curve.***

- Notice that the **History Window** is stating: **2 curves joined into one closed curve. ❷**

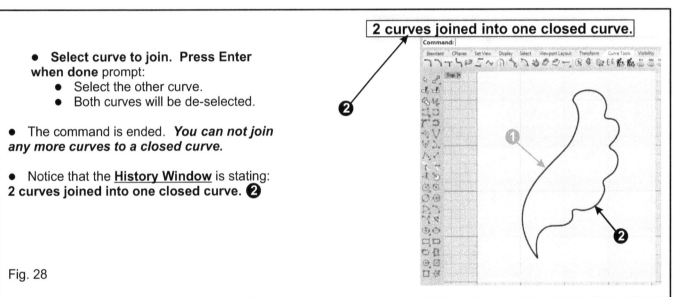

Fig. 28

- **Standard tabbed toolbar.** ⌐Standard⌐

- **Right-click** on the **Lock** command to unlock the picture plane.
  - The picture plane can now be selected because it is no longer locked.

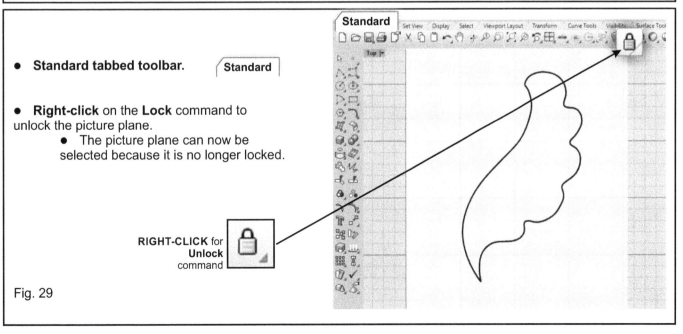

RIGHT-CLICK for
Unlock
command

Fig. 29

Scaling the Tracing and the Picture Plane
Scaling the traced design and the picture frame for accuracy.

- **Transform tabbed toolbar.**   Transform

- Click on the **Scale 2D** command in the **Scale** toolbar flyout.

  - **Select objects to scale** prompt:
    - Select both the line drawing and the picture plane. **❶**
    - Press **Enter.**

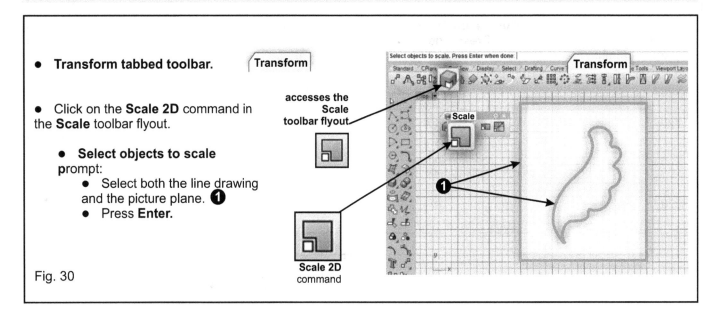

accesses the Scale toolbar flyout

Scale 2D command

Fig. 30

- **Origin Point** prompt:
  - Use **End osnap** to snap to the lower tip of the leaf as shown. **❷**
  - Click to set location.

Fig. 31

- **Scale factor or first reference point** prompt:
  - Use **Quad osnap** to snap to the top of the leaf as shown.
  - Click to set location. **❸**

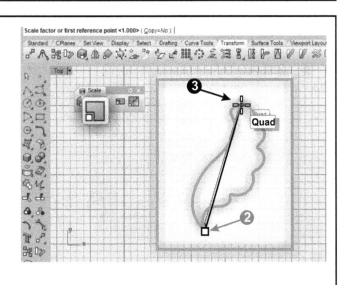

Fig. 32

- **Second reference point** prompt:
  - Type **"30"** in the **Command Line.**
  - Press **Enter.**

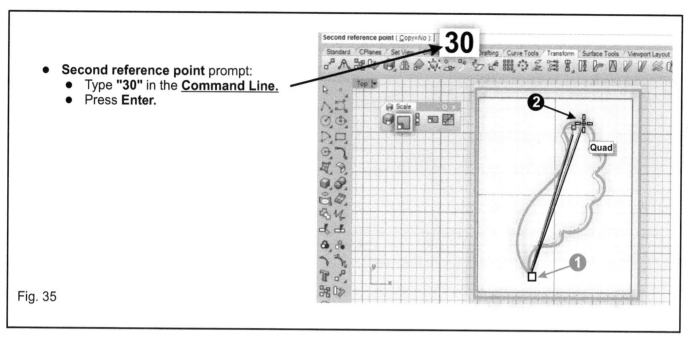

Fig. 35

- The command is ended.

- The dimension of the leaf drawing has now been accurately scaled to a length of 30mm.

- Save this file as: **leaf design.3dm.**

- When saving, be sure to click on the **Save Textures** option so that the image on the Picture Plane will be preserved.

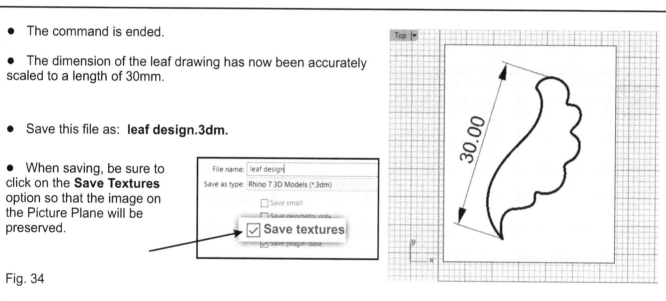

Fig. 34

If your Picture Plane Image is Missing
If you did not check **Save Textures** when saving, you may have to replace the image on your Picture Plane surface when you open the file again.

- If you re-open this file and see the **Missing Image files** box with the picture frame image listed, ❶ you need to re-introduce the image to the material properties of the picture frame surface.

- Click on the **Continue** button to complete the opening of the file. ❷

Fig. 35

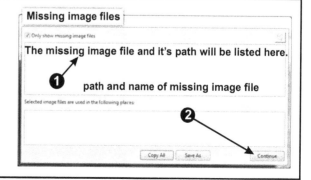

- If you turn off the layer for the linework, you will see a blank picture frame surface.

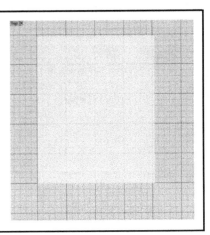

Fig. 36

- Click on the **Materials tab** ① to open the **Materials** panel.

- You will see a material listed for the picture frame. ②

- You will see the **leaf scan for bitmap trace.jpg** file listed under **Textures**. ③
  - Click on the browse button on the left of the listed texture. ④

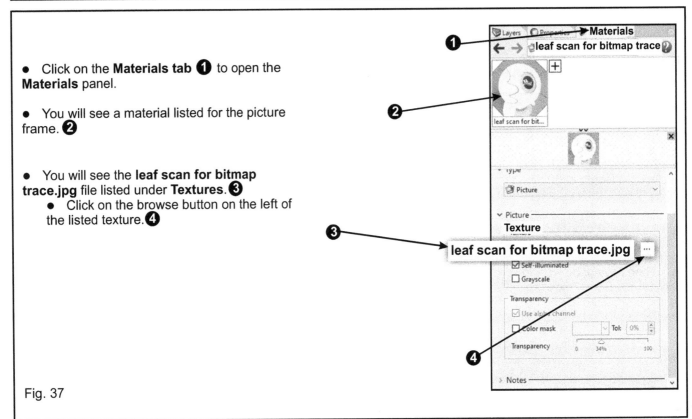

Fig. 37

- Navigate to the folder that contains the image you are using. Select that file ⑤ and click on the **Open** button. ⑥

- The image will be restored to your picture plane surface.

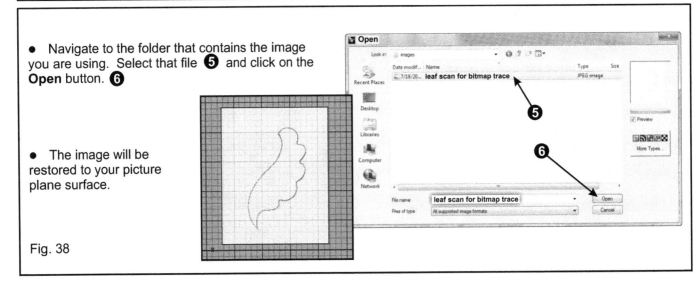

Fig. 38

Move Command
Moving the Picture Plane and Line Drawing

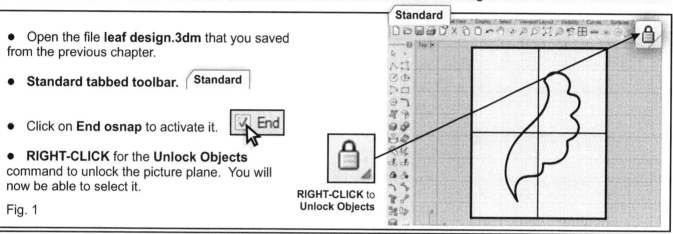

- Open the file **leaf design.3dm** that you saved from the previous chapter.

- **Standard tabbed toolbar.** | Standard |

- Click on **End osnap** to activate it. ☑ End

- **RIGHT-CLICK** for the **Unlock Objects** command to unlock the picture plane. You will now be able to select it.

RIGHT-CLICK to Unlock Objects

Fig. 1

- Click on the **Move** command.

  - **Select objects to move** prompt:
    - Select your Picture Plane and line drawing and press **Enter.**

Move command

Fig. 2

- **Point to move from** prompt:
  - Snap to the **Endpoint** of the bottom of the line drawing.
  - Click to set location.

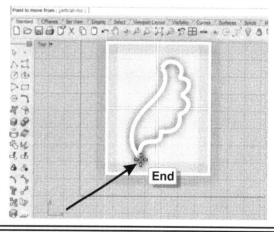

Fig. 3

- **Point to move to** prompt:
  - Type a "0" in the **Command Line** and press **Enter.**

Point to move to: **0**

Fig. 4

● The bottom tip of the leaf drawing has been accurately moved to sit on **0,0** which is the center of the grid, **the point where the X and Y axes, come together.**

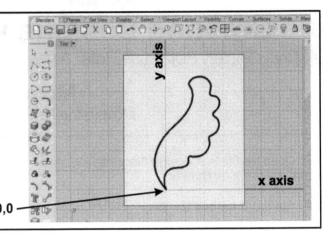

Fig. 5

Hide Objects/Show Objects Commands
Hiding and Showing the Picture Plane.

● **LEFT CLICK** on the **Hide Objects** command.

   ● **Select objects to hide. Press Enter when done** prompt:
      ● Select the Picture Plane and press **Enter.**

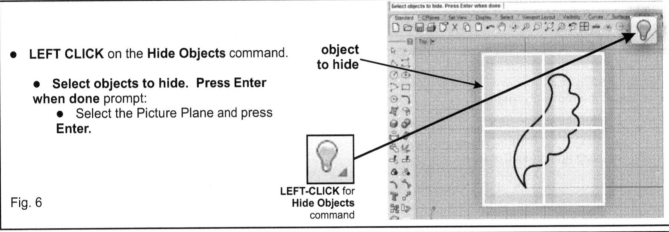

object to hide

LEFT-CLICK for
Hide Objects
command

Fig. 6

● The Picture Plane will be hidden from view.

● **RIGHT CLICK** on the same button for the **Show Objects** command.

RIGHT-CLICK for
Show Objects
command

Fig. 7

● The Picture Plane will once again be showing on the workspace.

● **Hide** the Picture Plane once again before proceeding to the next step.

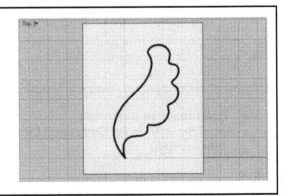

Fig. 8

Mirror Command
Creating Symmetry using the Mirror Command with the History function.

- Click on the **Record History** button at the bottom of the workspace.

Fig. 9

| Osnap | SmartTrack | Gumball | **Record History** |

- **Transform tabbed toolbar.** Transform

- Select the leaf drawing and **LEFT CLICK** on the **Mirror** command.

LEFT CLICK for the **Mirror** command

Fig. 10

- **Start of mirror plane** prompt:
  - Type "**0**" in the **Command Line** and press **Enter.** ❶

Mirror Plane starts at 0,0 ❶

Fig. 11

- **End of mirror plane** prompt:
  - Draw the cursor straight up, using **ORTHO** so that the mirror plane will be perfectly perpendicular.
  - Click anywhere on this plane to set the direction of the mirror plane. ❷

  - A perfect "mirror image" of the leaf will be created.

Fig. 12

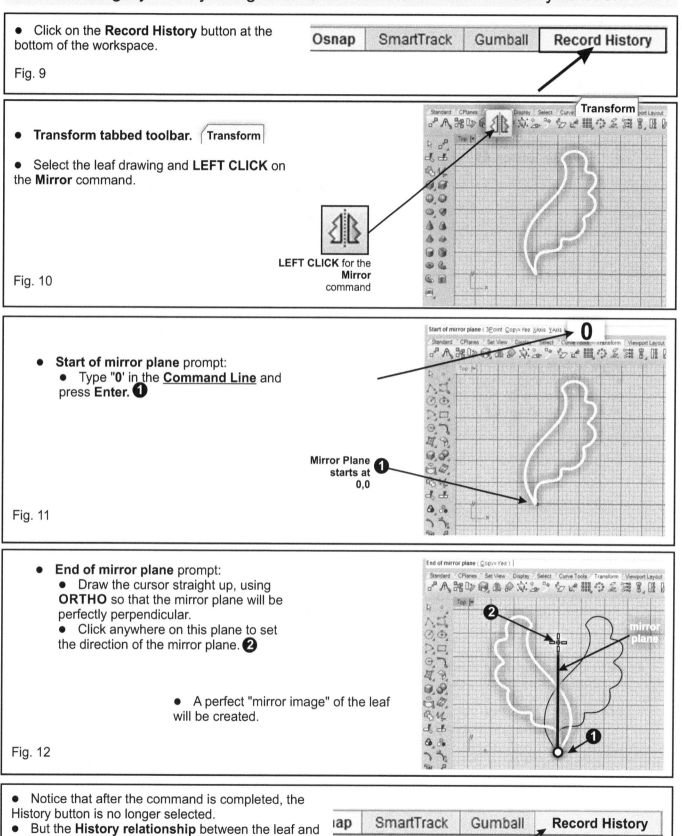

- Notice that after the command is completed, the History button is no longer selected.
- But the **History relationship** between the leaf and its mirrored copy has been established.

Fig. 13

| ap | SmartTrack | Gumball | **Record History** |

Rotate, Mirror, Point Editing with History Update
Continuing the design process.

- **LEFT CLICK** on the **Rotate 2-D** command.

  - **Center of rotation** prompt:
    - Snap to the **Endpoint** at the bottom of the parent object.
    - Click to set location. **1**

LEFT CLICK for the **Rotate 2-D** command

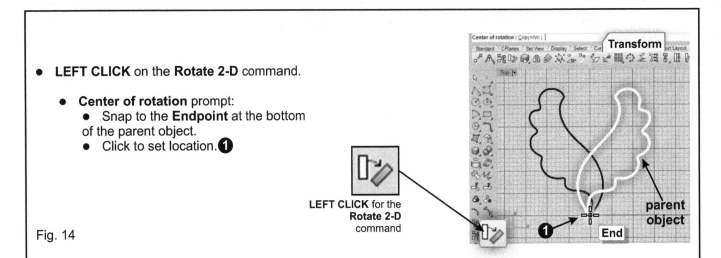

Fig. 14

- **Angle or first reference point** prompt:
  - Draw the cursor upward and click to set the first reference point somewhere on the grid as shown. **2**

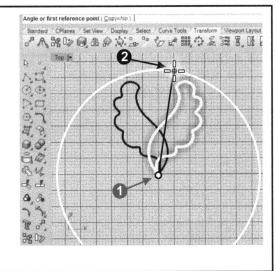

Fig. 15

- **Second reference point** prompt:
  - Draw the cursor around clockwise until the preview **3** of the new location of the leaf is in a position that you like.
  - Click to set this new location.

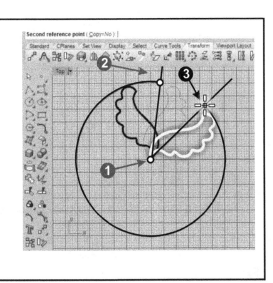

Fig. 16

- The leaf is now rotated into a new position.

- Note: **History** has updated the position of the leaf on the left so that it still is a mirror image of the original leaf that was rotated.
  - The original leaf on the right is called the **PARENT** and the mirror image on the left is called the **CHILD.**

Fig. 17

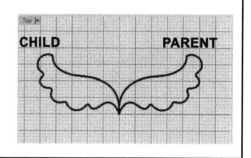

- See how many versions you can make from just point editing the **PARENT** object.

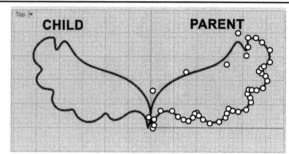

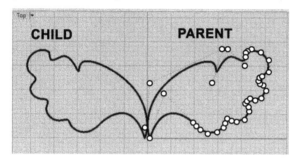

Fig. 18

- Click on the **Record History** button at the bottom of the workspace.

Fig. 19

| Osnap | SmartTrack | Gumball | **Record History** |

- Select both **CHILD** and **PARENT** and **LEFT CLICK** on the **Mirror** command.

  - **Start of mirror plane** prompt:
    - Type "**0**" in the **Command Line** and press **Enter.** ❶

LEFT CLICK for the **Mirror** command

Start of Mirror Plane "0"

Fig. 20

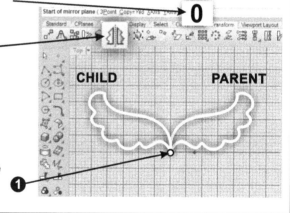

- **End of mirror plane** prompt:
  - Using **ORTHO,** draw the cursor straight over to the right or left and click to set location. ❷
  - Two mirror images have been created below the original 2 *and have a History relationship with them.*

Fig. 21

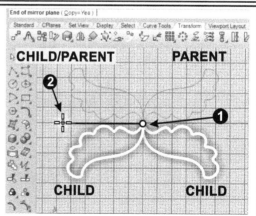

- Select the original **PARENT** object and **LEFT CLICK** on the **Rotate 2-D** command.

  - **Center of rotation** prompt.
    - Click in the middle of the leaf as shown. ❶

LEFT CLICK for
Rotate 2-D
command

Fig. 22

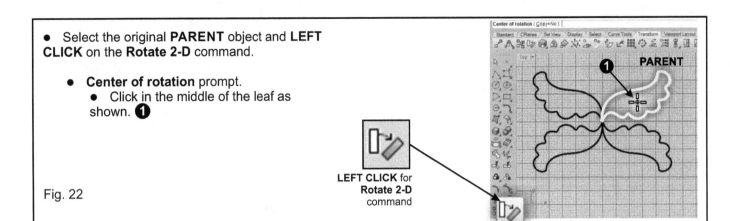

- **Angle or first reference point** prompt:
  - Draw the cursor out and click to set the first reference point as.❷

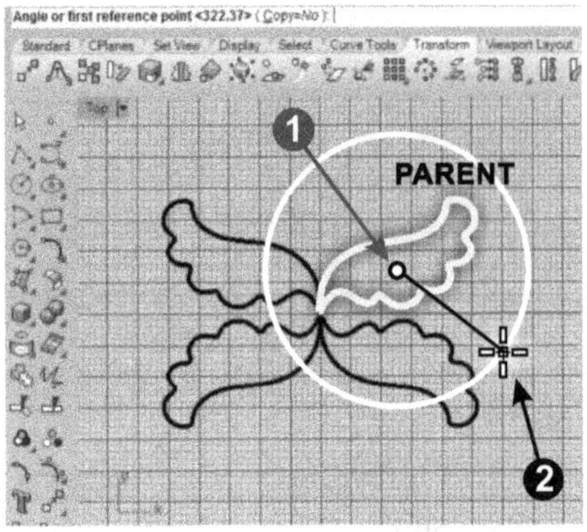

Fig. 23

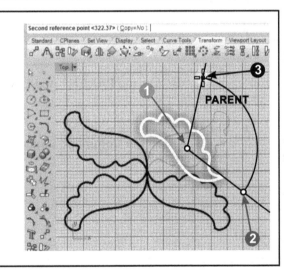

- **Second reference point** prompt:
  - Rotate the cursor around to the approximate position shown.❸
  - Click to set the location.

Fig. 24

- The other 3 elements have updated.

- Note how they intersect each other.

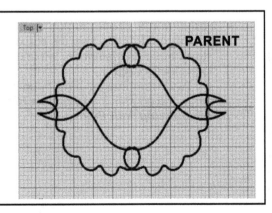

Fig. 25

- **Click and Drag** the original leaf out so that it is within the quadrant made by the X and Y axes as shown.
- Release the cursor.

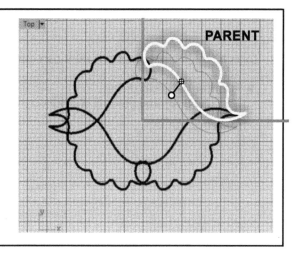

Fig. 26

- The three **CHILD** objects have updated.

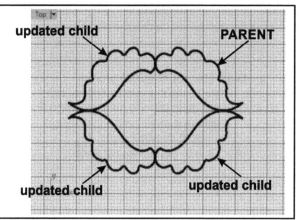

Fig. 27

- Click and drag one of the **CHILD** objects.

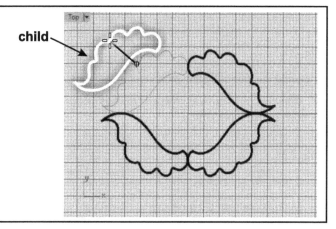

Fig. 28

- As soon as you release the cursor, the **Rhino 7 History Warning** box will appear.

- This will always happen if you edit a **CHILD** object.

- If you want to maintain the History relationship, click the **Cancel** button.

Fig. 29

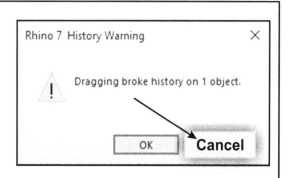

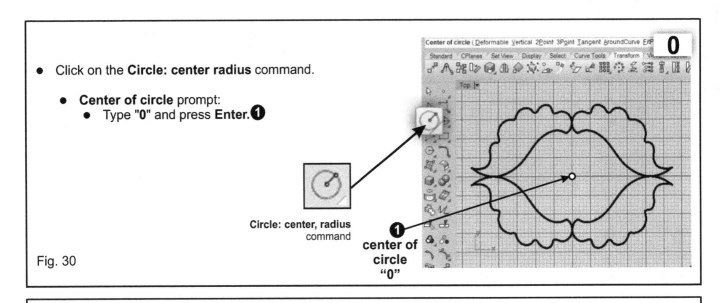

- Click on the **Circle: center radius** command.

  - **Center of circle** prompt:
    - Type "0" and press **Enter.**❶

Circle: center, radius
command

center of
circle
"0"

Fig. 30

- **Diameter (or Radius)** prompt:
  - Draw the cursor out so that it snaps to a point on the design that allows it to sit inside the design without overlapping it.
  - Click to set the location.❷

Fig. 31

- Click on the **Record History** button at the bottom of the workspace.

| Osnap | SmartTrack | Gumball | **Record History** |

Fig. 32

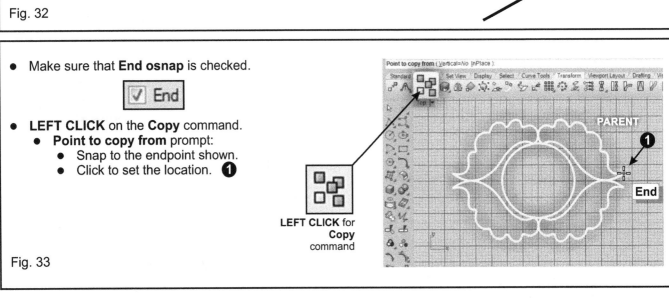

- Make sure that **End osnap** is checked.

☑ End

- **LEFT CLICK** on the **Copy** command.
  - **Point to copy from** prompt:
    - Snap to the endpoint shown.
    - Click to set the location. ❶

LEFT CLICK for
Copy
command

PARENT

Fig. 33

- **Point to copy to** prompt:
  - Click on the endpoint on the other side as shown to accurately place the copy. ❷

Fig. 34

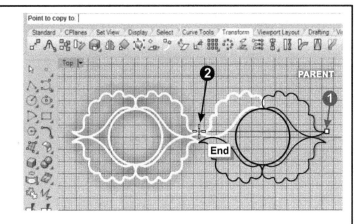

- Use the same strategy to create another copy.

- Press **Enter** when done.

Fig. 35

- Turn on **Edit Points** for the original **PARENT** object only.

Edit PointsOn
command

Fig. 36

- Click to turn on **Perp osnap**.

☑ Perp

- Select a point and drag it toward the circle until it snaps to a location **Perpendicular** to the original location of the point as shown.

- Release the cursor.

- Do some additional point editing of you want.

Fig. 37

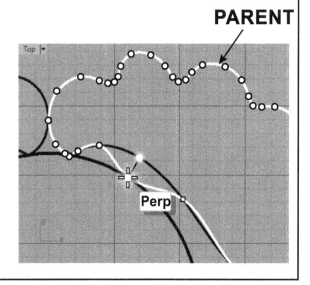

184

- All of the other leaves update as you drag control points on the parent object.

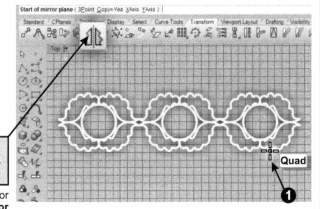

- History will continue to update the **CHILD** objects if you continue to edit the original **PARENT** object.

Fig. 38

- Make sure that **Quad osnap** is enabled.

- Select all of the design elements and **LEFT CLICK** on the **Mirror** command in the **Transform** toolbar flyout.

  - **Start of mirror plane** prompt:
    - Snap to the **Quad** point shown and click to set location. ❶

Fig. 39

LEFT CLICK for **Mirror** command

- Click on the **Record History** button at the bottom of the workspace.

| Osnap | SmartTrack | Gumball | Record History |

- *Note: Even though you have started the Mirror command, you can still decide to use History and enable it while the Mirror command is already in progress.*

Fig. 40

- **End of mirror plane** prompt:
  - Snap to one of the **Quad** points on one of the other leaves.
  - Click to set location. ❷

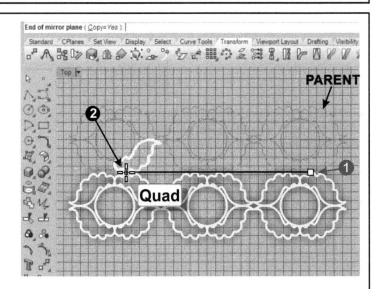

Fig. 41

- Use the **Mirror** command again to place another mirror copy on the other side of the original row.

- **Don't forget to enable History once again for this step.**

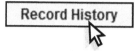

Fig. 42

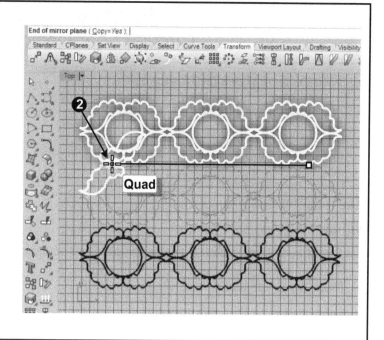

- If you continue to point edit the **PARENT** object, the rest of the leaves will update as shown.

- **Save** this file as **mirrored leaf designs.3dm.**

- *The original single leaf sketch will be used in the next section.*

Fig. 43

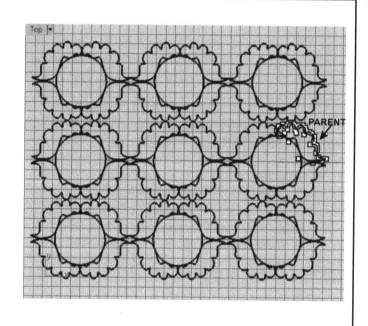

- **RIGHT-CLICK** on the **History** button ❶ at the bottom of the workspace.
    - Select the options ❷ shown in the context menu.
    - This will change the default setting that has History enabled all of the time.

- Note: Keeping History on all of the time can lead to complications as you don't always want to use it.

Fig. 44

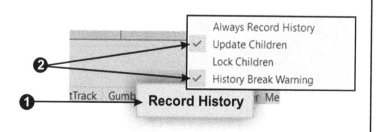

Polar Array Command
Circular Leaf Design using History

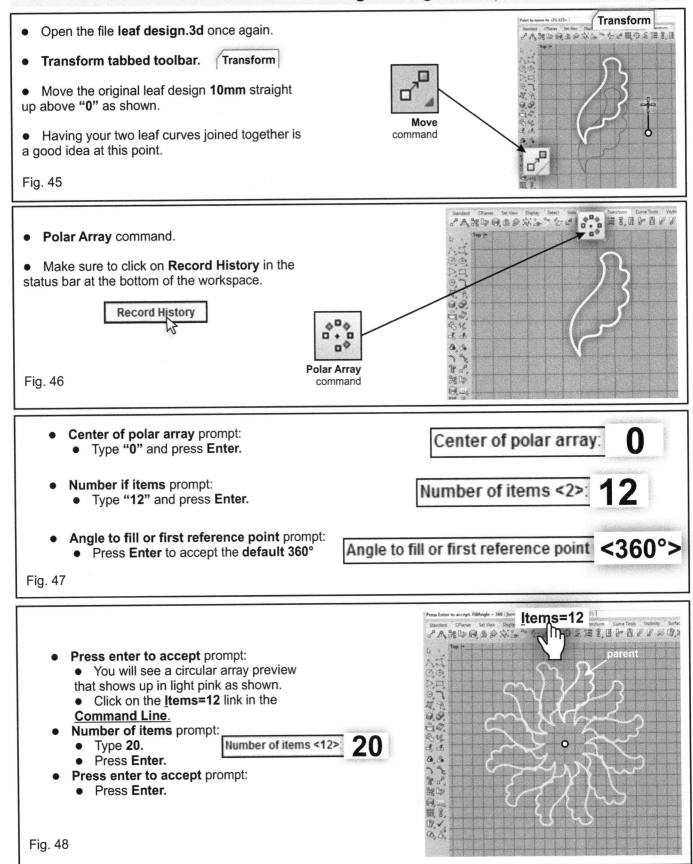

- Open the file **leaf design.3d** once again.

- **Transform tabbed toolbar.** ⌐Transform⌐

- Move the original leaf design **10mm** straight up above **"0"** as shown.

- Having your two leaf curves joined together is a good idea at this point.

Fig. 45

Move command

- **Polar Array** command.

- Make sure to click on **Record History** in the status bar at the bottom of the workspace.

Record History

Fig. 46

Polar Array command

- **Center of polar array** prompt:
  - Type **"0"** and press **Enter**.

- **Number if items** prompt:
  - Type **"12"** and press **Enter**.

- **Angle to fill or first reference point** prompt:
  - Press **Enter** to accept the **default 360°**

Fig. 47

Center of polar array: **0**

Number of items <2>: **12**

Angle to fill or first reference point **<360°>**

- **Press enter to accept** prompt:
  - You will see a circular array preview that shows up in light pink as shown.
  - Click on the **Items=12** link in the **Command Line**.
- **Number of items** prompt:
  - Type **20**.
  - Press **Enter**.
- **Press enter to accept** prompt:
  - Press **Enter**.

Number of items <12>: **20**

Items=12

parent

Fig. 48

• The command is ended. The polar array has created 20 copies around the designated center of array which, in this case, is **0**.

• Select the original parent object as shown.
• Click on the tab for the **Properties** window. ❶
  • Notice the **Display Color** line. ❷
  • The default setting is that the display color of the parent object is the same as the layer for the child objects - it is **By Layer** as shown.

Fig. 49

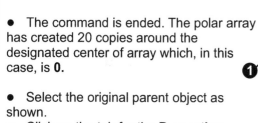
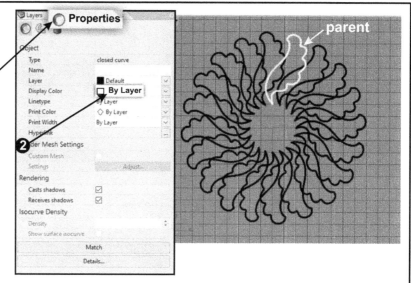

Changing the color of the Parent object will make it easier to locate among all of the other copies!

• Access the drop-down menu for the **Display Color** line ❶ and click on a color that is different from the color the parent is now - in this case, the color **Red** is selected. ❷

• The display color will now be seen as Red for the selected parent object.

Fig. 50

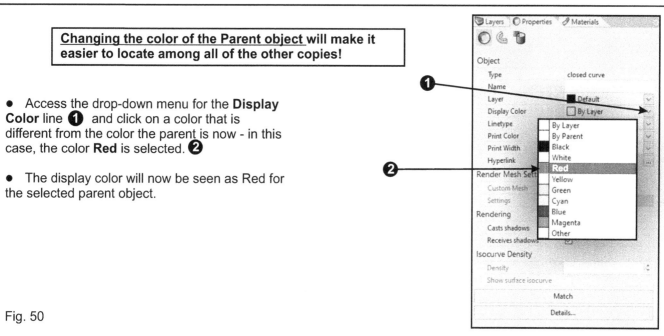

• Click on the grid to de-select the parent object and note that it is now red.

• *Note: it is still on the same layer as the rest of the objects in the array.*

Fig. 51

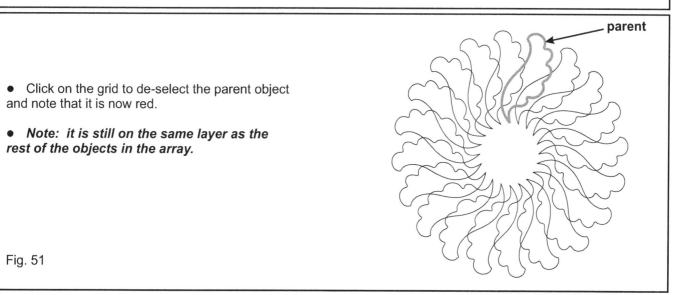

- Drag the **parent object** up about 5mm.

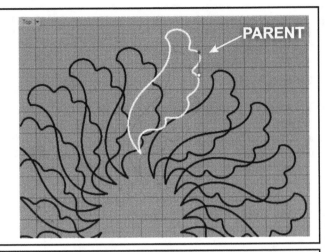

Fig. 52

- When you release the cursor, all of the other leaves will update to maintain the relationship to the parent object.

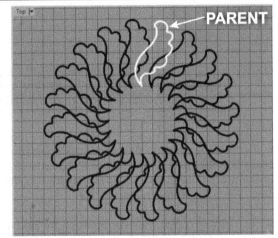

Fig. 53

- Use the **Rotate 2D** command to rotate the **parent object** clockwise as shown.

center of rotation

- When the Rotate command is finished, all of the **child objects** will update to match the rotation of the **parent object**.

PARENT

Fig. 54

- Select a Child object next to the Parent object and **LEFT CLICK** on the **Trim** command.

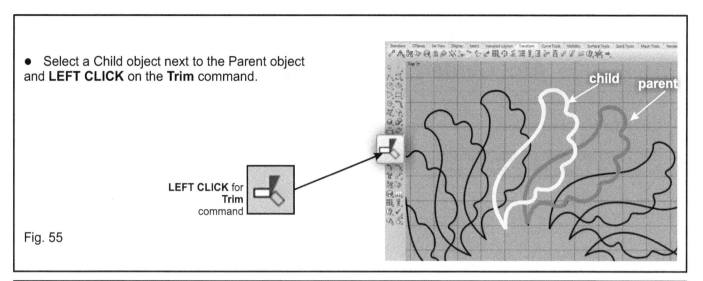

LEFT CLICK for
Trim
command

Fig. 55

- **Select object to trim** prompt:
  - Click on a part of the line of the Parent object that is inside the boundary of the selected Child object as shown.
  - When finished trimming, press **Enter**.

**click here
to trim**

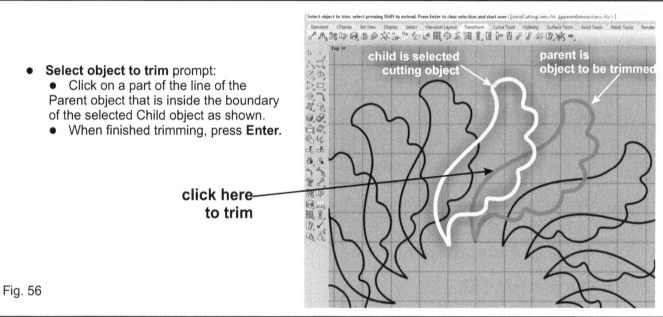

Fig. 56

- The **parent object** has been trimmed and the child objects have all updated.

- Suggestion: do all of your editing of the Parent object before doing this trimming step.

- You can save this design as **leaf design - polar array.3dm**

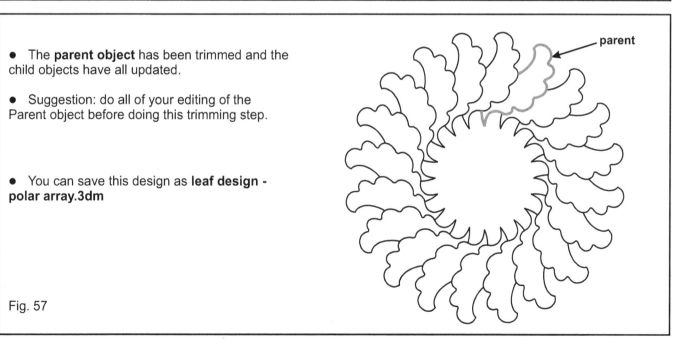

Fig. 57

Arc Commands

Arc: Center, Start, Angle command

- **Curve Tools tabbed toolbar.**   Curve Tools

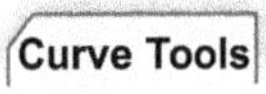

- Using **ORTHO,** draw two line segments,
15mm each, to create the polyline shown.

- Turn off **ORTHO.**

Fig. 1

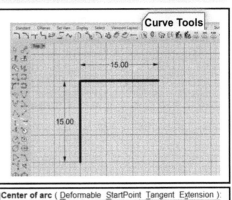

- Click on the **Arc: Center, Start, Angle**
command as shown.

  - **Center of arc** prompt:
    - Snap on the **Midpoint** of the line
    shown.
    - Click to set location. **1**

Fig. 2

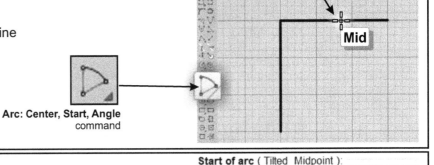

Arc: Center, Start, Angle
command

- **Start of arc** prompt:
  - Snap to one of the **Endpoints** of the
  line as shown.
  - Click to set location. **2**

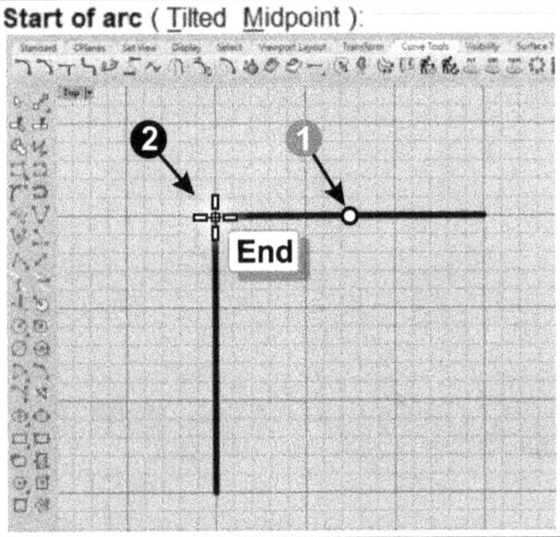

Fig. 3

- **End point or angle** prompt:
  - Draw the cursor around in a
  counterclockwise direction toward the
  other end other end of the line.
  - Notice preview arc and line.

- *If you turn ORTHO off, the cursor will
move smoothly around to the other side of
the line.*

Fig. 4

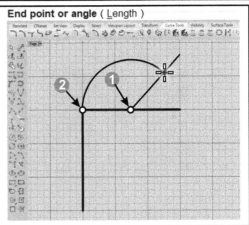

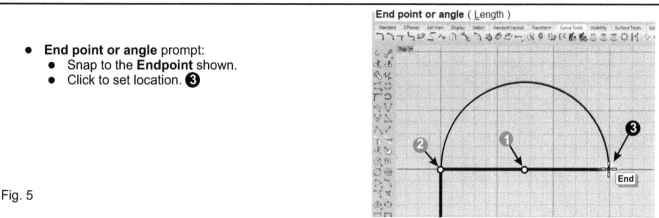

- **End point or angle** prompt:
  - Snap to the **Endpoint** shown.
  - Click to set location. ❸

Fig. 5

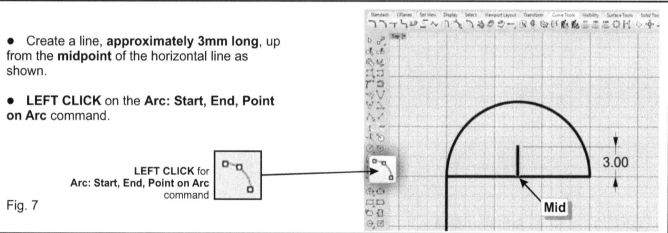

- The diameter of the new arc is exactly 15mm, the length of the line on which it was created.

Fig. 6

Arc: Start, End, Point on Arc command

- Create a line, **approximately 3mm long**, up from the **midpoint** of the horizontal line as shown.

- **LEFT CLICK** on the **Arc: Start, End, Point on Arc** command.

LEFT CLICK for
Arc: Start, End, Point on Arc
command

Fig. 7

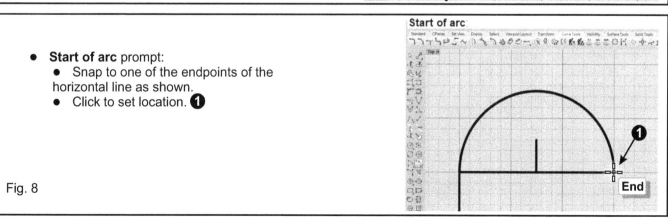

- **Start of arc** prompt:
  - Snap to one of the endpoints of the horizontal line as shown.
  - Click to set location. ❶

Fig. 8

- **End of arc** prompt:
  - Snap to the other end of the line.
  - Click to set location. ❷

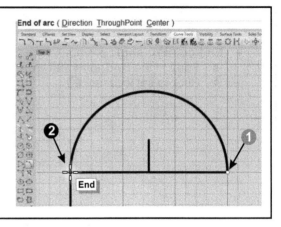

Fig. 9

- **Point on arc** prompt:
  - Snap to the **Endpoint** of the little 3mm perpendicular line.
  - Click to set location. ❸

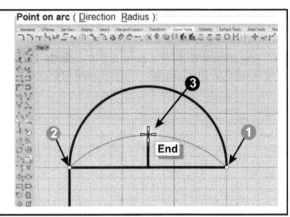

Fig. 10

- The finished arc has been created by clicking on 3 designated points.

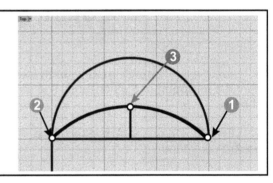

Fig. 11

Arc: Start, End, Direction at Start Command

- **LEFT CLICK** on the **Arc: Start, End, Direction at Start** command in the **Arc** toolbar flyout.

  - **Start of arc** prompt:
    - Snap to the lower endpoint of the vertical line. ❶
    - Click to set location.

LEFT CLICK for
Arc: Start, End, Direction at Start
command

Fig. 12

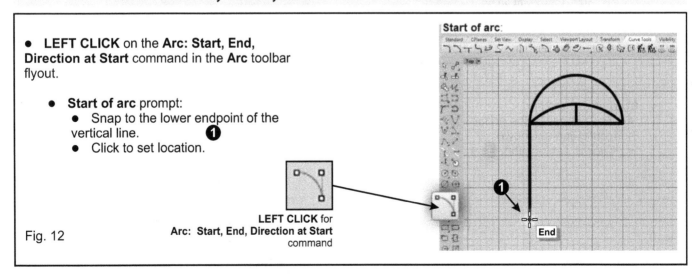

- **End of arc** prompt:
  - Snap to the endpoint of the horizontal line.
  - Click to set location. ❷

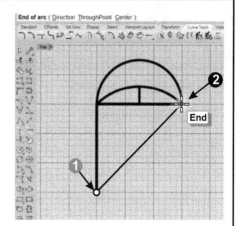

Fig. 13

- **Direction at start** prompt:
  - Draw the cursor down and see a preview of the arc and a straight direction guideline that follows the cursor.

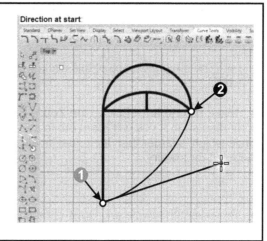

Fig. 14

- **Direction at start** prompt:
  - Use **ORTHO** to ensure that the arc direction guideline is perfectly horizontal.
  - Click to set location. ❸

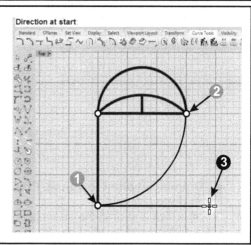

Fig. 15

- The finished arc touches two designated locations and the radius is determined by the direction control of the final location.

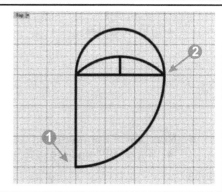

Fig. 16

- Create the layers shown.

- **ref geo** layer current.

Fig. 1

Creating the Basic Motif

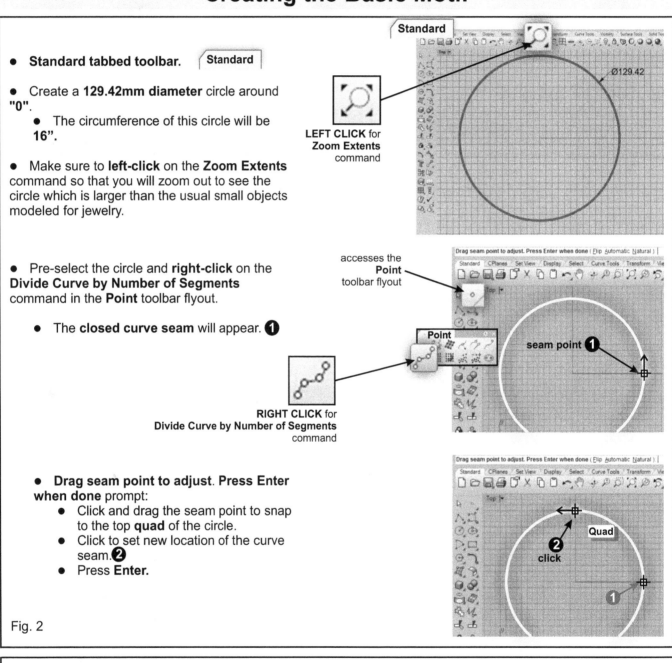

- **Standard tabbed toolbar.** ⌐Standard⌐

- Create a **129.42mm diameter** circle around **"0"**.
    - The circumference of this circle will be **16"**.

- Make sure to **left-click** on the **Zoom Extents** command so that you will zoom out to see the circle which is larger than the usual small objects modeled for jewelry.

LEFT CLICK for **Zoom Extents** command

- Pre-select the circle and **right-click** on the **Divide Curve by Number of Segments** command in the **Point** toolbar flyout.

    - The **closed curve seam** will appear. ❶

accesses the **Point** toolbar flyout

RIGHT CLICK for **Divide Curve by Number of Segments** command

seam point ❶

- **Drag seam point to adjust. Press Enter when done** prompt:
    - Click and drag the seam point to snap to the top **quad** of the circle.
    - Click to set new location of the curve seam. ❷
    - Press **Enter.**

Quad

❷ click

Fig. 2

- **Number of segments** prompt:
    - Type **"60"** and press **Enter.**

Number of segments <3> (Length Split=No MarkEnds=Yes GroupOutput=No) **60**

Fig. 3

- The circle will be divided into 60 equal segments by the placement of point objects.

- These are **"point objects"**, not control points.

Fig. 4

- **TECH LINES** layer current.

Fig. 5

current ──────▶ TECH LINES ✓ ■
ref geo
hidden lines

- Create a **Ø2mm diameter** circle around the second point from the top point.
  - Use **Point osnap** for accuracy.

Fig. 6

Ø2.00   top point

Point

- **Curve Tools tabbed toolbar.**   Curve Tools

- Use **Curve Offset** to offset the original Ø129.42 mm circle at a 1mm distance , using the **BothSides** option to put offsets inside and outside the circle.

LEFT CLICK for
Offset Curve
command

new 1mm offsets

Fig. 7

- **hidden lines** layer current.

current ──────▶
TECH LINES
ref geo
hidden lines ✓
Layer 04

- Use the **Offset Curve** command again to offset the original 129.42 diameter circle to a distance of **.5mm** with the **BothSides** option again.

new .5mm offsets

Fig. 8

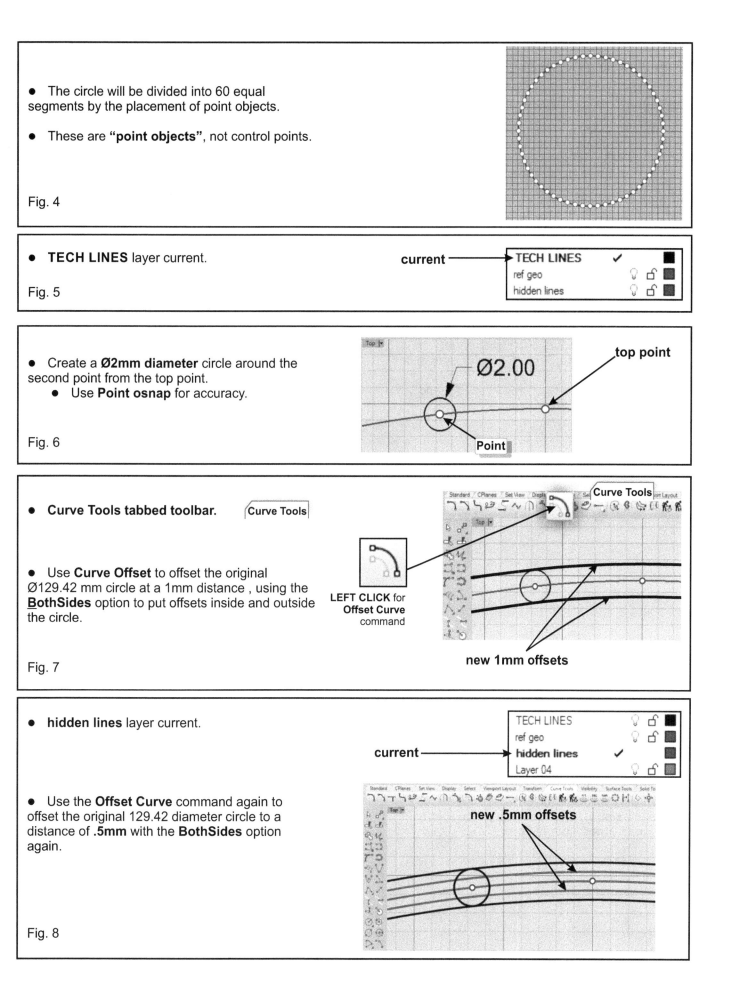

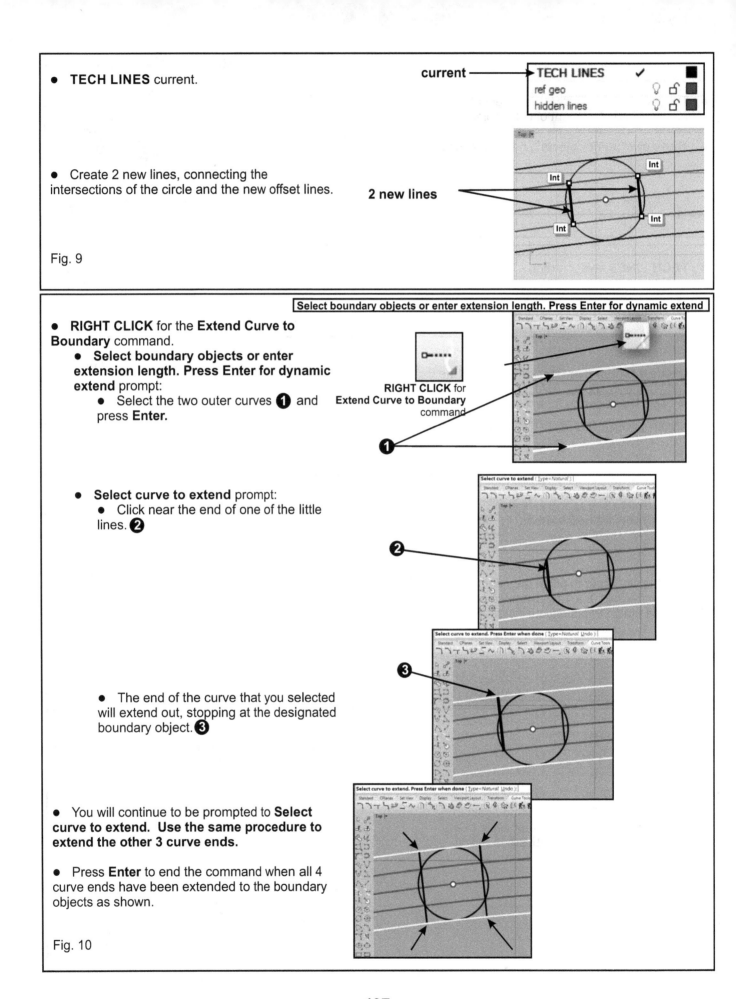

- **TECH LINES** current.

current ⟶ TECH LINES ✓
ref geo
hidden lines

- Create 2 new lines, connecting the intersections of the circle and the new offset lines.

2 new lines

Int
Int
Int
Int

Fig. 9

Select boundary objects or enter extension length. Press Enter for dynamic extend

- **RIGHT CLICK** for the **Extend Curve to Boundary** command.
  - **Select boundary objects or enter extension length. Press Enter for dynamic extend** prompt:
    - Select the two outer curves ❶ and press **Enter**.

RIGHT CLICK for **Extend Curve to Boundary** command

❶

- **Select curve to extend** prompt:
  - Click near the end of one of the little lines. ❷

❷

- The end of the curve that you selected will extend out, stopping at the designated boundary object. ❸

❸

- You will continue to be prompted to **Select curve to extend. Use the same procedure to extend the other 3 curve ends.**

- Press **Enter** to end the command when all 4 curve ends have been extended to the boundary objects as shown.

Fig. 10

197

- Select the circle and **LEFT CLICK** on the **Split** command.

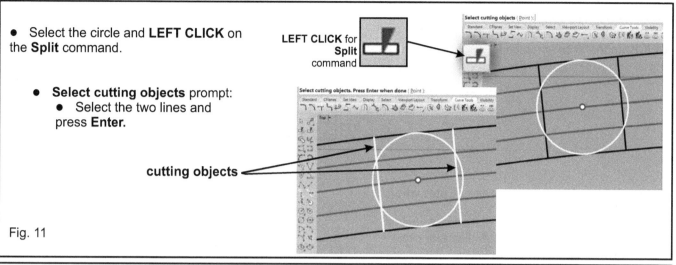

  - **Select cutting objects** prompt:
    - Select the two lines and press **Enter**.

cutting objects

Fig. 11

- Select the two split-off sides of the circle and change them to the **hidden lines** layer.

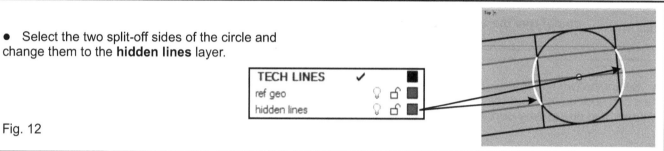

TECH LINES	✓	■
ref geo	♀ 🔓	■
hidden lines	♀ 🔓	■

Fig. 12

- **Transform tabbed toolbar.** ⟨Transform⟩

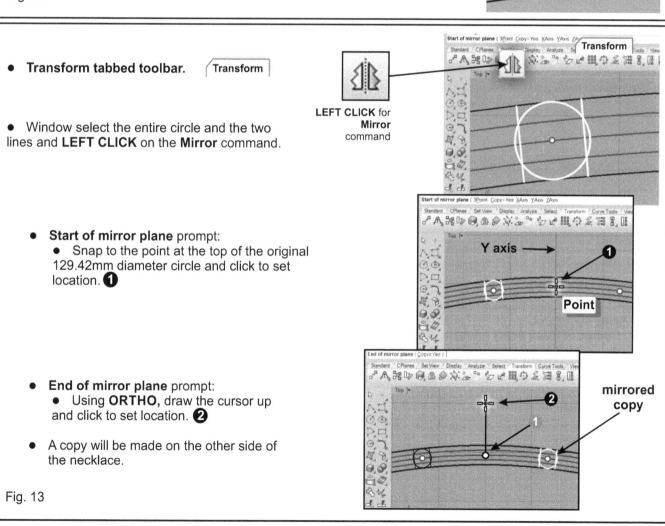

- Window select the entire circle and the two lines and **LEFT CLICK** on the **Mirror** command.

  - **Start of mirror plane** prompt:
    - Snap to the point at the top of the original 129.42mm diameter circle and click to set location. ❶

  - **End of mirror plane** prompt:
    - Using **ORTHO,** draw the cursor up and click to set location. ❷

  - A copy will be made on the other side of the necklace.

Fig. 13

198

- Select the two little inner lines and **LEFT CLICK** on the **Trim** command.

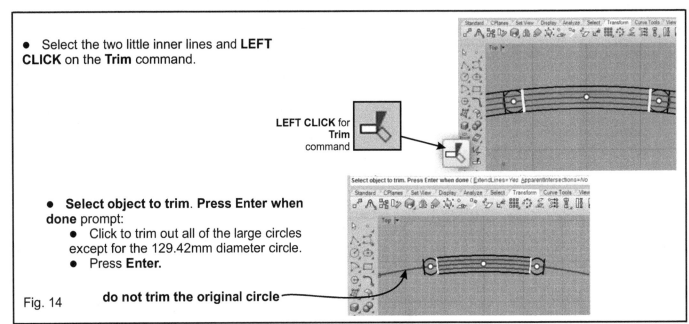

LEFT CLICK for **Trim** command

- **Select object to trim. Press Enter when done** prompt:
  - Click to trim out all of the large circles except for the 129.42mm diameter circle.
  - Press **Enter.**

Fig. 14   **do not trim the original circle**

- Select the two larger arcs and the two little lines and click on the **Join** command to join these 4 curves into one **closed curve**.

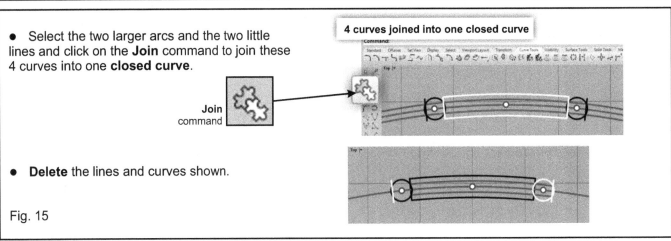

4 curves joined into one closed curve

Join command

- **Delete** the lines and curves shown.

Fig. 15

- Turn off the **ref geo** layer.

Fig. 16

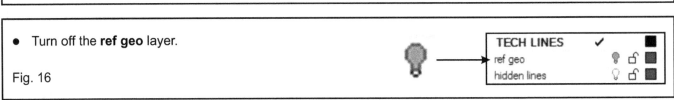

TECH LINES	✓	■
ref geo	♀ 🔓	■
hidden lines	♀ 🔓	■

- Select all of the objects shown and click on the **Polar Array** command.
  - **Center of Polar Array** prompt:
    - Type **"0"** and press **Enter.**
  - **Number of items** prompt:
    - Type **"30"** and press **Enter.**
  - **Angle to fill or first reference point <360>** prompt:
    - Press **Enter** to accept the default **360° angle to fill.**
  - **Press Enter to accept** prompt:
    - Press **Enter.**

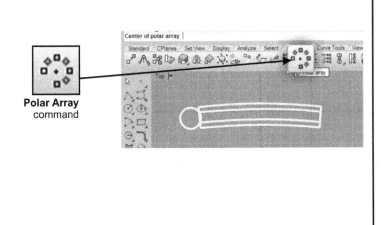

Polar Array command

Fig. 17

- **ref geo** layer current.

- Turn off **hidden lines** layer.

current ➝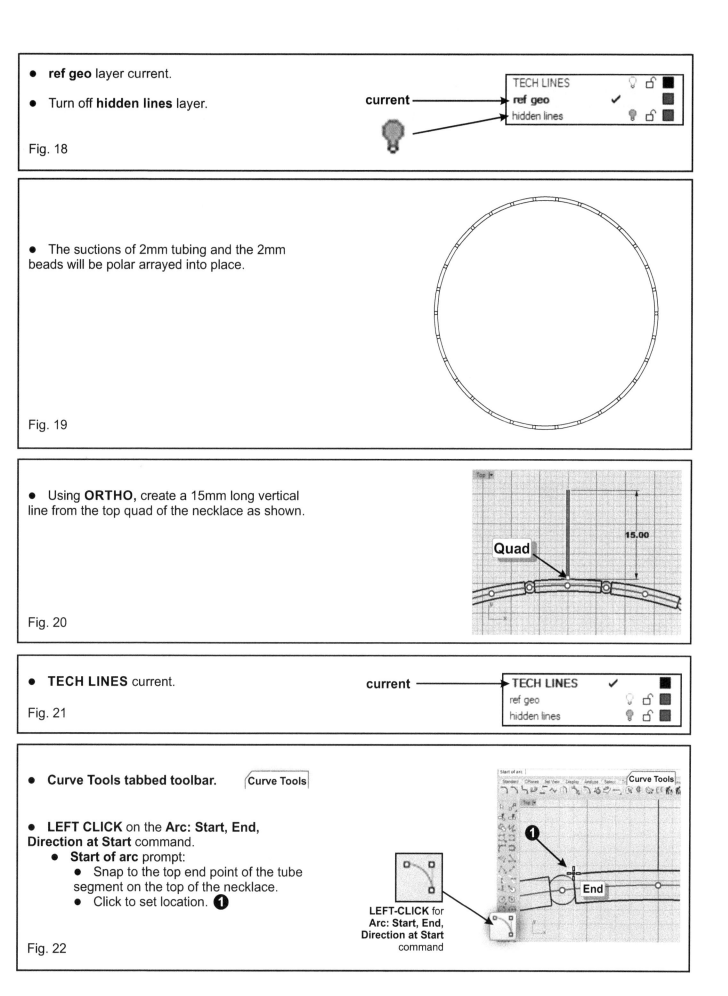

Fig. 18

- The suctions of 2mm tubing and the 2mm beads will be polar arrayed into place.

Fig. 19

- Using **ORTHO,** create a 15mm long vertical line from the top quad of the necklace as shown.

Fig. 20

- **TECH LINES** current.

current ➝

Fig. 21

- **Curve Tools tabbed toolbar.**   Curve Tools

- **LEFT CLICK** on the **Arc: Start, End, Direction at Start** command.
  - **Start of arc** prompt:
    - Snap to the top end point of the tube segment on the top of the necklace.
    - Click to set location. ❶

LEFT-CLICK for
**Arc: Start, End,
Direction at Start**
command

Fig. 22

- **End of arc** prompt:
  - Snap to the top **End** of the new 15mm line.
  - Click to set location. **②**

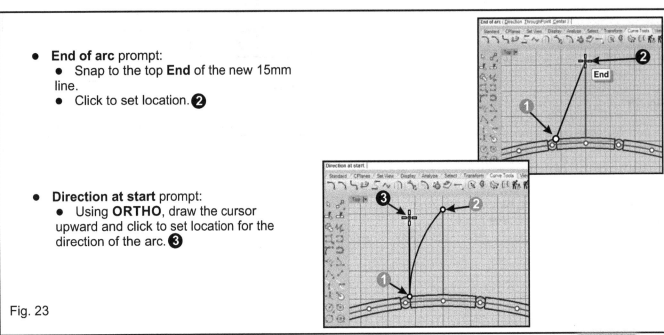

- **Direction at start** prompt:
  - Using **ORTHO**, draw the cursor upward and click to set location for the direction of the arc. **③**

Fig. 23

- **Transform tabbed toolbar.** [Transform]

- **Mirror** the new arc over to the other side.
  - The 15mm vertical line will be the **mirror plane.**

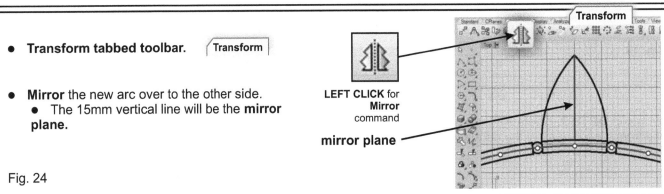

LEFT CLICK for **Mirror** command

mirror plane

Fig. 24

- Select the two arcs and click on the **Join** command to create a single open curve.

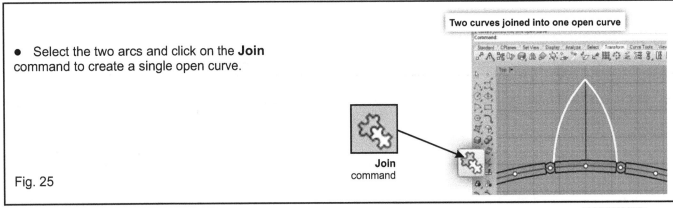

Two curves joined into one open curve

Join command

Fig. 25

- Select the new design motif and click on the **Polar Array** command.

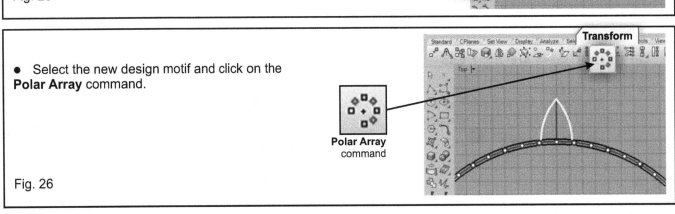

Transform

Polar Array command

Fig. 26

- **Center of polar array** prompt:
  - Type **"0"** and press **Enter**.
- **Number of items** prompt:
  - Type **"30"** and press **Enter**.
- **Angle to fill or first reference point <360>** prompt:
  - Press **Enter** to accept the default **360°** **angle to fill**.
- **Press Enter to accept** prompt:
  - Press **Enter**.

- The design motif will be Polar Arrayed into place, in proper alignment with the tubing sections.

Fig. 27

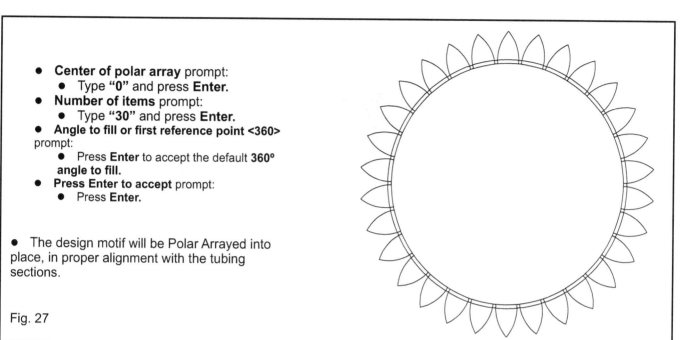

- Create a new layer called **ref geo 2** and make that layer current.
- This layer will be a reference for the scaling of the design motifs.

Fig. 28

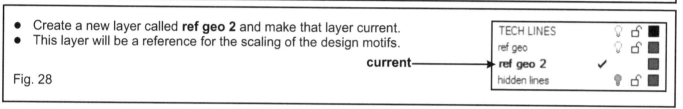

- **Curve Tools tabbed toolbar.**   Curve Tools

- Create a **Line** between the **end points** of the arcs of the new motif.

Single Line command

Fig. 29

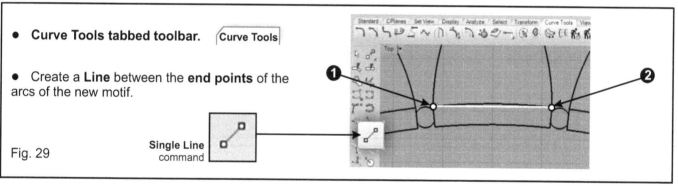

- **Transform tabbed toolbar.**   Transform

- **Polar Array** the new line.
  - **Center of polar array** prompt:
    - Type **"0"** and press **Enter**.
  - **Number if items** prompt:
    - Type **"30"** and press **Enter**.
  - **Angle to fill or first reference point** prompt:
    - Press **Enter** to accept the default **360°**.
  - **Press Enter to accept** prompt:
    - Press **Enter**.

Polar Array command

line to be arrayed

Fig. 30

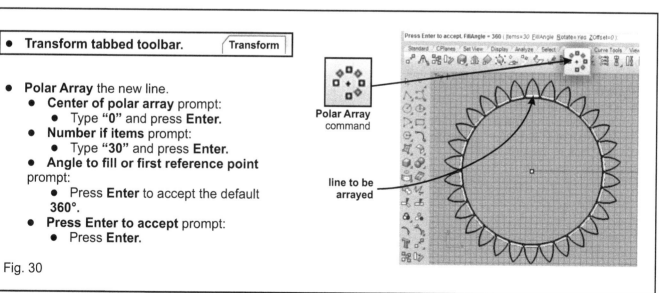

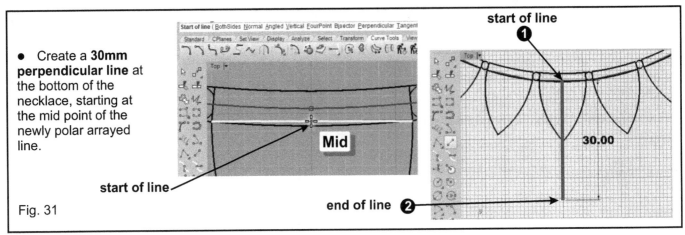

- Create a **30mm perpendicular line** at the bottom of the necklace, starting at the mid point of the newly polar arrayed line.

start of line

Mid

start of line

start of line ①

30.00

end of line ②

Fig. 31

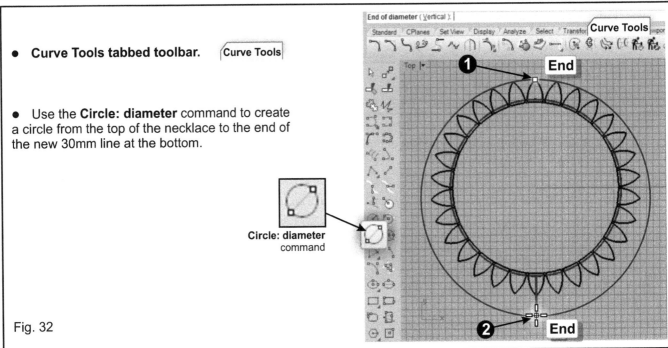

- **Curve Tools tabbed toolbar.** Curve Tools

- Use the **Circle: diameter** command to create a circle from the top of the necklace to the end of the new 30mm line at the bottom.

Circle: diameter
command

End ①

End ②

Fig. 32

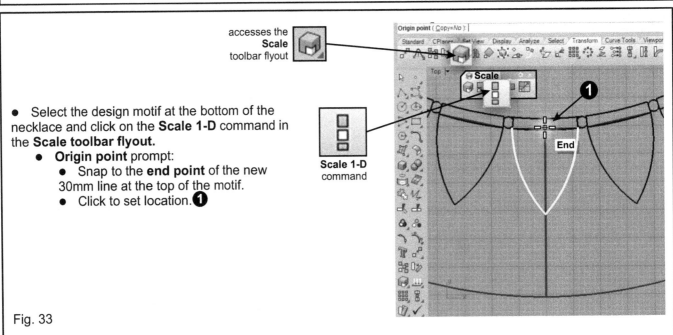

accesses the **Scale** toolbar flyout

- Select the design motif at the bottom of the necklace and click on the **Scale 1-D** command in the **Scale toolbar flyout.**
  - **Origin point** prompt:
    - Snap to the **end point** of the new 30mm line at the top of the motif.
    - Click to set location. ①

Scale 1-D
command

End

Fig. 33

- **Scale factor or first reference point** prompt:
  - Draw the cursor down and snap to the **End point** of the design motif.
  - Click to set location. ❷

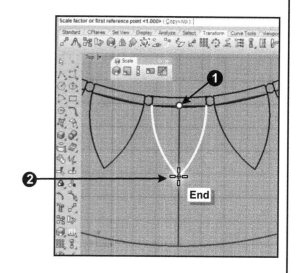

- **Second reference point** prompt:
  - Draw the cursor down and snap to the **end point** of the **30mm line**.
  - Click to set location. ❸

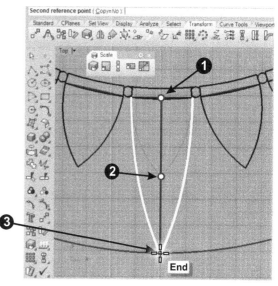

Fig. 34

- Select the next design motif up from the one just scaled and click on the **Scale 1-D command** again.
  - **Origin point** prompt:
    - Snap to the **mid point** of the straight line that was polar arrayed previously in Fig. 30.
    - Click to set location. ❶

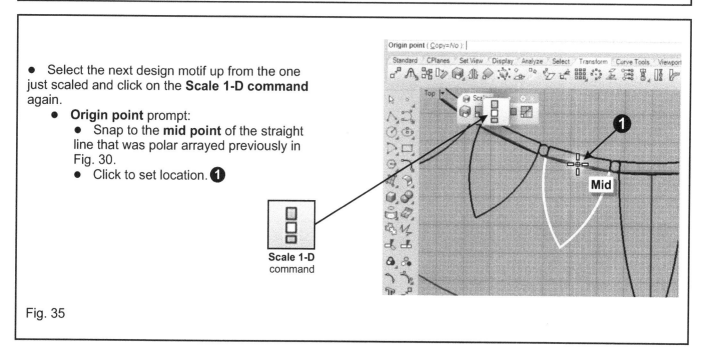

Scale 1-D
command

Fig. 35

- **Scale factor or first reference point**
prompt:
    - Draw the cursor down and snap to the
    End point of the design motif.
    - Click to set location. ❷

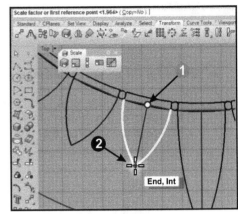

- **Second reference point** prompt:
    - Draw the cursor down and snap to the
    intersection with the outer circle.
    - Click to set location. ❸

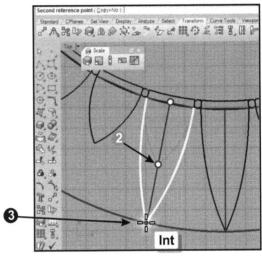

Fig. 36

- The rest of the design motifs have been
scaled, using the same technique.

- The motifs on the other side of the necklace
have been deleted.

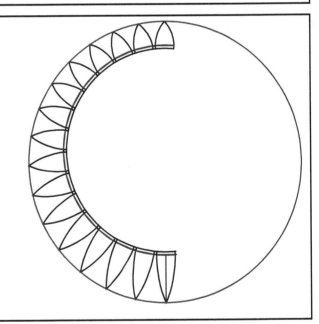

Fig. 37

- Turn off the **ref geo 2** layer.

- **TECH LINES** layer current.

Fig. 38

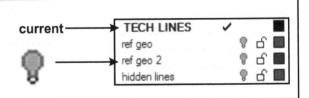

- Select all of the design motifs, tubing sections, and beads, *except for the motifs and tubing sections on the top and bottom of the necklace* and click on the **Mirror** command.

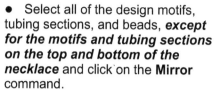

LEFT CLICK for **Mirror** command

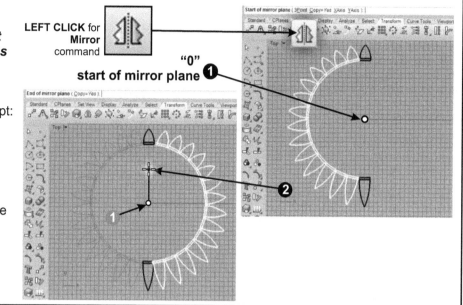

"0"
start of mirror plane ❶

- **Start of mirror plane** prompt:
  - Type **"0"** and press **Enter.** ❶

- **End of mirror plane** prompt:
  - Using **ORTHO**, draw the cursor up and click to set location. ❷

Fig. 39

- **Curve Tools tabbed toolbar.** [Curve Tools]

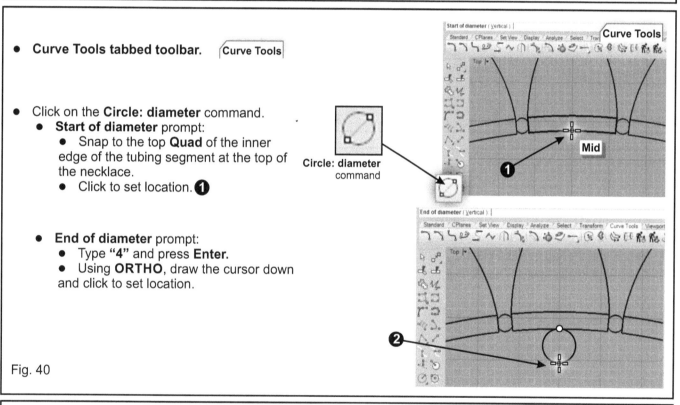

Curve Tools

- Click on the **Circle: diameter** command.
  - **Start of diameter** prompt:
    - Snap to the top **Quad** of the inner edge of the tubing segment at the top of the necklace.
    - Click to set location. ❶

  Circle: diameter command

  Mid

  - **End of diameter** prompt:
    - Type **"4"** and press **Enter.**
    - Using **ORTHO**, draw the cursor down and click to set location.

Fig. 40

- **LEFT CLICK** for the **Offset Curve** command.
  - **Select curve to offset** prompt:
    - Select the **4mm circle** just created.
  - **Offset distance: .5**
  - **Side to offset** prompt:
    - Offset to the inside of the circle.

- A top view technical of a 3mm stone with a .5mm bezel has been created.

Fig. 41

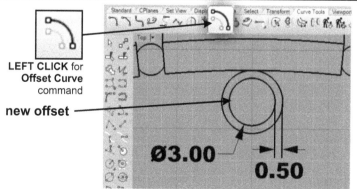

LEFT CLICK for **Offset Curve** command

new offset

Ø3.00

0.50

- **Polar Array** the new bezel with stone around the inside of the necklace, creating 30 copies that align with the tubing sections.

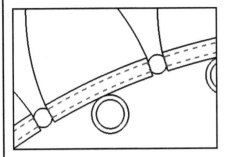

- You can turn on the **hidden lines** layer for a detail view.
  - The hidden lines layer has been assigned a custom linetype of .5.00,.5.00.

Fig. 42

- In this version, an additional circle allows for alternate scaling.

- Notice that the top motif has been replaced by a basic shape for a clasp.

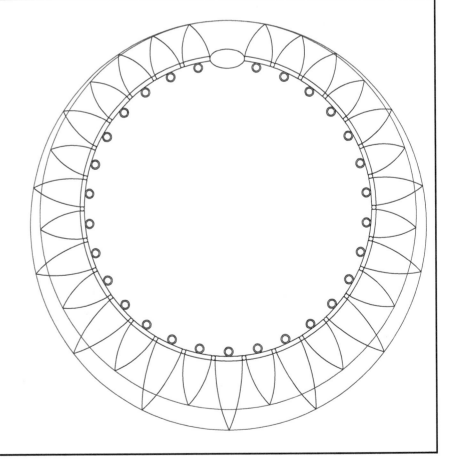

Fig. 43

Arraying Around a Square

Array Along Curve and Polar Array Commands

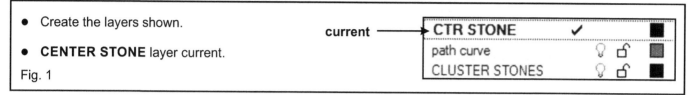

- Create the layers shown.

- **CENTER STONE** layer current.

Fig. 1

- **Curve Tools tabbed toolbar.** ⌐Curve Tools⌐

- Click on the **Circumscribed Square: center, radius** command in the **Polygon** toolbar flyout.
  - **Center of circumscribed polygon** prompt:
    - Type **"0"** and press **Enter.** ❶
  - **Midpoint of polygon edge** prompt:
    - Type **"5.25"** and press **Enter.**
    - Using **ortho**, move the cursor straight up and click to set location. ❷

Circumscribed Square: center, radius command

accesses the **Polygon** toolbar flyout

Fig. 2

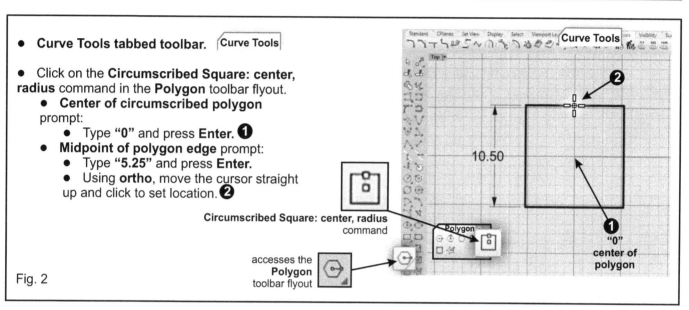

- Select the square ❶ and **LEFT CLICK** on the **Offset Curve** command.
  - **Side to offset** prompt:
    - Type **"1.25"** and press **Enter.**
    - Click to create a new offset around the outside of the square. ❷

Fig. 3

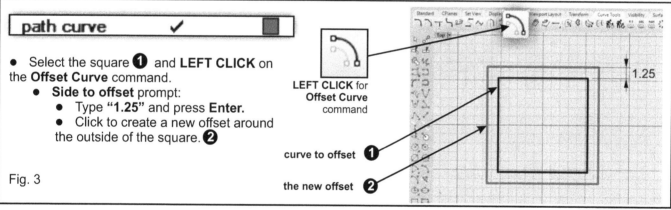

LEFT CLICK for **Offset Curve** command

curve to offset ❶

the new offset ❷

- Select the new offset and **left-click** on the **Explode** command.

- The offset square will be exploded into 4 separate line segments.

left-click for the **Explode command**

Fig. 4

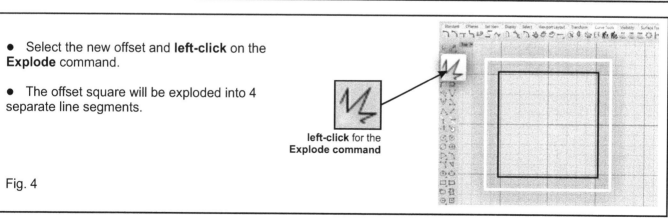

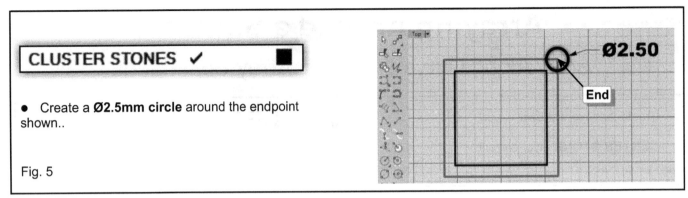

CLUSTER STONES ✓ ■

- Create a **Ø2.5mm circle** around the endpoint shown..

Fig. 5

- **Transform tabbed toolbar.** ⌐Transform⌐

- Click on the **Array Along Curve** command in the **Array** toolbar flyout.

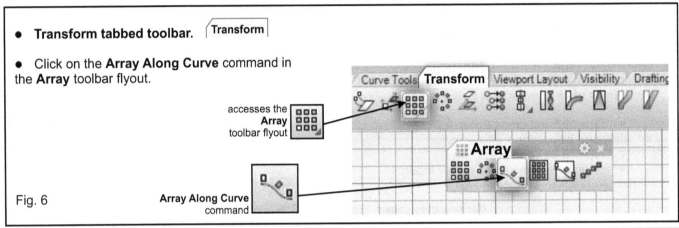

accesses the
Array
toolbar flyout

Array Along Curve
command

Fig. 6

- **Select objects to array** prompt:
  - Select the circle. ❶
  - Press **Enter.**
- **Select path curve** prompt:
  - **Click near the right end** of the horizontal line at the top as shown. ❷

Fig. 7

- As soon at the **path curve** is selected, the **Array Along Curve Options** box will appear.

  - Type the number **"6"** in the **Number of Items** category as shown. ❸
  - Click on the **OK** button to exit the dialog box. ❹

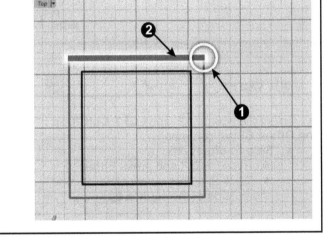

Fig. 8

- After you exit the dialog box, 6 circles will appear evenly spaced along the assigned path curve.

- **Delete** the circle on the far left.

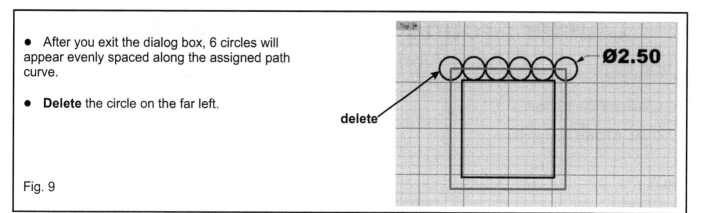

Fig. 9

- Click on the **Polar Array** command.
  - **Select objects to array** prompt:
    - Select all of the circles and press **Enter.**

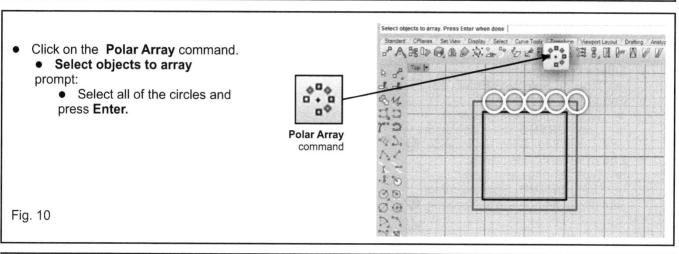

Polar Array
command

Fig. 10

- **Center of polar array** prompt:
  - Type **"0"** and press **Enter.**
- **Number of items** prompt:
  - Type **"4"** and press **Enter.**
- **Angle or first reference point** prompt:
  - Press **Enter** to accept the **360°** default or type **"360"** in the **Command Line** and press **Enter.**

Center of polar array: **0**

Number of items **4**

Angle to fill or first reference point <360> (

- A number of pink **preview circles** appear.

- Press **Enter** to accept.

- The finished array.

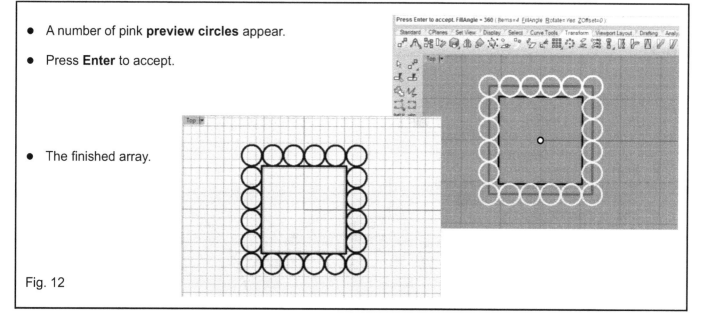

Fig. 12

Cluster Around an Oval Center Stone
Array Along Curve command

- Create the layers shown.

- **OVAL STONE** layer current.

Fig. 1

OVAL STONE	✓		■
ref geo		♀ 🔓	▨
CLUSTER STONES		♀ 🔓	▨
PRONGS		♀ 🔓	■
prong ref		♀ 🔓	▨

- **Curve Tools tabbed toolbar.**   ⌐Curve Tools⌐

- Click on the **Ellipse: from center** command.
    - **Ellipse center** prompt:
        - Type **"0"** and press **Enter.** ❶
    - **End of first axis** prompt:
        - Type **"4"** and press **Enter.**
        - Using **ORTHO**, draw the cursor over to the right and click to set location. ❷
    - **End of second axis** prompt:
        - Type **"5"** and press **Enter.**
        - Using **ORTHO**, draw the cursor straight up and click to set location. ❸

Ellipse: from center command

Fig. 2

- The finished 8mm x 10mm oval.

⟵ 8.00 ⟶

10.00

Fig. 3

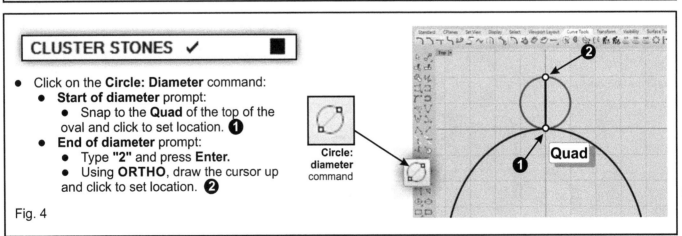

CLUSTER STONES ✓   ■

- Click on the **Circle: Diameter** command:
    - **Start of diameter** prompt:
        - Snap to the **Quad** of the top of the oval and click to set location. ❶
    - **End of diameter** prompt:
        - Type **"2"** and press **Enter.**
        - Using **ORTHO**, draw the cursor up and click to set location. ❷

Circle: diameter command

Quad

Fig. 4

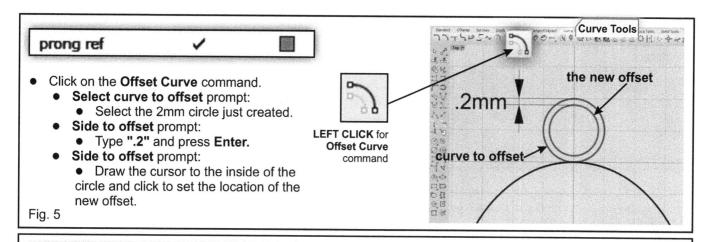

prong ref ✓ ▢

- Click on the **Offset Curve** command.
  - **Select curve to offset** prompt:
    - Select the 2mm circle just created.
  - **Side to offset** prompt:
    - Type "**.2**" and press **Enter**.
  - **Side to offset** prompt:
    - Draw the cursor to the inside of the circle and click to set the location of the new offset.

LEFT CLICK for **Offset Curve** command

.2mm

the new offset

curve to offset

Fig. 5

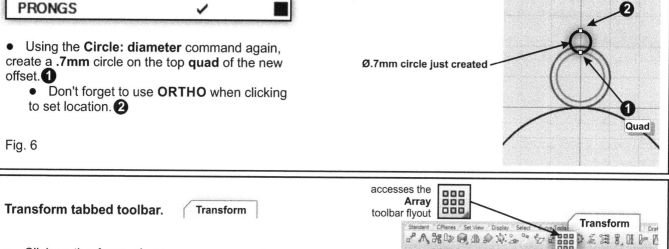

PRONGS ✓ ■

- Using the **Circle: diameter** command again, create a **.7mm** circle on the top **quad** of the new offset. ❶
  - Don't forget to use **ORTHO** when clicking to set location. ❷

Ø.7mm circle just created

Quad

Fig. 6

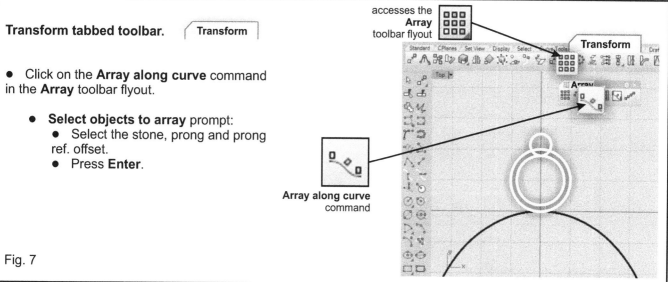

Transform tabbed toolbar. ⌐ Transform

- Click on the **Array along curve** command in the **Array** toolbar flyout.

  - **Select objects to array** prompt:
    - Select the stone, prong and prong ref. offset.
    - Press **Enter**.

accesses the **Array** toolbar flyout

Transform

Array along curve command

Fig. 7

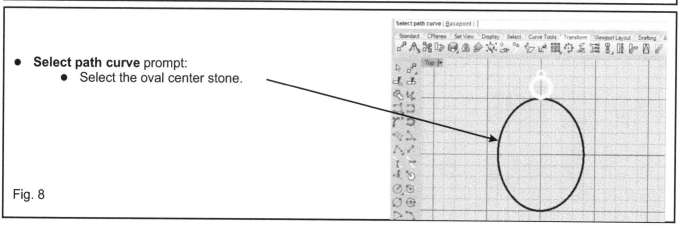

- **Select path curve** prompt:
  - Select the oval center stone.

Fig. 8

- **Array Along Curve. Press Enter to accept** prompt:
  - Click on the **Items=2** option ❶ in the **Command Line.**
    - **Number of items** prompt:
      - Type **"16"** and press Enter. ❷

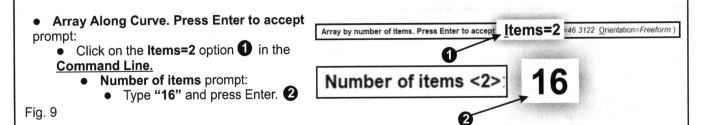

Array by number of items. Press Enter to accept **Items=2** =46.3122 Orientation=Freeform)

❶

Number of items <2> **16**

❷

Fig. 9

- The array is completed - 16 items have been arrayed around the oval center stone.

- **But this is not an accurate spacing of stones - the gaps between them are inconsistent.**

- **Undo** this array (Ctrl + Z on your keyboard or click on the **Undo** button in **Standard tabbed toolbar**.)

Undo command

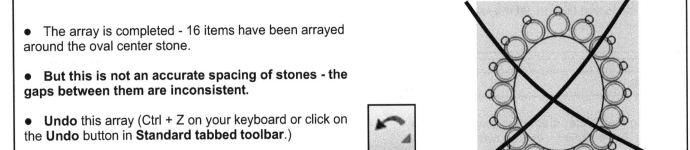

Fig. 10

---

prong ref ✓ ■

- **Curve Tools tabbed toolbar.**   Curve Tools

- Select the **Oval** ❶ and **LEFT CLICK** on the **Offset Curve** command.

  - **Side to offset** prompt:
    - Click on the **ThroughPoint** option ❷ in the **Command Line.**

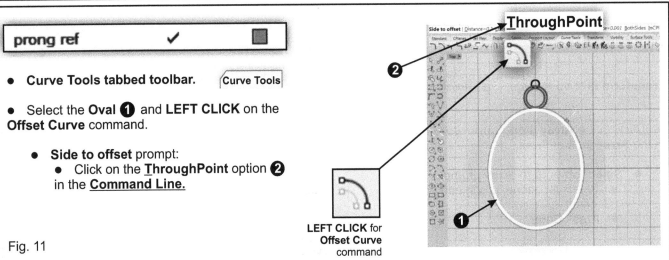

ThroughPoint

❷

LEFT CLICK for **Offset Curve** command

❶

Fig. 11

- **Through point** prompt:
  - Draw the offset out until it snaps to the **center of the circle** at the top of the oval as shown.
    - Remember that the cursor has to be hovered over the curve of a circle to deploy **Center snap.**
  - Click to set location.

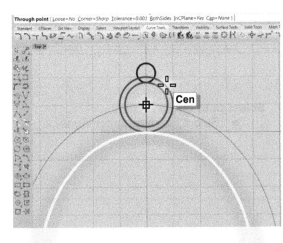

Through point (Loose=No Corner=Sharp Tolerance=0.001 BothSides InCPlane=Yes Cap=None):

Cen

Fig. 12

- Use the **Array Along Curve** command again to array the little circles as before.

    - This time, use the new offset as the **path curve.**

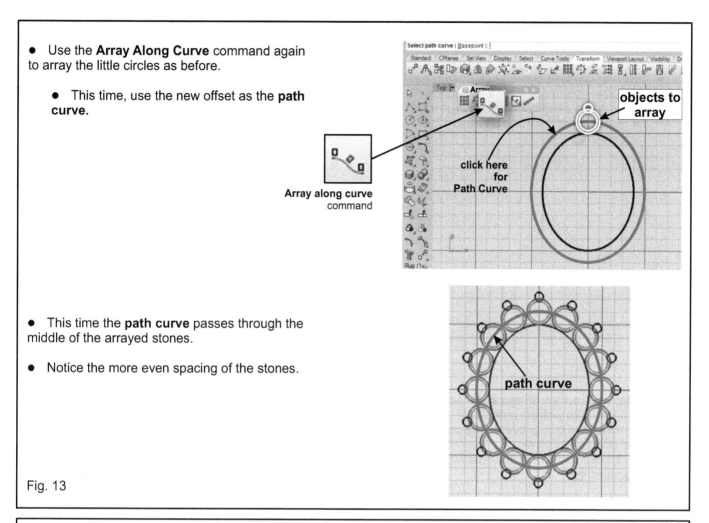

Array along curve
command

- This time the **path curve** passes through the middle of the arrayed stones.

- Notice the more even spacing of the stones.

Fig. 13

PRONGS ✓ ■

ref geo

- Turn off ref geo layer.

- **Curve Tools tabbed toolbar.** `Curve Tools`

- Zoom in on the top round stone and it's neighbor to the left as shown.

- Click on the **Circle: tangent to 3 curves** command in the **Circle** toolbar flyout.

    - **First tangent curve** prompt:
        - Draw the cursor over the prong curve shown.
        - Click to set this first location when the white constraint line appears as shown. **1**

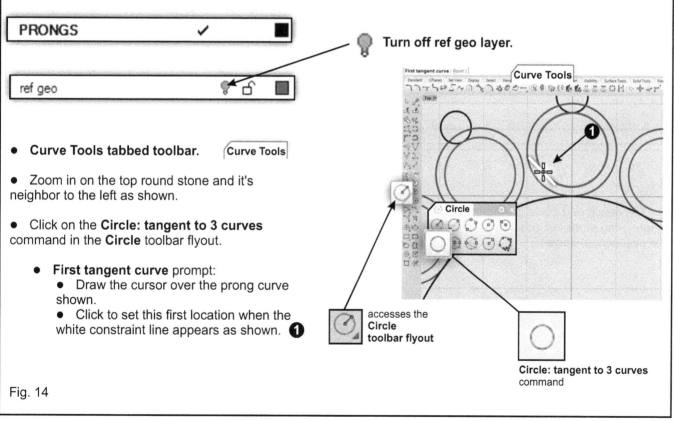

accesses the
Circle
toolbar flyout

Circle: tangent to 3 curves
command

Fig. 14

- **Second tangent curve or radius** prompt:
  - Draw the cursor across to the inner offset of the neighboring circle as shown.
  - Click when the white constraint line appears. **❷**

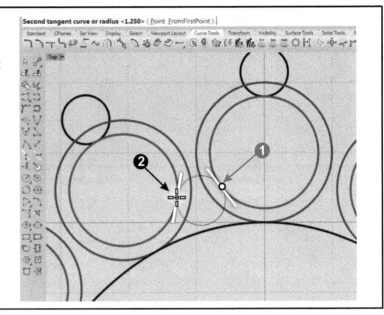

Fig. 15

- **Third tangent curve. Press Enter to draw circle from first two points.** prompt:
  - Draw the cursor over to the curve of the oval center stone.
  - Click when the white constraint line appears. **❸**

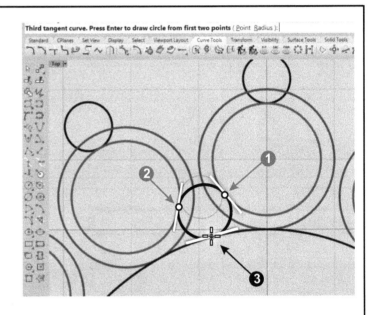

Fig. 16

- The new prong curve is tangent to both neighboring prong ref geo curves as well as to the oval center stone.

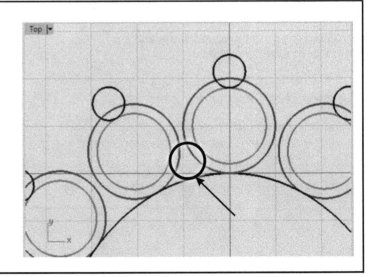

Fig. 17

215

- Create 3 more prongs, using the same technique.

- **Stop with these prongs.** *You do not have to create prongs for the rest of the stones.*

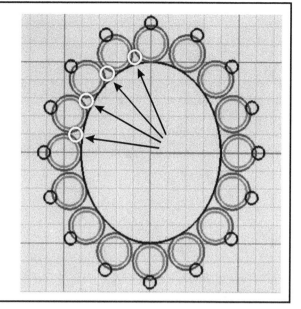

Fig. 18

---

left-click for **Trim** command

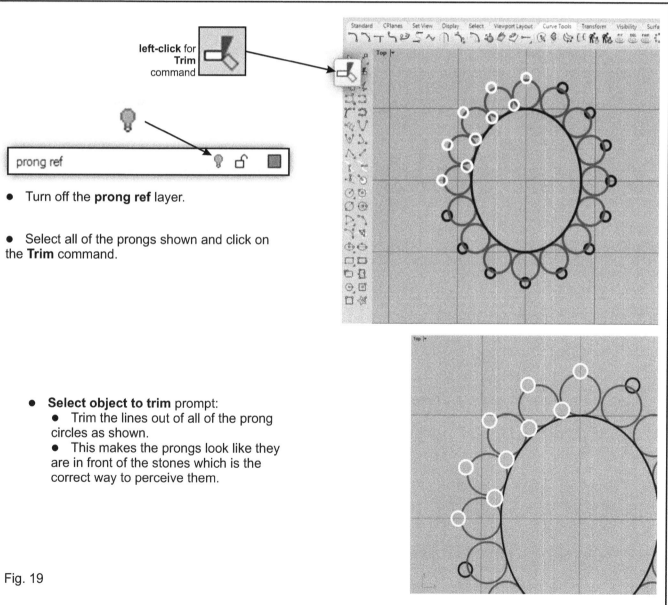

prong ref

- Turn off the **prong ref** layer.

- Select all of the prongs shown and click on the **Trim** command.

- **Select object to trim** prompt:
  - Trim the lines out of all of the prong circles as shown.
  - This makes the prongs look like they are in front of the stones which is the correct way to perceive them.

Fig. 19

- Using **Grid Snap** mode, draw a polyline along the X and Y axes on the grid as shown.

- The angle of this polyline is at **0** and the lines are perfectly vertical and horizontal.

- Turn off **grid snap**.

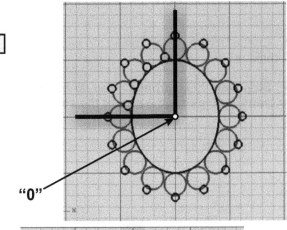

"0"

- Select all stones and prongs that are outside of the angle of the polyline as shown.

- **Delete** these selected objects.

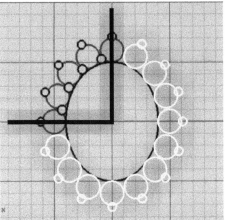

- Select the polyline and click on the **Trim** command.

Trim
command

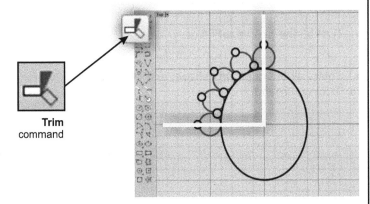

- Trim away or delete everything that is on the outside of the angle of the polyline as shown.

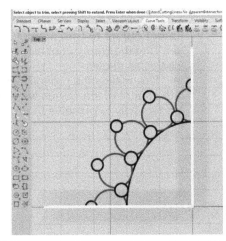

Fig. 20

- **Transform tabbed toolbar.** `Transform`

- **Hide** or **Delete** the polyline.

- Select all remaining objects and **Mirror** them across the Y axis to make a **horizontal mirror copy** as shown.

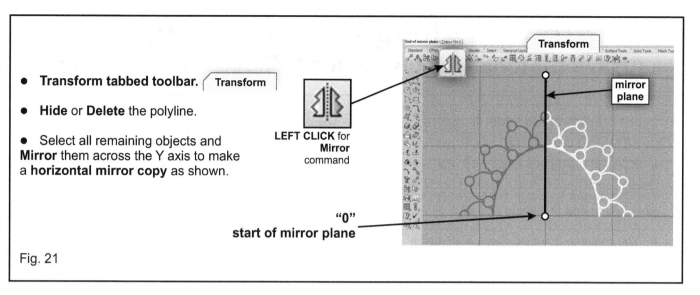

LEFT CLICK for **Mirror** command

mirror plane

"0"
start of mirror plane

Fig. 21

- Select all objects again and **Mirror** across the X axis to create a **vertical mirror copy** as shown.

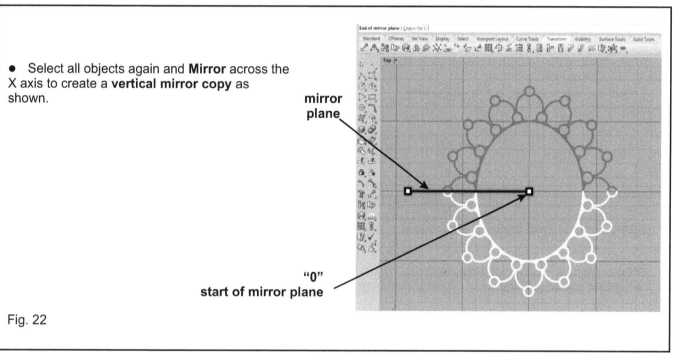

mirror plane

"0"
start of mirror plane

Fig. 22

- The finished oval cluster.

- Remember, you can toggle the grid on and off by pressing the F7 key. **F7**

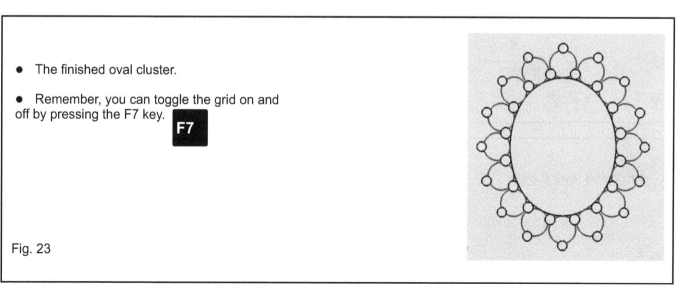

Fig. 23

Arraying Along a Freeform Curve
Arraying Stones Around a Heart Shape for Micropave

- Open the **freeform heart.3dm** file that you made in the **Freeform Curves** chapter.

  - If you do not have this file, use freeform curves to create the heart shown, making sure to use **End osnap** so that the curves touch each other end to end at top and bottom.

  - You can also open the **heart & teardrop shapes for array along curve** file on the www.rhinoforjewelry.com website:
    - support files for textbook/files for textbook.

Fig. 1

- Create the layers shown with the **heart ref** layer current.

current ⟶

HEART		
heart ref ✓		
path curve		
STONES		
PRONGS		
prong ref		

Fig. 2

- **Curve Tools tabbed toolbar.** | Curve Tools |

- **Offset** the heart curve to the outside.
  - **offset distance: .25mm**.

LEFT CLICK for **Offset Curve** command

new offset

.25

.25

Fig. 3

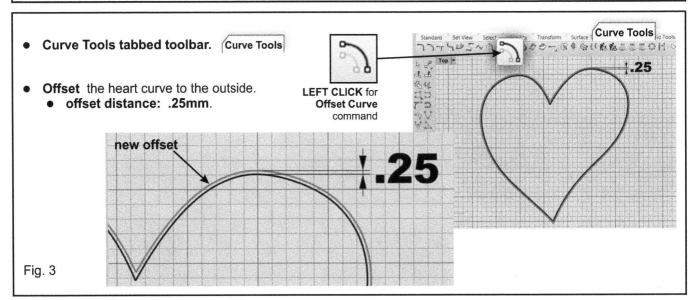

- **path curve** layer current.

current ⟶

HEART		
heart ref		
path curve ✓		
STONES		
PRONGS		
prong ref		

Fig. 4

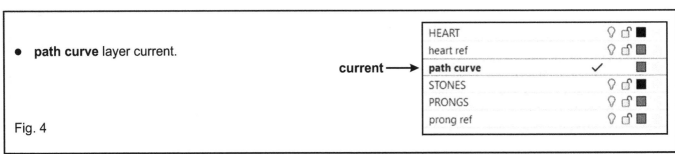

- Select the new offset and offset again to the outside.
- **offset distance: 1mm**.

1mm offset

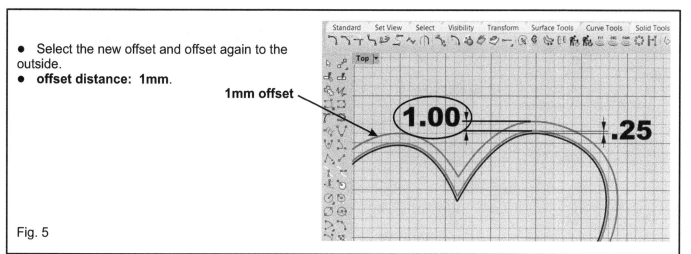

Fig. 5

- Select the new offset and offset again to the outside.
- **offset distance: 1mm**.

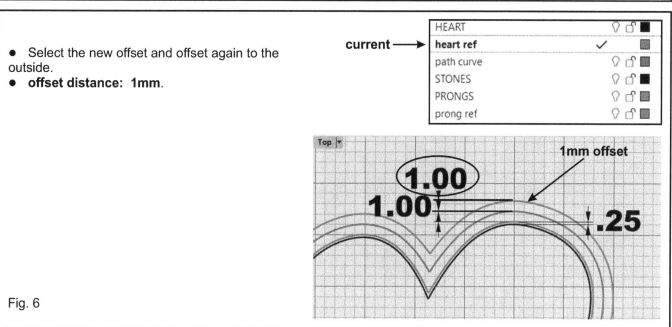

Fig. 6

- Select the last offset and offset again to the outside.
- **offset distance: .25mm**.

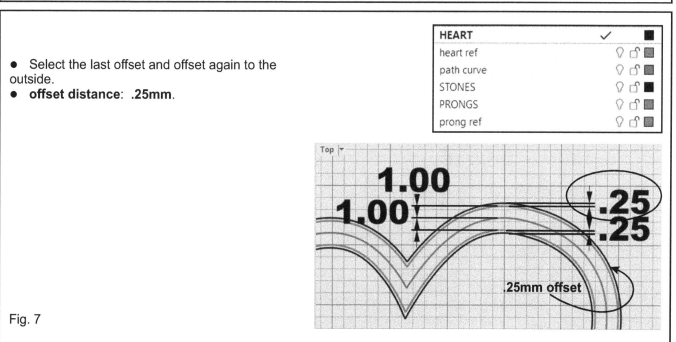

Fig. 7

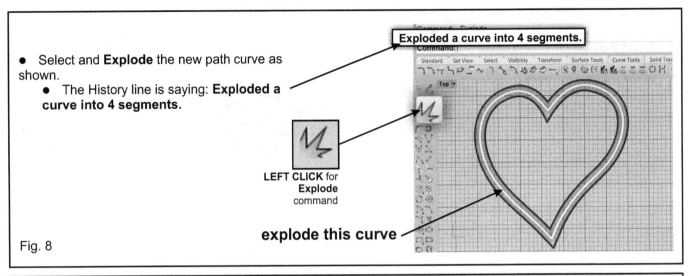

- Select and **Explode** the new path curve as shown.
    - The History line is saying: **Exploded a curve into 4 segments.**

Exploded a curve into 4 segments.

LEFT CLICK for
Explode
command

explode this curve

Fig. 8

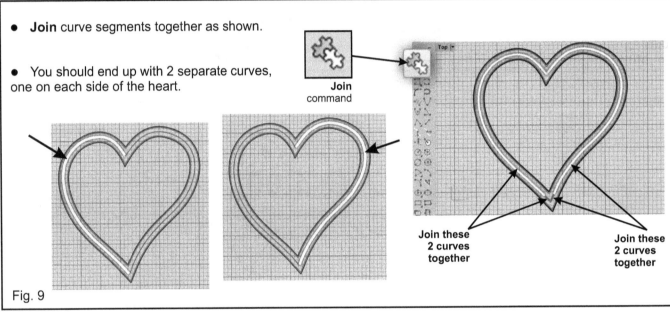

- **Join** curve segments together as shown.

- You should end up with 2 separate curves, one on each side of the heart.

Join
command

Join these
2 curves
together

Join these
2 curves
together

Fig. 9

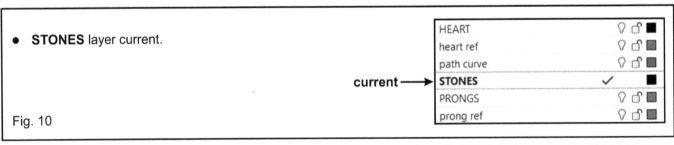

- **STONES** layer current.

current ——▶

HEART		
heart ref		
path curve		
STONES	✓	
PRONGS		
prong ref		

Fig. 10

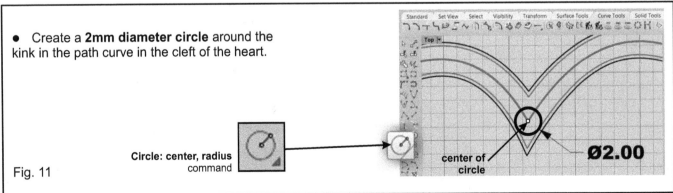

- Create a **2mm diameter circle** around the kink in the path curve in the cleft of the heart.

Circle: center, radius
command

center of
circle

Ø2.00

Fig. 11

- **prong ref** layer current.

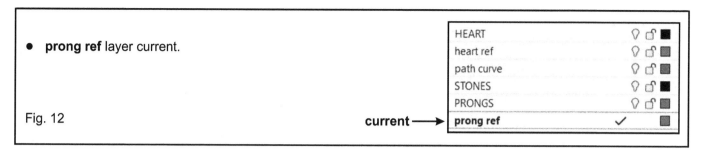

Fig. 12

LEFT CLICK for **Offset Curve** command

- **Offset** the 2mm circle to the inside.
  - **offset distance .1mm**.

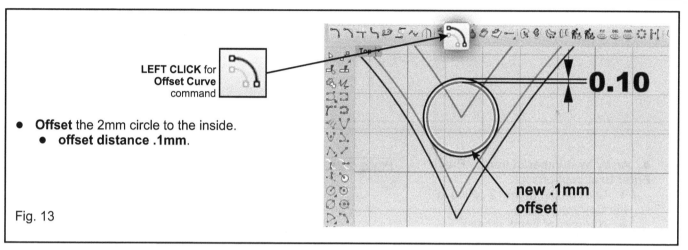

0.10

new .1mm offset

Fig. 13

Arraying the Stones Along the Path Curves

- **Transform tabbed toolbar.**   Transform

- Click on the **Array Along Curve** command in the **Array** toolbar flyout.

accesses the **Array** toolbar flyout

Array Along Curve command

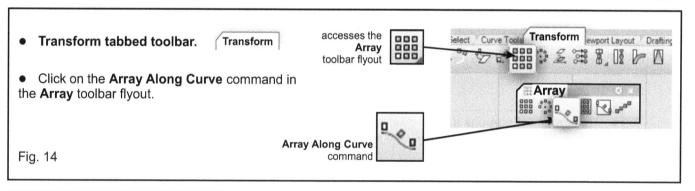

Fig. 14

- **Select objects to array** prompt:
  - Select the 2 circles shown. ❶
  - Press **Enter**.

Select objects to array. Press Enter when done:

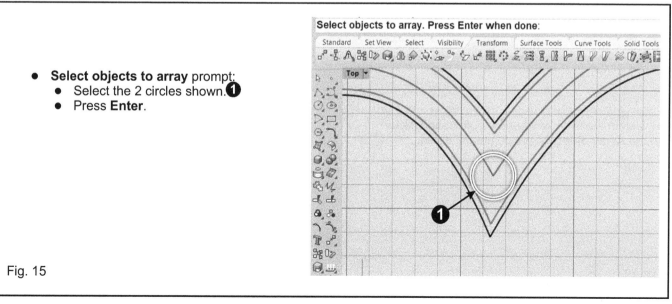

Fig. 15

- **Select path curve** prompt:
  - Select the **path curve** on the right, clicking on the approximate location shown. ❷

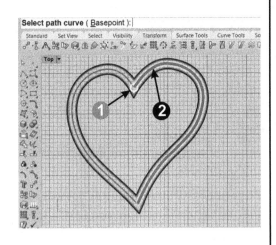

Fig. 16

- **Array by number of items. Press Enter to accept** prompt:
  - Click on the **Items=2** option in the **Command Line**.
  - **Number of Items** prompt:
    - Try **"26"** and press **Enter**.

Fig. 17

- The stone will array evenly along the specified path curve.

> - **Remember! Everyone's heart design will be different unless you are using the one provided.**
>
> - **You may have to undo the array and then repeat it, trying another number of items until you have a good number for your own original design.**

Fig. 18

- Delete the two circles at the bottom and click on the **Array along Curve** command again.

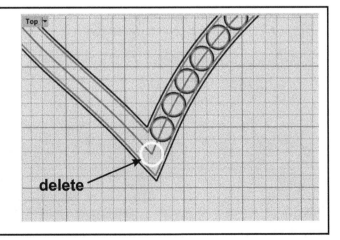

Fig. 19

- **Select objects to array** prompt:
  - Select the stone and its offset **1** at the beginning of the **path curve** as shown and press **Enter**.

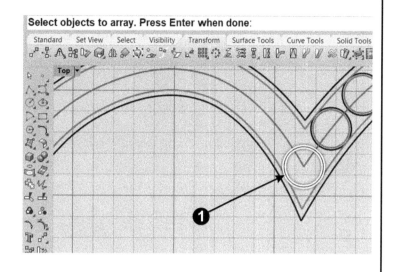

Fig. 20

- **Select path curve** prompt:
  - Select the **path curve, 1** this time on the left of the heart as shown.
  - *Make sure to select near the top* as shown.**2**

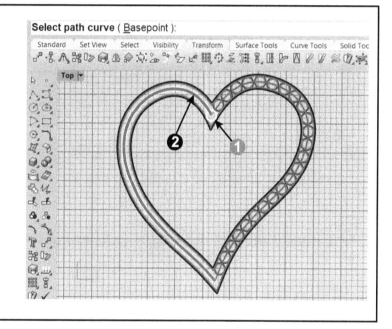

Fig. 21

- **Array by number of items. Press Enter to accept** prompt:
  - Click on the **Items=26** option in the **Command Line**.
  - **Number of Items** prompt:
    - Try **"25"** and press **Enter**.

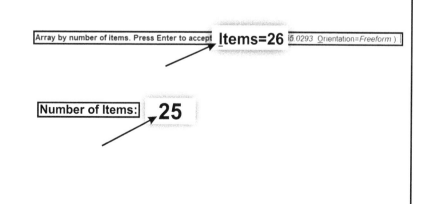

Fig. 22

- The finished arrays.

Fig. 23

Creating the Prongs

- **PRONGS** layer current.

Fig. 24

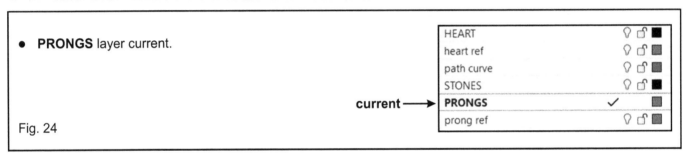

- **Curve Tools tabbed toolbar.**

- Use the **Circle: tangent to 3 curves** command to create the prong shown, coming in contact with the 3 curves bordering it.
  - [Ref: **Cluster Around an] Oval Center Stone** chapter, Figs. 14 - 17]

Circle Tangent to 3 Curves command

Fig. 25

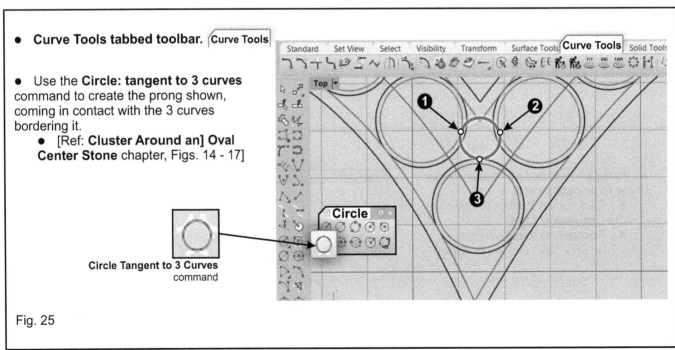

- Use the **Circle: tangent to 3 curves** command to create the prong directly below, coming in contact with the 3 curves bordering it.
  - [Ref: **Cluster Around an] Oval Center Stone** chapter, Figs. 14 - 17

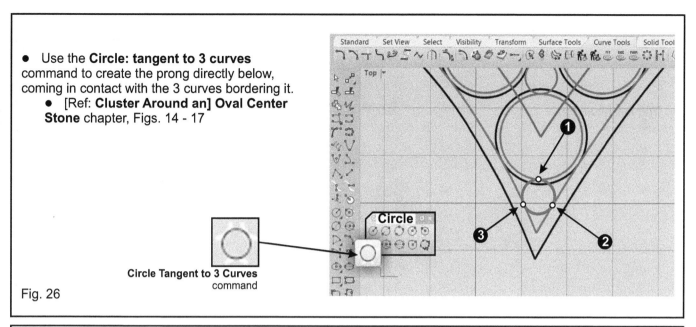

Fig. 26

Circle Tangent to 3 Curves
command

- Turn off the **path curve** layer.

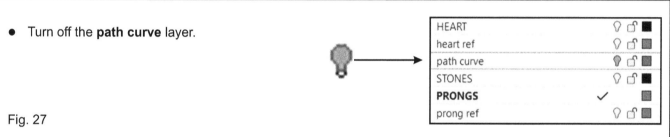

Fig. 27

- 3 new prongs have been created in the inner and outer rows of prongs, using the **Circle: tangent to 3 curves** command as before.

- Continue to create prongs for the rest of the drawing.

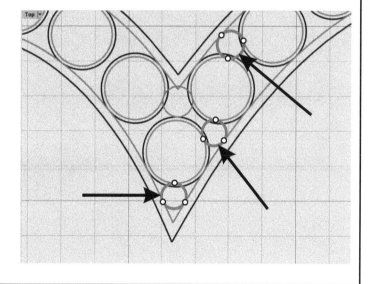

Fig. 28

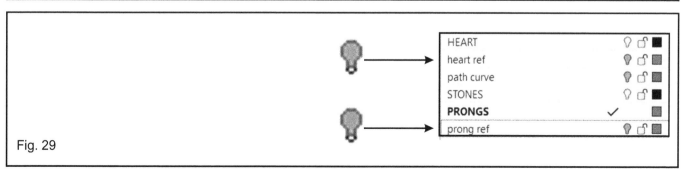

Fig. 29

226

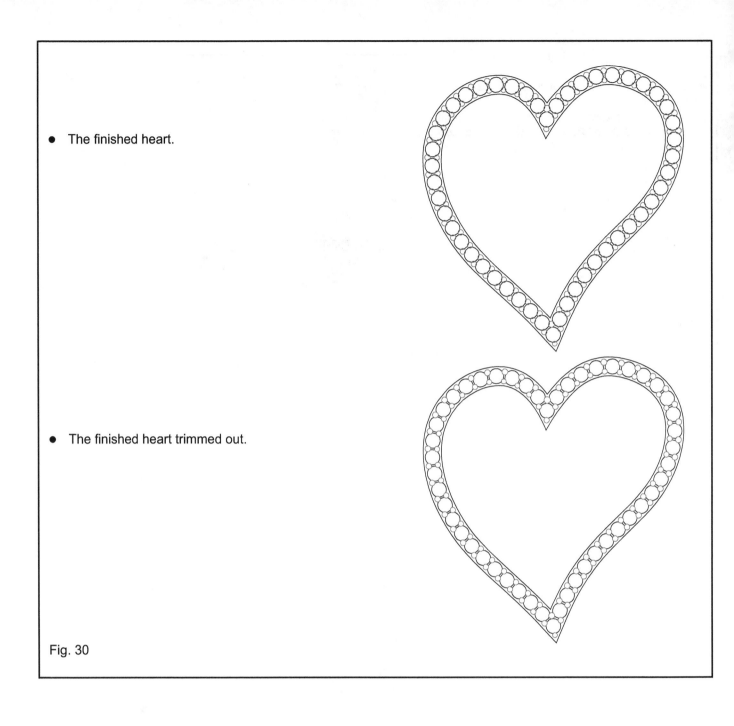

● The finished heart.

● The finished heart trimmed out.

Fig. 30

Printing

- Open your Rhino file: **pearl ring technical drawing.3dm.**

- **Top** viewport.
  - Rhino will print in the active viewport so make sure that the **Top Viewport** is active by clicking anywhere in it.

- The **construction lines** layer is turned off.

Fig. 1

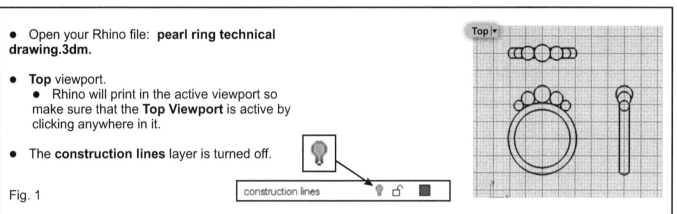

- Select the **construction lines** layer. ❶

- Click on the **New Layer** button. ❷

- A new layer will appear under the selected **construction lines** layer.
  - Name this new layer **display construction lines.** ❸
  - Assign the color **red.**

Fig. 2

- **display construction lines** layer current.

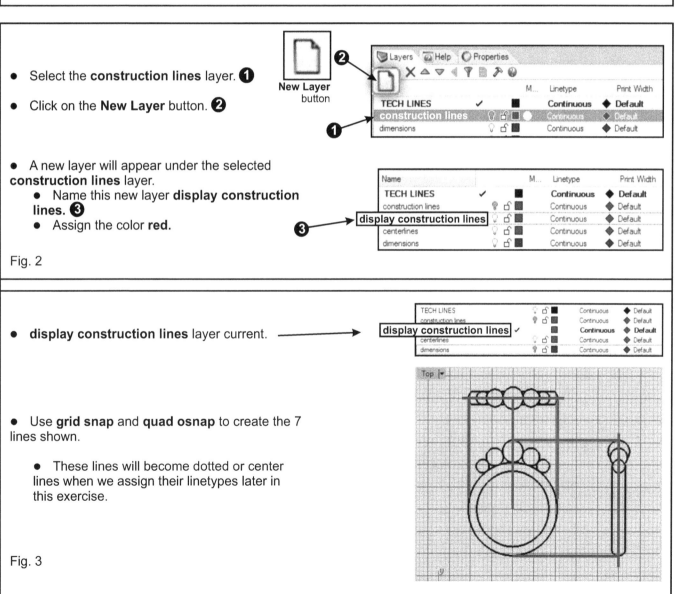

- Use **grid snap** and **quad osnap** to create the 7 lines shown.

  - These lines will become dotted or center lines when we assign their linetypes later in this exercise.

Fig. 3

- **Standard tabbed toolbar.** | Standard |

- Click on the **Print** command as shown.
    - *You can also type the shortcut **Ctrl + P** to activate the **Print** command.*

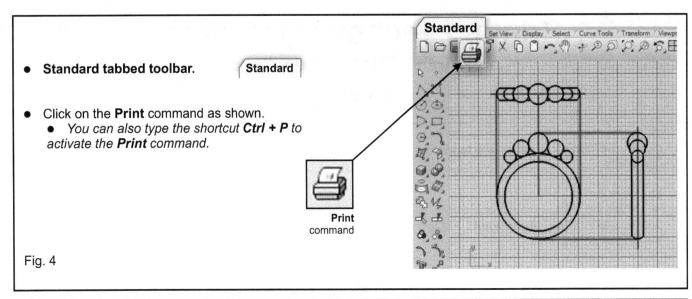

Print
command

Fig. 4

- The **Print Setup** box will open.

Fig. 5

- **Destination: ❶**
    - Your designated printer will be the default destination.
    - Click on the **Properties** button for familiar settings associated with your printer. ❷
- **Output Type: ❸**
    - This should be set at **Vector Output** because you are printing lines and don't need pixels until you get into rendered images in 3D modeling.
- **Output Color: ❹**
    - The default **Print Color** is the color of the layers you used.
    - Display color refers to colors assigned by you for printing.

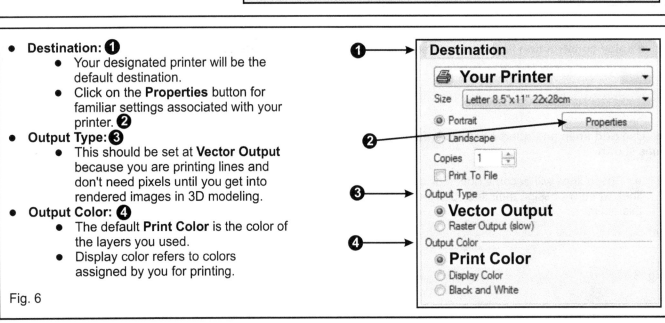

Fig. 6

- **View and Output Scale** category:
  - Select the **Extents** option.

- Notice that the default scale setting is **Scale to Fit.**
  - Click on the little triangle to open up a drop-down list of scale settings. **1**

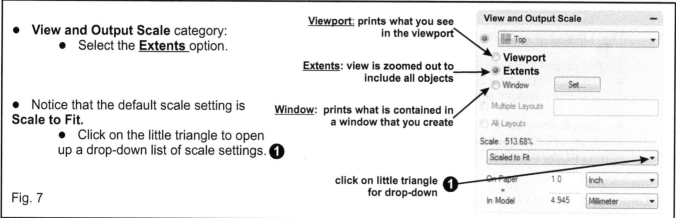

Fig. 7

- A drop-down list will appear, showing different Scale settings.

- Scroll up to the top of the drop-down list and click on the **1:1** setting. **2**
  - Your printed image will be *scaled to the exact size of the drawing.*

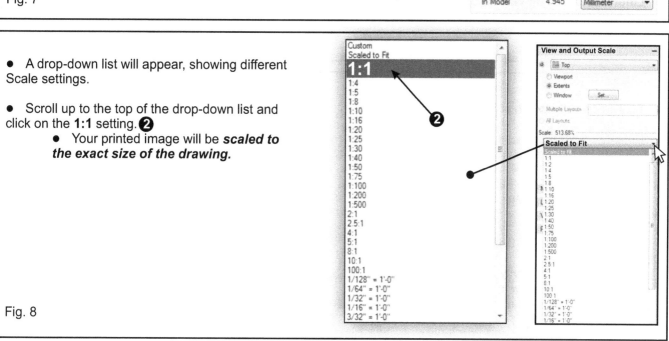

Fig. 8

- Close the previous categories by clicking in their upper right corners.

- Open the **Margins and Position** category as shown. **1**
  - Notice that the **Centered** option is selected. **2**
  - The drawing is centered on the print preview as shown.

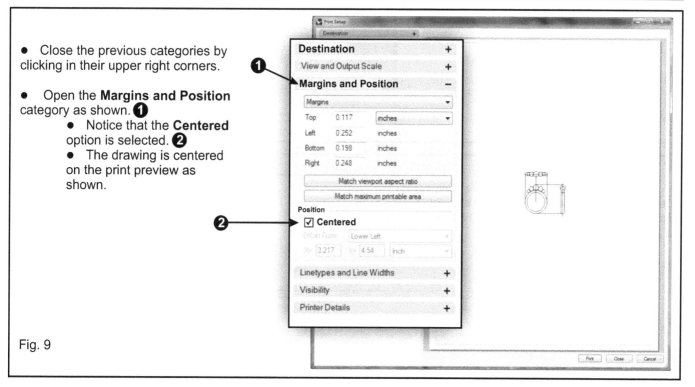

Fig. 9

230

- Open the **Linetypes and Line Widths** category. ❶
    - The default line width is a hairline. ❷
    - The default line type is a continuous line until more specific linetypes are assigned.
        - *We will soon cover how to adjust Linetype settings to enhance the impact of the drawing.*

- Click in the upper right corner to close the **Linetypes and Line Widths** category.

Fig. 10

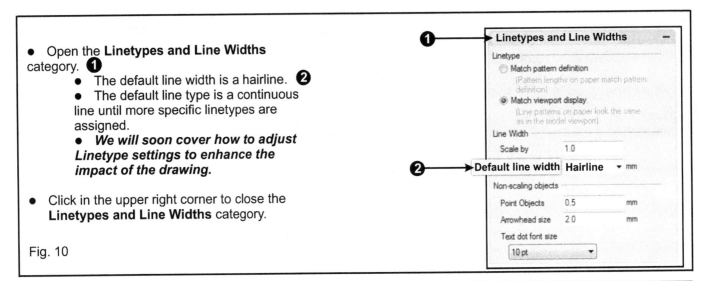

- Click to open the **Visibility** category.

- Note that different options allow other elements to be printed, such as the background color of the viewport, the grid, grid axes, and any picture frame or other background bitmap that may be in the viewport.

- Note the option called **Only Selected Object.**
    - This means that **only objects that are selected** will show in the preview window and be printed.
        - *If you do not see anything in the preview pane and you have not selected anything, check to see if this option is checked!*

Fig. 11

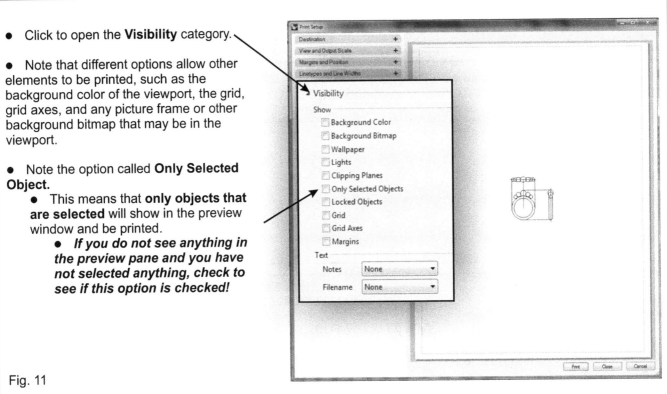

- The final category, **Printer Details,** describes the printer you will be using, it's port into your computer, the paper type and the printable area of the image.

Fig. 12

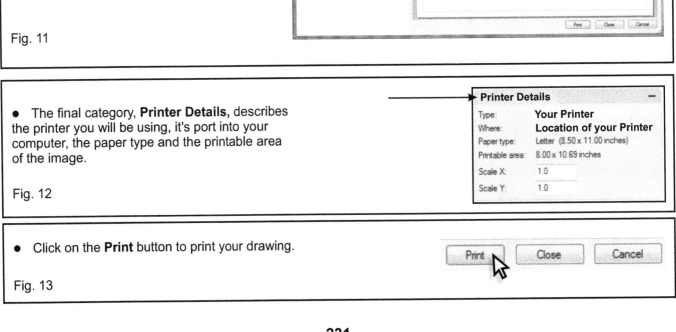

- Click on the **Print** button to print your drawing.

Fig. 13

Linetypes, Colors, & Print Width

- Notice that the line widths are, by default, hairlines and all lines are "continuous", rather than being "dotted" or "dashed".

- Now is the time to assign linetypes, colors, and line widths for a more dynamic presentation.

Fig. 14

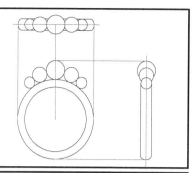

- Use the cursor to pull the Layers box and column widths out so that you can see all of the column headings.

- We will be working with these categories:
  - **Linetype**
  - **Print Color ②**
  - **Print Width ③**

Fig. 15

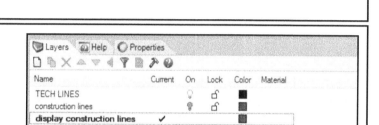

- If you see something like this, it means that some of the category columns need to be made visible.

Fig. 16

- **Right-click** on the line that shows the column names as shown. ❶

- A drop-down context menu will appear as shown. ❷

Fig. 17

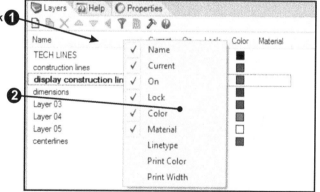

- Draw the cursor down and click on **Linetype.**❶

- The **Linetype** column will now be showing in the **Layers** box.❷

Fig. 18

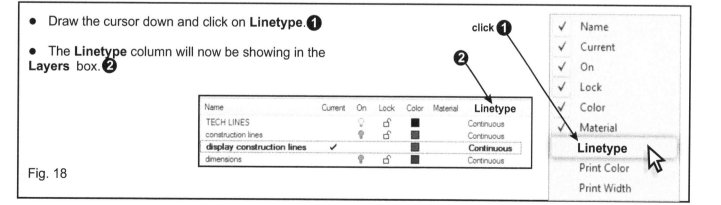

- Use this process again to make the **Print Color** and **Print Width** category columns visible.

Fig. 19

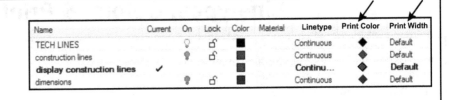

Dotted Linetype

- Click on the word **Continuous** ❶ in the **Linetype** column of the **display construction lines** layer line. ❷

Fig. 20

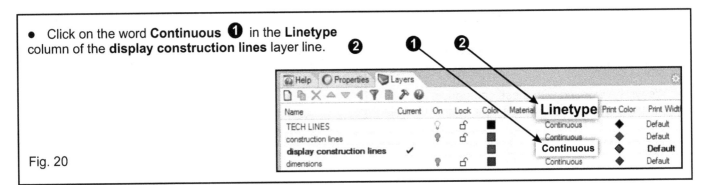

- When the **Select Linetype** box appears, select the **dots** linetype. ❶

- Click the OK button to exit the box. ❷

Fig. 21

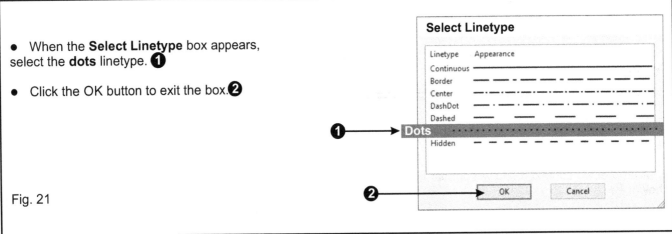

- The **display construction lines** in the drawing now have a dotted linetype.

- note: You can toggle the grid off by pressing the **F7 Hotkey.** Press again to toggle the grid on again.

F7   **press to toggle grid off**

F7   **press to toggle grid on again**

Fig. 22

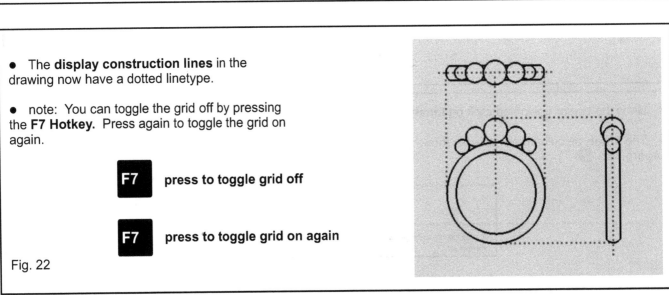

Centerline Linetype

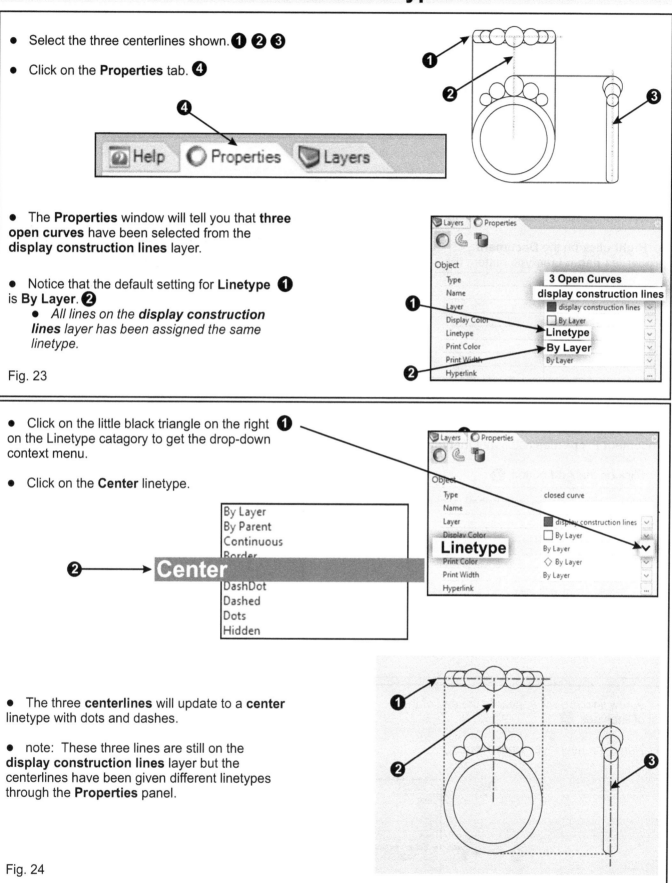

- Select the three centerlines shown. ❶ ❷ ❸

- Click on the **Properties** tab. ❹

❹

- The **Properties** window will tell you that **three open curves** have been selected from the **display construction lines** layer.

- Notice that the default setting for **Linetype** ❶ is **By Layer**. ❷
  - *All lines on the **display construction lines** layer has been assigned the same linetype.*

Fig. 23

- Click on the little black triangle on the right ❶ on the Linetype catagory to get the drop-down context menu.

- Click on the **Center** linetype.

By Layer
By Parent
Continuous
Border
❷ ➞ **Center**
DashDot
Dashed
Dots
Hidden

- The three **centerlines** will update to a **center** linetype with dots and dashes.

- note: These three lines are still on the **display construction lines** layer but the centerlines have been given different linetypes through the **Properties** panel.

Fig. 24

Creating a Custom Linetype

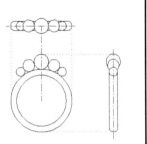

- The default **dots** linetype may be very faint in the printing.

- In this exercise, a new custom linetype will be created that may show up better in the printed technical drawing.

Fig. 25

- **Drafting tabbed toolbar.**

- **Right-click** on the **Document properties page: Linetype** button.

RIGHT-CLICK for
Document properties page: Linetype

Fig. 26

- The **Rhino Options** box will open to the **Document Properties** category **Linetypes**. ❶

- Click on the **Add** button. ❷

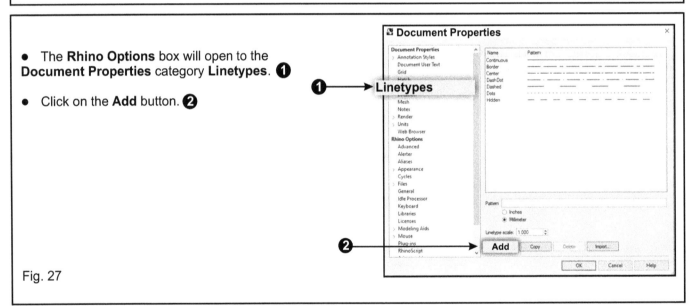

Fig. 27

- A new linetype will appear at the end of the list of linetypes. ❸

- Name the new layer **1mm-1mm**. ❹

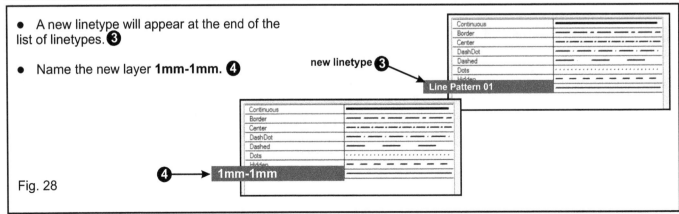

new linetype ❸

Fig. 28

- Change the **Pattern** setting to read <u>**1.00**</u>, **1.00** ❹

- <u>**1.00**</u> is the **length of each dash**
- **1.00** is the **length of the spaces between the dashes.**

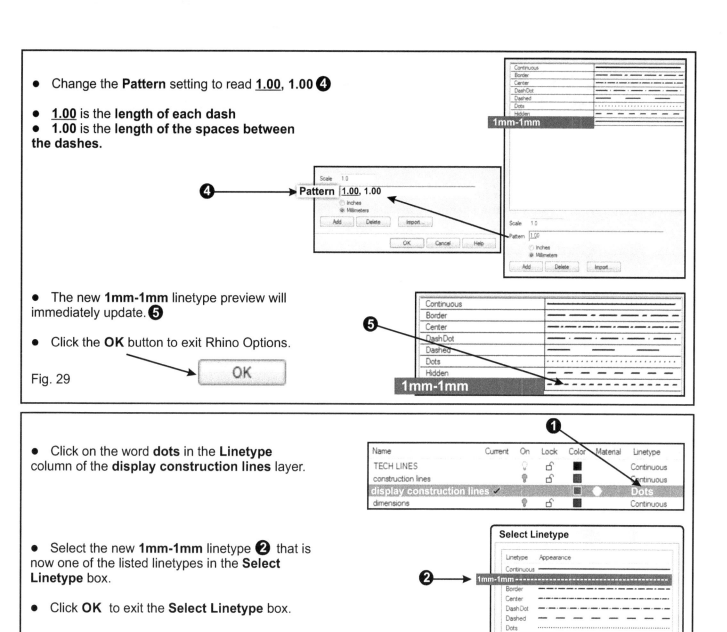

❹ → **Pattern** | 1.00, 1.00

- The new **1mm-1mm** linetype preview will immediately update. ❺

- Click the **OK** button to exit Rhino Options.

Fig. 29

OK

- Click on the word **dots** in the **Linetype** column of the **display construction lines** layer.

- Select the new **1mm-1mm** linetype ❷ that is now one of the listed linetypes in the **Select Linetype** box.

- Click **OK** to exit the **Select Linetype** box.

Fig. 30

- The new linetype is more visually clear than the dotted line.

- Shown here both in the workspace display and in the print preview.

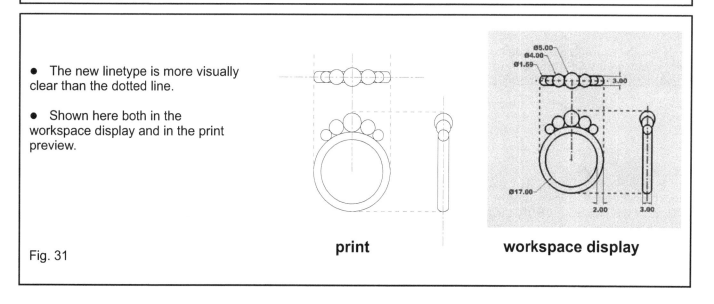

print   **workspace display**

Fig. 31

Print Color

- Default **Print color** will be the same color as the layer.**❶**

- In this example, the layer color of red will also be the **Print Color. ❷**

- **If you want to change a color for printing, click on the Print Color block for a specific layer.**

Fig. 32

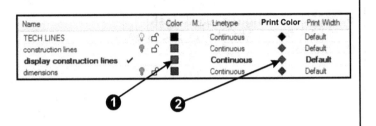

Assigning Print Width

- Click on the word, **default** in the **Print Width** column of the **TECH LINES** layer**❶**

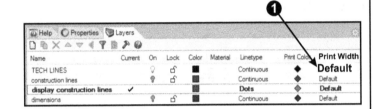

- The **Select Print Width** box will appear.

- Click on the **0.18 width** and click the OK button. **❷**

- This will result in the **TECH LINES being printed heavier than the construction lines.**

> - Note: The change in line widths will not show on your workspace display. **They will only show in the printing.**

Fig. 33

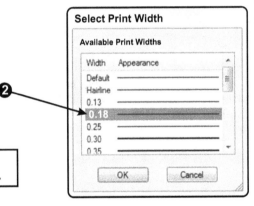

- Print the drawing again, adding dimensions and changing the **Output Color** in the **Destination** category to **Display Color.**

- Looking at the print preview may not show you the difference in line widths but the print itself will show that the main **TECH LINES** are wider than the **construction lines**.

Fig. 34

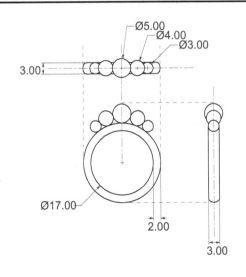

Index

Dana Buscaglia has had many years of experience as a designer and a model maker for the jewelry industry.

Dana has been teaching CAD for jewelry at the Fashion Institute of Technology since 2004.